V-WEAPONS HUNT

V-WEAPONS HUNT

Defeating German Secret Weapons

Colonel Roy M. Stanley II, USAF (ret.)

Pen & Sword
MILITARY

Other Books By The Author

World War II Photo Intelligence
Prelude To Pearl Harbor
To Fool A Glass Eye
Asia From Above

First published in Great Britain in 2010 by
Pen & Sword Military
An imprint of
Pen & Sword Books Ltd
47 Church Street
Barnsley
South Yorkshire
S70 2AS

ISBN 978 1 84884 259 5

A CIP catalogue record for this book is
available from the British Library

Printed and bound in England
By CPI UK

Pen & Sword Books Ltd incorporates the Imprints of Pen & Sword Aviation,
Pen & Sword Family History, Pen & Sword Maritime, Pen & Sword Military,
Wharncliffe Local History, Pen & Sword Select, Pen & Sword Military Classics, Leo
Cooper, Remember When, Seaforth Publishing and Frontline Publishing

For a complete list of Pen & Sword titles please contact
PEN & SWORD BOOKS LIMITED
47 Church Street, Barnsley, South Yorkshire, S70 2AS, England
E-mail: enquiries@pen-and-sword.co.uk
Website: www.pen-and-sword.co.uk

DEDICATION

With deepest respect and admiration,
this book is dedicated to Second World War reconnaissance collectors and photo interpreters
who had to win these battles and, at the same time, invent all the skills and techniques
that to this day make a Photo Interpretation Report something a wise commander relies upon.

ACKNOWLEDGEMENTS

One of the best things about being a PI is that you develop a good memory for details, and you are part of an exclusive "inner circle" of other PIs who are willing to share thoughts and materials. I was honored to be allowed to join the Medmenham Club, and I have fellow members Wing Commander M D (Mike) Mockford, OBE, RAF (Ret'd), and Major ACL (Chris) Halsall, Intelligence Corps (Ret'd) to thank for some of the most significant photos in this book — and particularly for access to Douglas Kendall's unpublished memoirs. I also had fine cooperation from the National Air and Space Museum (NASM), Defence Audio Visual Agency (DAVA), Imperial War Museum, US National Archives, Bundesarchiv and several private collectors of Second World War imagery. Some of my sense of what was going on and how people felt at the time comes from years of taking every chance I had to talk with former bomber and fighter pilots during unit Reunions, Squadron parties and coffee breaks during various military assignments. I have also talked with people who heard the buzz-bombs overhead as children. They were there and lived through the critical months this book documents.

The opinions that follow are mine alone, and if I got any of the story wrong, I hope the friends who helped me, and those who served at Medmenham, will forgive.

Lastly, I want to thank the publishers (noted in the Bibliography) who so graciously granted permission to quote from their copyright material, and the folk at Pen & Sword for making this such a comfortable experience--particularly Brigadier Henry Wilson and David Hemingway.

CONTENTS

INTRODUCTION

When my son (a USAFR Lt. Col serving in Intelligence) learned what I was writing he asked how it would add to an oft told story. I replied that conventional wisdom on the topic wasn't always correct and I didn't believe most people knew the important nuances. I would write the whole truth and nothing but the truth, setting the record straight in this saga of photo interpretation (PI)[1] that was the core of an intelligence triumph that played an important role in the outcome of the Second World War.

It is one thing to go back through archives to analyze the capability of a given weapon, but how and when the weapon is used, and how it is answered, is determined by people who act within a situation as they understand it. People living in critical times act based upon what they believe to be true, not upon what some researcher later learns. Hindsight is always correct but people under stress aren't. It is one thing five decades later to opine for various reasons that "the V-weapons were too few and too inaccurate to be decisive", but those about to be on the receiving end of the weapons didn't know that. After sixty years of living and reading military history I believe military history is best written by people who lived it, or understand what the major players were doing and thinking. "Been there, done that" trumps "read about it". I prefer to assess the impact of the V-weapons on the progress and outcome of the Second World War by relying upon the words of those who lived through the assault: Churchill, Eisenhower, Montgomery, and various intelligence personnel quoted in this text. They certainly feared the V-weapons and worried that they could decisively influence the conduct of the war. No one can ever be certain how decisive the V-weapons might have been without timely Allied discovery and intervention.

A number of books have touched on the Allied search for the V-weapons, and many included a few of the most notable aerial photographs involved in the hunt. For all but three of those authors,[2] the aerial photos were not a primary source of information. As a trained photo interpreter, aerial photos were invaluable to my understanding the full story of the victories and mistakes in the race to find and stop new German long-range weapons.

I never met the people who lived this tale — I wish I had — but I feel as though I know them. Their words are familiar. I've lived them! I learned to PI on black and white prints from the Second World War and the Korean War. An RAF Officer taught the "Weapons Bloc" in USAF PI School where I learned to recognize a Giant Wurzburg radar and the difference between a panzer, a sturmgeschutz and a half-track from their tracks and different aspect ratios—though none of those had been in the field for fifteen years. I learned to use stereo, marks on the ground and shadows to find and identify objects and activities. My first assignment was to PI on prints, so I know what those Second World War PIs did, how they did it, what they felt. I know what you can and can't do with prints. I know the pressure they were under to finish a stack of prints as the missions kept rolling in. The only thing I didn't experience was the added pressure of imminent threat of attack. I don't envy them that experience, but having heard B-40 rockets and mortars overhead in South Vietnam, I think I can understand that too.

When I began looking at aerial imagery in the late 1950s, we had better cameras, faster collection aircraft and photo lab equipment, finer grain aerial film and better enlargers, but we used a stereoscope Second World War PIs would have recognized, and we still lived by the Three Phase photo interpretation cycle pioneered at the Central Interpretation Unit (CIU) at RAF Medmenham, Buckinghamshire, later the Allied Central Interpretation Unit (ACIU) after the Americans joined the effort.

We used comparative (earlier) coverage to detect change; another important legacy of the CIU. Intelligence is a process of building one piece upon another until the whole is understood and Third Phase PI techniques developed at Medmenham resulted in forensic dissection of a target. Most of this story takes place in that realm. My own PI experience was in First and Second Phase but I have the background to understand the imagery and unravel details of what really happened in the complex tale and crucial epic of how the German V-weapons were found and delayed enough to prevent them from having more of an impact on the war.

Success in the hunt for German V-weapons was a great achievement for Allied Intelligence, a great story — a story worth retelling and understanding.

---

1 PI can be used in many ways: "He is a PI." "We must PI the film." "He is PI-ing the film." "The mission has been PI-ed."

2 Constance Babington Smith, Ursula Powys-Lybbe and Douglas Kendall (work unpublished). A fourth author with first hand experience in the all-important hunt, Professor Reginald V Jones, used the photos but only at very specific points in the search. Not a trained PI, his contributions were sometimes helpful, sometimes misleading, even meddlesome.

Chapter I

BACKGROUND

THE SETTING

For over half a century we have lived in The Nuclear Age with the threat of long-range ballistic missiles. In 1939-1945 that era was anticipated…it was actually dawning but no one could know where or how, much less how it would progress. In Second World War the machines of war were improving at an accelerating rate. The Allies had several ground-breaking aircraft; heavy-hauling long-range bombers and high-performance fighters, even jet-powered versions in the air. The Third Reich had proven to be quite innovative in weapons development. The Germans had several operational jet fighters and reconnaissance aircraft in use by 1944. Some of their submarines and armored vehicles were outstanding. Their 88mm anti-aircraft gun was so good it was in demand for other uses, particularly as a tank-killer. German radar was as good, or better, than anything the Allies had and we basically copied their "blind bombing" system of intersecting electronic bombing beams. Early in the war both the Allies and the Axis were known to be working on a nuclear bomb. The obvious conclusion was that if the Allies were working on something new, so was the enemy. Their scientists, engineers and workers were just as good and just as dedicated, and the obvious conclusion was that if we could do something, so could they. The quest for intelligence was to find out what the enemy was doing, how far along were they, where were they doing it, and how could that progress be disrupted. The darkest fear was that the enemy would create a weapon that was significantly better, worse yet, something the Allies hadn't thought of.

British and Commonwealth forces, later joined by the Americans, had first withstood, then beaten the worst Hitler could hurl at them, then begun to give back more destruction than they took but until the invasion of the continent there was no way to change the proximity of the Axis enemy just twenty-two miles away in France. Nor was there an easy, much less comprehensive, way to discover what was going on behind the German "Iron Curtain" of the early 1940s, and there were persistent rumors from different sources of strange new long-range weapons of terrible effectiveness—weapons against which there would be no defense.

At first these new weapons were discounted as German propaganda designed to boost morale at home, keep neutrals neutral and frighten or intimidate the Allies. Thinking of extreme long range surface-to-surface weapons, people remembered the "Paris Gun" in The Great War,[1] and it was known that the Germans had built an 800mm monster gun, "Schwerer Gustav," in the late 1930s.[2] No one on the Allied side doubted that there were new weapons in secret development that would fall into the same category of unique and far reaching, but there were indications that the new Nazi weapons would have greater range and be employed in large quantities. Indications were that the new weapons were specifically intended to punish England in retaliation for the bombing of Germany (which was itself a retaliation for the bombing of England in 1940), and to divert Allied bomber sorties from German targets. The new secret weapons were originally named Versuchmuster (experimental type). German propaganda later relabelled them Vergeltungswaffen (weapons of reprisal). Hitler expected that there would be "such a storm of protest and war-weariness (in Britain) that the Government will be overthrown following V-weapons strikes" (The Air War 1939-1945, p. 155. The author cites USSBSS and two other authors as authority for this).

To accomplish either purpose, at a minimum the threat would have to be credible. Intelligence Services can never discount anything, but a threat 'in being' is obviously more significant than one on the drawing board. If the new weapons existed, they had to be found; but where to look and what to look for? What might the new weapons look like? Were there characteristics of the weapons or their firing sites that would help identify them? The firing/launching sites had to be found, but at what range did one search for them? Every stone had to be turned over to see what lay beneath, and there were a lot of stones. The classic struggle of intelligence is to sort through a mountain of information on some topics and a dearth of information on others, separating the wheat from the chaff, avoiding "circular confirmations" where multiple reports from the same original event seem to validate the information. This task of discrimination is never-ending but has special urgency during periods of actual fighting. The specific problem of German "wonder weapons" was compounded because no one in Allied Military Intelligence, and few of their covert sources, had the background necessary to assess observations or information on rockets and exotic propellants. They had to learn as they went, and they had to learn fast.

On the German side, it appears to me that they never evolved a strategic bombing concept that could have been applied to the V-weapons, instead viewing and treating them as long-range artillery.

THE GREAT SEARCH

Seldom in the history of warfare did intelligence contribute to, and shape, the military campaigns of a war as it did between 1939 and 1945. There are numerous pinnacles in the struggle between intelligence and enemy operational forces: chasing down *Bismarck*; the Battle of the Atlantic; planning the Normandy Invasion; long term application of Allied bombing against German petroleum and aircraft production; the moves and counter-moves on radar and blind bombing; and the Battle of Midway come readily to mind. But for me the essence of Intelligence in Second World War is demonstrated in the incredible race between German efforts to field a family of unstoppable "wonder weapons" and the Allies' methodical process to discover them, understand them and destroy them.

That this race involved risk and loss of life, enormous levels of expenditure and human effort over a relatively short period of time, and ranged from the Baltic to mid-coastal France and from England to Poland only makes the story the more exciting. Had the Germans won the contest and been able to fire on England with the schedule and numbers intended, it is possible to question if the invasion of Europe through Normandy would have been possible. Certainly it would not have been possible in early June 1944. That might have caused the war in Europe to drag on into 1946, or longer, by which time Nazi Germany would have expanded use of jet interceptors and ultra-long range aircraft, possibly even a nuclear device. In short, everything we know about the latter half of this century might have been dramatically changed if British and American intelligence had been even a few days slower in laying bare to overwhelming air superiority the high-tech "V-weapons" upon which Hitler counted so heavily to turn the tide of battle in his favor.

What a challenge this race became. The Axis side knew what they wanted to do and when they wanted to do it. They had to overcome incredible technical problems to develop and deploy the weapons that were on the "cutting edge" for their day. For the Allies, it was like playing "Where's Waldo" when you don't if Waldo exists; how many Waldo's there might be; where to look, or what "Waldo" looks like—meanwhile he is going to try hard to kill you if you get caught searching, or if you fail to find him.

WHAT WEAPONS?

There was nothing new about armies trying to develop weapons that outranged the prevailing weapons of the day. The Chinese had used rockets as early as the thirteenth century, British Congreve Rockets provided the "rockets' red glare" over Fort McHenry in 1814,[3] the Soviets were using large quantities of "Katyusha" rockets, Germans had the "Nebelwerfer" and the United States had 200mm rockets, sometimes fired in large numbers from specially configured support ships for pre-landing beach preparation. All of these were short ranged, aimed but unguided, and had relatively small warheads.[4] They were essentially a different form of artillery—tactical weapons fired on a ballistic trajectory, depending upon high volume of fire to blanket a target area for success. They were more akin to strategic aerial bombing and it was expected that they would have the same targets: cities, marshalling areas and production facilities. The Germans had several air-to-surface guided bombs that demonstrated considerable accuracy but were short ranged, depending upon the launching aircraft keeping a line-of-sight on the target. Only limited numbers of those weapons were available, and Allied fighters fending the launch aircraft out of range limited continuing success of the first "smart bombs".[5] The Allies quickly followed suit with two air-to-ground "guided" bombs; Azon and Grapefruit, both of which promised much but accomplished little.[6]

Azimuth only controlled AZON drops of gravity bombs on the bridge at Precy, Fr., 31 May 1944. Smoke showed bomb to air crewman steering the weapon. One has hit and another is on the way.

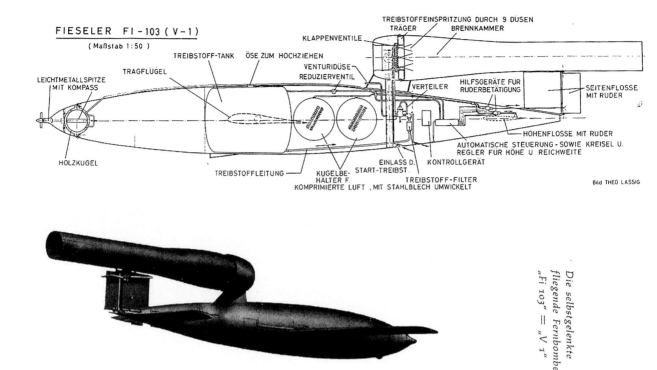

FIESELER FI - 103 (V-1)
(Maßstab 1:50)

LEICHTMETALLSPITZE MIT KOMPASS
TRAGFLÜGEL
TREIBSTOFF-TANK
ÖSE ZUM HOCHZIEHEN
KLAPPENVENTILE
TREIBSTOFFEINSPRITZUNG DURCH 9 DÜSEN
TRÄGER
BRENNKAMMER
VENTURIDÜSE
REDUZIERVENTIL
VERTEILER
HILFSGERÄTE FÜR RUDERBETÄTIGUNG
SEITENFLOSSE MIT RUDER
HÖHENFLOSSE MIT RUDER
AUTOMATISCHE STEUERUNG - SOWIE KREISEL U. REGLER FÜR HÖHE U. REICHWEITE
HOLZKUGEL
TREIBSTOFFLEITUNG
KUGELBE-HALTER F. KOMPRIMIERTE LUFT , MIT STAHLBLECH UMWICKELT
EINLASS D. START-TREIBST.
KONTROLLGERÄT
TREIBSTOFF-FILTER

Bild THEO LASSIG

Die selbstgelenkte fliegende Fernbombe „Fi 103" = „V 1"

The Fiesler Fi 103, known to Allies as the V-1 "buzz bomb" was produced first and in large numbers. (Bundesarchiv)

Still, the Allies couldn't ignore the possibility that something like a larger version of the German "smart bombs" was about to appear, something more destructive and with greater range. The German "wonder weapons" that Allied Intelligence was searching for were said to be strategic surface-to-surface weapons—ranging far beyond the battlefield and with larger warheads and possessing some sort of guidance. In many respects, the V-weapons were needed because the Luftwaffe had never developed a bomber capability with range, payload and numbers similar to RAF Bomber Command and the USAAF Eighth Air Force. Unlike all the other weapons, these new systems would have the capability to launch themselves. But through the summer of 1943, nothing was identified that could threaten large targets at long range.

The English people had suffered through the Blitz and stood fast until the RAF (and the invasion of the Soviet Union) made wholesale aerial bombing infeasible for the Germans. No one in the UK wanted to go through another period like that. In 1944, with the Allied invasion of Normandy imminent, German attacks on ports, dumps and troop concentrations in southern England would make an already difficult endeavor even more difficult.

The world was about to change forever. At all costs, the Allies wanted to deny any new initiative to the enemy. A critical stage of the war was just months away and the nuclear and missile genies were about to come out of the bottle, but only a few elites on either side knew anything about that—and none of them could guess how it might turn out or what it could mean. It was the job of Allied Intelligence to understand and hold back that dawn, or at least to insure that the enemy did not control it…and there wasn't much time left.

It was a struggle of epic scope and moment—a hunt the Allies couldn't afford to lose.

---

1 The 210mm "Pariskanone" fired a 70lb round a maximum of eighty-two miles. Just over 200 rounds were fired in the summer of 1918.

2 Heavy Gustav was a railroad gun that fired a seven-ton shell up to twenty-nine miles. It fired forty-eight rounds destroying several forts in the Crimea in July 1942, then was dismantled and sent back to Krupp for refurbishing, where it languished for want of a target. Depending upon what source you use, a sister gun, "Dora", was never used or was briefly deployed to Stalingrad, never fired, then was dismantled in Germany.

3 Sir William Congreve's "war rocket" came from an idea picked up in India and was first used in the siege of Boulogne in 1806. These rockets had warheads from three to twenty-four pounds and were launched at a high angle, ranging to 3,000 yards.

4 The "Katyusha" came in various sizes. The launcher was a simple metal rack holding as many as thirty-six rockets of from 75mm to 132mm. The US systems mounted racks holding sixteen to sixty 4.5-inch rockets and ranged out to nearly three miles. The "Nebelwerfer" came in 150mm and 210mm versions, both large enough to hold chemical as well as high explosive loads. It had a range of just under five miles and was fired on a relatively flat trajectory.

5 The PC1400X, "Fritz-X," was a 400kg armour piercing bomb with radio (later wire) control. A sister weapon, the Henschel 293 was a 550kg HE bomb with a rocket motor and radio control. Both were first used in August 1943. (See Hallion article.)

6 Azon was an "azimuth only" radio guidance system that could be applied to any large gravity bomb. It was used with some success in Italy and CBI in 1944 though *Combat Chronology* (p. 357) says attacks on five bridges in France on 31 May 1944 were "unsuccessful". Grapefruit was a 2000lb. bomb fitted with small wooden wings and tail, dropped on a preset glide path. On 28 May 1944, 116 of them were dropped on Cologne, Germany. Some thirty-five hit within Cologne. Others wound up as much as seventeen miles from their target.

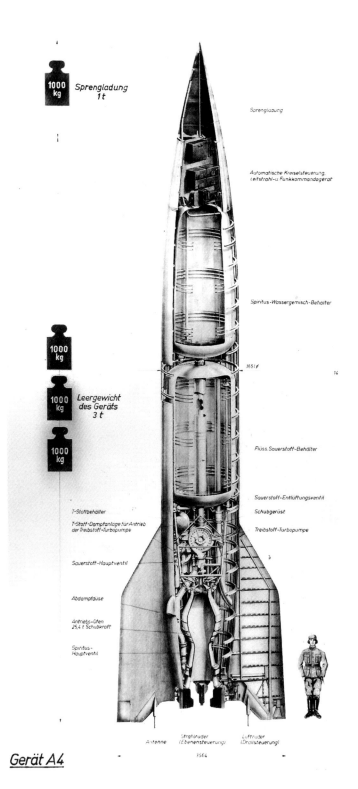

Sprengladung
1t

1000 kg

1000 kg

Leergewicht
des Geräts
3 t

1000 kg

Sprengladung

Automatische Kreiselsteuerung,
Leitstrahl-u Funkkommandogerat

Spiritus-Wassergemisch-Behälter

1651 f

14

T-Stoffbehälter

T-Stoff-Dampfanlage fur Antrieb
der Treibstoff-Turbopumpe

Sauerstoff-Hauptventil

Abdampfdüse

Antriebs-Öfen
25,4 t Schubkraft

Spiritus-
Hauptventil

Flüss.Sauerstoff-Behälter

Sauerstoff-Entlüftungsventil

Schubgerüst

Treibstoff-Turbopumpe

Antenne

Strahlruder
(Ebenensteuerung)

Luftruder
(Drallsteuerung)

3564

Gerät A4

The A4 rocket, known to the Allies as the V-2. (NASM)

16

Chapter II

TOOLS OF THE HUNT

ORIGINS

In the First World War aerial photography had been used to map enemy trench lines, look for indications of an offensive, or occasionally venture to the rear far enough to locate depots. As the Second World War loomed it was realized that the whole of an enemy "war-making structure" had to be exposed. Both the Germans and the French were ahead of England in concepts and practices of strategic photoreconnaissance. Britain (and the US) began World War II with aerial photography aircraft, equipment, skills and mind-sets oriented to mapping or purely tactical "front line" applications (*Eye of Intelligence*, p. 19-21. Hereafter noted as *Eye*).

A leisurely training of PIs began again in 1925, but by 1935 they were still "salvaging stereoscopic equipment left over from World War One." These were quickly proven to be utterly inadequate for the three major tasks of Photo Intelligence: determining threat; identifying targets[1]; and reporting battle results. By the middle of January 1940 the RAF had lost forty aircraft (mostly Blenheim bombers carrying cameras) photographing 2,500 square miles of the continent. The Blenheim had a range of nearly 2,000 miles and was faster than most fighters in 1935, but its 260mph top speed and 27K altitude were no longer good enough by 1940. While used for tactical photo work until 1944, the aircraft was utterly outclassed for deep penetration missions. In the opening months of the war, ten Blenheims were lost trying to photograph the Ruhr factories from 10K altitude in support target selection by Bomber Command, without returning a single photo (Douglas Kendall's unpublished memoirs, quoted in the Autumn 2007 Medmenham Club Newsletter, p. 25 and *Air Spy*, p. 30). The RAF also had the 90mph Lysander intended for use photographing the "front lines" and hopelessly inadequate for survival in defended airspace. The French had lost sixty photographing 6,000 square miles. It was obvious that as the Germans gained control of the ground and air, the Allies would soon be denied visual confirmation of anything they wanted to know about occupied Europe.

A pioneer RAF photo interpreter, Wing Commander Douglas Kendall, wrote, "On the British side, there was virtually no P.I. unit when war broke out, although one existed on paper as a branch of the Air Ministry. Accordingly in September, 1939, a small number of civilians were picked somewhat at random, put in uniform and instructed to interpret photographs. As they had no idea what to look for, no photographs to interpret, and would not have been listened to even if they had found anything, it was hardly surprising that PR/PI played no part in the 1940 battle

One of the first PR "Spitfires", a Mk 1 with Sidney Cotton's innovative modifications, painted "duck-egg green". Seclin, France sometime between Nov 1939 and Apr 1940. (Medmenham Club)

for France and that in consequence no one knew where the enemy were or when they would strike"(Kendall, Autumn 2007 Medmenham Club Newsletter, p. 24. RAF hierarchy is Flight-Squadron-Wing-Group).

Fortunately, just before the start of the war an "unofficial" photo reconnaissance effort had begun under partnership between Britain's Secret Intelligence Service (MI6) and a unique and visionary aviator and inventor, Australian Frederick Sidney Cotton. Cotton had worked with MI6 before the war began, taking covert aerial photographs of industries and military build-ups in Germany. Details of those flights and the early days of PI in the Second World War are well told in both *Air Spy* and *Eye of Intelligence*. Cotton flew his own twin-engine Lockheed 12A Electra Jr., fitted with extra tanks, secret camera windows and painted duck-egg green so it virtually disappeared when at altitude, to covertly photograph industrial targets deep inside Germany and Italian territory in the Mediterranean.[2]

Cotton's efforts were so productive that his operation was absorbed into the RAF on 22 September 1939. Cotton's only demand was that he have a free hand because he was going to have to quickly do a lot of "unorthodox" things in organization, procurement and operations. The unit was to be administered by Fighter Command because they wouldn't be a 'client' for the photographs and thus probably wouldn't interfere (*Air Spy*, p. 19). Meanwhile, Cotton had

RAF Supermarine "Spitfire" stripped of guns and painted a deep gloss blue were given cameras and larger fuel tanks for high altitude, long-range photorecon work. This is probably from 1943. The slight "notch" under the roundel is a window for a vertical camera. (NASM)

18

The birthplace of modern photoreconnaissance, Heston Aerodrome, southwest of London, probably from about the time Prime Minister Chamberlain returned here from his October 1938 Munich meeting with Hitler—about a year before Cotton's covert operation began. (Medmenham Club)

determined that to get the imagery Britain needed, he required the highest flying, longest ranging, fastest aircraft he could lay hands on—establishing the model for photo recce aircraft for the next half-century.

The German Target Graphic on the next page shows no indication that the Luftwaffe was aware of Cotton's secret aerial reconnaissance flying from Heston. The Aerodrome, photographed on 15 August 1940, was labelled a civilian field (Zivilflugplatz). The quality of imagery isn't good enough for all the annotations to be the result of photo interpretation—particularly details like the "iron construction" noted on annotation #2. Identification of hangars, workshops and administrative/billeting facilities probably came from pre-war German "tourists" freely going through Heston's terminal. The M4 now runs east-west through the landing ground.

The air war over England had just begun and Heston's grass landing area had been marked with dark lines to break up the open area, probably not so much to camouflage the field as to keep it from being a navigational marker for important targets closer to London. Note the

Maßstab etwa 1:9 200

500 0 500 1000 m
(1cm = 92 m)

Southall

Heston

GB 10 105
(2.Ang.)

Bild:
0663/40/120(V)
(Lfl 2)
vom
15.8.40.

Karte GB/E
1:100 000
Blatt 34

Länge
(westl.Greenw.):
0 ° 23' 40 "
Nördl. Breite:
51 ° 29' 10 "
(   )

Mißweisung:
– 10 ° 55'
(Mitte 1938)

Zielhöhe
über N N 30 m

1956

nach London (Mitte)
21 Km Luftlinie

Ⓐ GB 10 105 Zivilflugplatz

1)	8 Flugzeughallen, 6 eng zusammengebaut , verschiedene Dacharten	etwa	10 800 qm
2)	Werfthalle, Eisenkonstruktion	etwa	4 300 qm
3)	Flugzeugfabrikhalle, massiv, Satteldach	etwa	2 500 qm
4)	Werkstattgebäude, an 1) angebaut	etwa	1 200 qm
5)	Unterkunfts-u. Verwaltungsgebäude, massiv, versch. "	etwa	1 900 qm
6)	Nebengebäude	etwa	1 800 qm

Gleisanschluß nicht vorhanden   bebaute Fläche   etwa 22 500 qm
Erweiterung des Platzes möglich.   ==

disruptive lines pretending to be hedges aren't seen on the oblique photo from a year or two earlier.

August 15th was "Eagle Day" and airfields were a major objective as the Luftwaffe tried to saturate British air defenses. I may be wrong but it looks to me like the base imagery for this graphic was taken during a strike. Those ragged puffs (see arrows) starting just to the left of the annotation "A" and running up and left to just beyond the Terminal (annotation "5") look like bomb

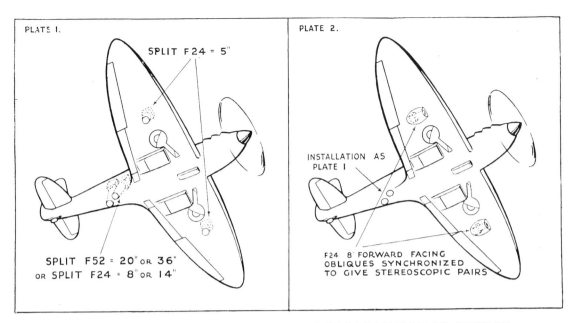

PLATE I.

SPLIT F24 = 5"

SPLIT F52 = 20" OR 36"
OR SPLIT F24 = 8" OR 14"

PLATE 2.

INSTALLATION AS
PLATE I

F24 8" FORWARD FACING
OBLIQUES SYNCHRONIZED
TO GIVE STEREOSCOPIC PAIRS

CAMERA INSTALLATIONS IN THE RECONNAISSANCE SPITFIRE

The diagrams above are typical camera installations in the reconnaissance Spitfire. Plate I : High altitude split vertical layout. Plate 2 : Low altitude forward facing oblique, F.24-8" cameras are used for this installation. Below : The first F.24 camera with 5" lens to be installed in a Spitfire wing by the R.A.E. during October, 1939.

CAMERA MOTOR

F24 CAMERA

impacts. It looks like another stick of bombs running up toward the small hangar on the far left end of the facilities. Within a few weeks Luftwaffe destruction of the facilities drove Cotton's operation (probably in the large hangar at annotation #3) from Heston to Benson in Oxfordshire.

Pulling every string he knew, Cotton obtained two priceless Mark I Spitfires on 16 October 1939. Cockpits were given a sliding hood and the aircraft were stripped of all excess weight (including guns) to increase speed, ceiling and range. Cotton then added cameras and rigged the aircraft to keep the lenses, film and batteries from freezing at altitudes up to 35,000 feet— something no one else was doing in those days. Unlike the Luftwaffe Ju 86P high-altitude reconnaissance aircraft, aircrew in RAF Spitfires and Mosquitoes routinely operated at 30,000 to 40,000 feet without a pressurized cockpit. The planes were later painted a dark "PR Blue", making them hard to see at altitude.

The first operational PR mission of a Cotton modified "Spit" occurred on 18 November 1939. Prior to April 1940, some of the early missions were flown from Seclin, near Lille, France.

Flying out of Heston Aerodrome, eleven miles WSW of Charing Cross, a lone Cotton Spitfire successfully photographed 5,000 square miles of German Europe by mid-1940 (*Air Spy*, p. 30). The 5" square exposures were of very small scale (1:65-70,000) and provided little intelligence but were far better than nothing and fine for maps. Film processing, plotting and initial interpretation occurred at Heston, but the cameras and lenses were designed to get a reasonable 1:10,000 scale image from below 10,000 feet altitude. With Cotton's Spits three or four times higher, the imagery scale was very small. Kendall wrote that the scale was 1:35,000. Actually, with the 3.25" and 5" lenses in use at the time the scale was more like 1:80,000 to 1:120,000, much too small for detailed analysis (Kendall, Spring 2008 Medmenham Club Newsletter, p. 21). True, the cameras collected about twelve times the ground coverage but seeing all but the most obvious things required considerable magnification and stereoscopic viewing for any sort of detailed interpretation. This resulted in creation of an equally unofficial activity to exploit the film using the facilities and enlargement equipment of the Aircraft Operating Company, a mapping business in Wembley, north of Heston Aerodrome. This Company had optics and machines designed for precise measurement on very small-scale aerial photos. Getting larger scale imagery from high altitude was months in the future, after longer focal-length lenses (such as 36") were developed and fitted into the aircraft.

Originally all photo interpretation was done at Wembley, but within a few months Wick, St. Eval and Heston got First Phase sections (*Air Spy*, p. 50 & 54). RAF and WAAF interpreters joined those of the Air Operating Company at Wembley and, in an anagram of PDU and AOC the Wembley PI operation was grandly named PADUOC HOUSE.

Everyone knew it wasn't an ideal situation, but you fight with what you have. Those early missions concentrated upon "finding out what was going on", following known enemy assets (aircraft and ships), and assessing damage (mostly from bombing); in modern terms, creating a data base. The Damage Assessment missions were some of the most dangerous since when Bomber Command came at night, the Germans quickly learned that a lone Spit would visit the same target within a day or two.

There were mistakes and failures along with the experimentation and successes, but modern PR/PI was beginning. Military historian John Keegan has written: "The intelligence of imagery is frustratingly rich—many needles but in a vast haystack" (Intelligence in War, p. 22). Cotton's efforts were beginning a systematic sorting through that haystack.

Based upon their early success, the Cotton organization, initially known as the "Heston Special

Flight" (for experimental PR purposes), added Spits though every one of those aircraft was like gold to the RAF. For security reasons, the name of the Heston Special Flight was changed to Number 2 Camouflage Unit in November and to the Photographic Development Unit in January 1940 (*Air Spy*, p. 28). By July 1940 it had grown into the Photo Reconnaissance Unit (PRU). Cotton's success "was based on the unexpected – in other words, on his non-conformity. He hated red tape and had no qualms about cutting it. This worked wonders in getting the unit going but was the despair of the RAF administrative channels. Consequently the Heston Special Flight became an ugly duckling which was thrown from one RAF Command to another at about monthly intervals as senior officers sought to rid themselves of the headache" (Kendall, Spring 2008 Medmenham Club Newsletter, p. 20-21). Others involved have written that uncontested success eventually made the PRU and its infant PI effort something everyone wanted to claim—there weren't many successes to boast in those days. In the unseemly bureaucratic scramble to assume military control of an obviously thriving Intelligence operation, Cotton was commissioned, promoted to Wing Commander, then shuffled aside in June. Bomber Command, the Army and the Royal Navy all wanted the unit, each knowing it would be a major consumer of the product and not wanting to have their requirements filtered through another organization. A clever compromise assigned the unit to RAF Costal Command (not a customer), giving the unit a priceless degree of autonomy during the early days of growth. By July there were PRU detachments in Scotland and Cornwall. In September 1940, German bombing of Heston destroyed five Spitfires and Cotton's Lockheed, forcing the PRU to relocate west to RAF Benson, a few miles south of Oxford (*Air Spy*, p. 58). The original photo flight was expanded to form 106 Group at Benson on 19 October 1942. Squadrons 541 (the original PRU), 542 and 543 flew Spitfires while 540 and 544 Squadrons flew de Havilland Mosquitoes from Leuchars, Scotland and Benson respectively.

Only late in the war did 106 Group operate from one place. The 540 Squadron didn't move

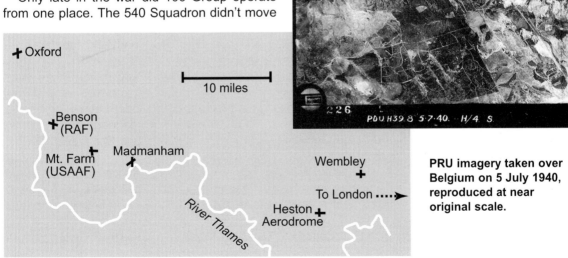

PRU imagery taken over Belgium on 5 July 1940, reproduced at near original scale.

to Benson until 29 Feb 1944 (by this time it was flying Spitfires). Dedicated to cover of France, 543Sq converted to Mosquitoes in 1943 and disbanded on 18 October 1943. Based at Benson, 544Sq operated a detachment of Mosquitoes from Leuchars in Scotland.

When the USAAF 13th Photo Squadron moved into Mount Farm, a few miles from Benson, in March 1943, their F-4s (photo version of the Lockheed P-38) routinely carried five cameras, bringing back 2,000 feet of large-scale film or more on each sortie. Col. Elliott Roosevelt (third child of FDR) had made a name for himself commanding the Allied Photo Wing and 3rd Photo Group in North Africa during Operation Torch.[3] In the summer of 1943 he was moved to Mount Farm to head the 7th Photo Group and 325th Recce Wing.[4] "The US photographic squadrons were among the earliest to reach Europe after Pearl Harbour and established themselves initially

USAAF Lockheed "Lightning" F4, photo version of the P-38E/F. Note camera windows and solid "PR Blue" paint job devised by the RAF PRU to make an aircraft harder to see at high altitude.

Technicians loading 24" K-17 Split Verts in an F5. A pair of 6" K-17s and a 24" K-18 are waiting on the stand. Note large magazines holding 500' of film. USAAF reconnaissance film was 9.5" wide. Some film in "strike cameras" placed in bombers, was narrower.

With guns removed, the "Lightning's" large open nose permitted installation of multiple cameras—in this case six (three K-17 6" lens Tri-Met cameras look left, right and down; a 24" vertical, and two 24" split verticals). Hoses take air and heated fluids to operate cameras and keep them from freezing at high altitude.

at Mount Farm, an airfield five miles away from Benson, the main RAF photographic base. The nearness contributed to close co-operation. Initially they arrived with P.38 (Lockheed Lightning) aircraft. It was soon found that this aircraft, when loaded, would not fly high enough and crew losses started to run too high. To overcome this, Elliott borrowed Spitfires and Mosquitoes from the RAF and meanwhile put pressure on Washington to improve the performance of the P.38s. He even took a team of leading reconnaissance pilots back to the USA for a short trip to give manufacturers a chance to build into the aircraft the specifications dictated by operational experience. As a result of Elliott's efforts the performance of the P.38s was improved greatly and they gave excellent service during the closing years of the war" *(Douglas* Kendall *Unpublished Memoirs,* p. 75. Hereafter noted as Kendall). Kendall may actually be referring to two different events. The USAAF 3rd PG was in England at Membury and Steeple Morden from June to November 1942—on the way to Operation Torch. Part of this time it was commanded by Major Elliott Roosevelt who returned to England as a Colonel to command the 7th PG. The first US photo planes at Mount Farm were in March 1943. Author Glen Infield quotes the CO of 13th PRS saying Roosevelt's

Benson Airdrome south of Oxford, 23 July 1945. The larger planes (upper right) are Mosquitoes, the smaller are Spitfires, and two four-engine aircraft near the hangars I can't ID. (Medmenham Club)

predecessor, Col. Homer Sanders, was the one who got the Spits and Roosevelt insisted that "American pilots were going to fly American planes" (*Unarmed and Unafraid*, p. 87).

By the spring of 1943, all the photoreconnaissance assets employed for deep penetration missions were in place and ready, among other high priority tasks, to perform the search for the German "secret weapons."

Right: USAAF Photo reconnaissance base, Mount Farm, Oxfordshire, 18 April 1944. Aircraft present are F-5 "Lightning's" a few PR Spitfires, a B-25 and Eliot Roosevelt's personal B-17 (center left).

Below: One of my all time favorite aerial photos of the war, an enlagement of April 1944 "local" coverage shows "reverse lend-lease" with three PR Spitfire Mk XI getting their roundels repainted to USAAF livery for use by 7PG.

Danesfield House, Oxfordshire. Work done in trailers (arrow) included inventing almost all the techniques, systems and procedures that would be used in aerial photo interpretation for years to come. Photo taken in 1945 by a low-flying F5 from the USAAF 325th Recon Wing.

MEDMENHAM

The PI operation was bombed out of Wembley on 2 October 1940 and initial interpretation followed the aircraft to Benson. Detailed and follow-on interpretation was relocated west along the Thames to Danesfield House. Initially named the Photo Interpretation Unit (PIU), the activity was renamed Central Interpretation Unit (CIU) in January 1941 (*Eye*, p. 36). The story is much more complicated than related above (see *Eye of Intelligence* for the best detailed relation of these events).

    "The unit was housed in a large country house on the banks of the River Thames near a village called Medmenham. The great advantage of the house was that it was very large and modern. In other words, it had plumbing that worked and was centrally heated" (Kendall, p. 80). This location was conveniently six miles SSW of a major customer, Bomber Command Hq at High Wycombe, and twelve miles ESE of the major supplier at Benson. Nissen huts were added in the open space between the house and river to provide additional space for PI and photo lab work and the place was designated RAF Station Medmenham with Group Captain Peter Stewart as Station Commander.

"Continuous processing machines were erected for the development of duplicate negatives. Duplicating machines had been brought into use and the latest type Multiprinters with automatic exposure control became available to the Section together with rectifying enlargers[5] for the production of controlled mosaics. In addition considerable facilities were introduced for making very big enlargements required, in particular, for the production of photographic skins needed for model making. An efficient Rotaprint Section was also installed for the production of target maps.

By the time all this apparatus was installed, the Photographic Section became the equivalent of a large and efficient commercial photographic organization. Much of the apparatus was non-standard RAF and required some "robbing" of commercial establishments" (Medmenham Collection Archive). The urgency of the situation resulted in intelligence being "turned loose" to get the answers needed. No longer hampered by the bureaucratic procurement system, the photo lab and PI shops were probably better equipped for rapidly handling a large volume of aerial imagery than any other similar operation in the world. One time as many as 250 personnel worked in the Medmenham photo lab.

Lab work could also be done in the collection squadrons, speeding up the first critical PI reporting. That meant the main lab could concentrate on making all the copies of prints needed for subsequent PI and distribution to other customers.

Creating a cadre of photo interpreters was another task entirely. Those skills came only with experience. "The success of PR was, of course, based in the first instance on the ability of our air forces to secure the necessary photographs, without

WILLIAMSON MANUFACTURING CO. LTD. *Photographic Engineers*

WILLIAMSON

PHOTOGRAPHIC LORRIES

The Williamson Manufacturing Company can supply all types of mobile photographic units. Lorries can be equipped with developing and printing apparatus to the requirements of the user. The Multiprinter machines have been specially designed for operation in vehicles. Specifications and drawings can be supplied on request.

The illustration shows the interior of standard Photographic Lorries with developing, enlarging and printing equipment.

Prices and sizes vary according to equipment required.

LITCHFIELD GARDENS, WILLESDEN, LONDON, N.W.10
PAGE 26

the enemy being able to deny any target to us. However these would have been useless without an effective interpretation organization to extract information and to put it into intelligible form in the right channels.

"The PI Unit that came into being in July 1940, immediately following the collapse of France was such an organization, its success being based on the combined ability of the remarkable group of interpreters in the central unit. They were all carefully selected and had to pass a

29

rigorous training course. Large numbers of the officers were famous university professors; professional men and engineers of almost every type were also included in the group. The theatrical profession contributed five or six members and we even had a famous choreographer. We recruited en bloc the whole archaeological school from Cambridge on the grounds that they knew how to piece together information from scraps of evidence. We had a tobacco grower from Rhodesia, a Coptic scholar from the Sudan and a famous British brass rubber who specialized in studying old tombstones.

"Typical of our university professors was Dr Hamshaw-Thomas, from Cambridge. He was one of our senior officers and for the purposes of the war had abandoned his gown and assumed the guise of an air force officer with the rank of Wing Commander. I well remember on one occasion taking Field Marshall Smuts, the South African Prime Minister, into Hamshaw-Thomas' office for a discussion. After it was over and we were out of earshot, the Field Marshall turned to me and said, 'Do you know, that fellow is the world's leading palaeobotanist', no mean compliment from someone who was a renowned botanist in his own right" (Kendall, p. 74). Wing Commander Hugh Hamshaw-Thomas had been an RFC photographic officer in 1917. As Chief of Third Phase Interpretation in 1943, it was he and his Army opposite number, Major Norman Falcon, who set up Flight Lieutenant Andre Kenny and Army Captain Robert Rowell in Third Phase sub-sections to investigate Peenemünde (*Eye*, p. 189, and *Air Spy*, p. 148-149).

The new organization was staffed by both RAF and WAAF personnel (including some female Section Officers) and operated on a 24-hour basis with three shifts. Anyone who did the job well was accepted in this open integration that demonstrated attitudes rather ahead of their time in the military. Apparently an invasion threat can also be the "mother of invention". Other services, Canadians and Americans were gradually added to expand the unit capability. The Prime Minister's daughter, Sarah, was a WAAF officer at Medmenham, and Major John Churchill, son of Winston's brother, also worked there.

"The various people in the unit were so well integrated that it made little difference whether a British, Canadian or American officer was charge of each section. Since (the ACIU) supplied information to all services, it had proved impossible to place it under a routine military formation and still satisfy all units that they were getting equal priority in the use of its services. In any case, the unit was made up of sub-units loaned from all three services of the various allies. A compromise was therefore reached whereby the RAF administered the base, while the

Recce pilots reviewing film of a mission with an Intel Officer. The roll of RAF 5.5" imagery shows how few exposures the small, wing-mounted cameras could return. With each frame so valuable, recon planes flew missions with cameras off between objectives, but an experienced pilot would divert from course and click off a few exposures if something caught his eye.

Typical First or Second Phase PI shop, this one USAAF. Drafting tables and fluorescent lights were ideal for working on prints. Prints from earlier missions were stored in the boxes seen on the right. (USAF)

operations came under the Allied Joint Chiefs of Staff. While it is normally unwise to split operational and administrative responsibility, it worked well in this case, thanks to the personalities involved" (Kendall, p. 77-78). Kendall added, "Needless to say, there were minor problems. For instance, placing all services and all allies in one unit under RAF administration automatically condemned the US and Canadian components to RAF rations, with the consequent overdose of Brussels sprouts. It also created a crisis amongst the batmen, or more correctly, batwomen, since all the batmen had been replaced by WAAFs. RAF units perform the same function either each man for himself or by detailing some of the GIs. Batmen or batwomen just do not exist in US units. The US units attached to us seemed to be very short of GIs and consequently we never found that we could call on them for their share of batmen. Our ration of batwomen had to be spread very thinly therefore to cover US as well as British officers. This was all taken in good heart."

Another near-by country house (Nuneham Park) was appropriated to serve as a PI school. Initially billeted with the surrounding populace, eventually a camp was created under the trees near the house to serve the fast-growing compliment. Apparently mildew was a serious problem in the huts under the trees for camouflage. "The camp came as quite a shock to the US personnel, not to mention the Canadians, who had been used to living in dry centrally heated atmospheres" (Kendall, p. 80). In March 1942 the new Ally recognizing the urgent need for combat use of aerial imagery, The Army Air Forces created an Intelligence School at Harrisburg,

Pennsylvania (*Air Spy*, p. 110-111). This was about the same time the USAAF realized that the aircraft they had for photo collection were too "low and slow" to survive in contested air and quickly adapted the P-38 for aerial recon work. They realized that learning from the best in the business would be beneficial and by June American Army and Navy personnel were being trained by Medmenham, changing the US aerial imagery emphasis from mapping to intelligence. The techniques they learned were quickly spread to US forces throughout the world.

HOW IT WORKED

Photo reconnaissance missions were flown for one or both of two reasons: to get coverage of an area to see what was there; or, to get pre- or post-strike or specific coverage of one or more designated targets. Early in the war a Cottonized Spitfire could carry two cameras (in the gun compartments of each wing). Each camera brought back about 150 feet of very small scale imagery ("Evidence In Camera," ACIU magazine, March 1945, p. 10-11). Initial use was Williamson F.24 camera with a 5" lens and 125 exposures in the magazine. Exposures were typically 7" x 8" and imagery scales ranged from 1:79,000 to 1:82,000.

True to their movie heritage, early British cameras used sprocketed film. The example presented earlier in this book was taken by a PDU Spitfire over Belgium on 5 July 1940. It is a contact print, exactly the same size that came out of the aircraft, and shows the scale of collection with a short focal-length lens and 5" film. The reader can see how hard it was, even with considerable magnification, to get anything detailed without highly specialized equipment and training. Those cameras were designed for a taking altitude of 10,000 feet, but there wasn't much choice. The small cameras were available and they fit into the wing chord of the Spitfire. Burning a gallon of fuel a minute, weight was precious for long-range Spitfires and they had to remain at

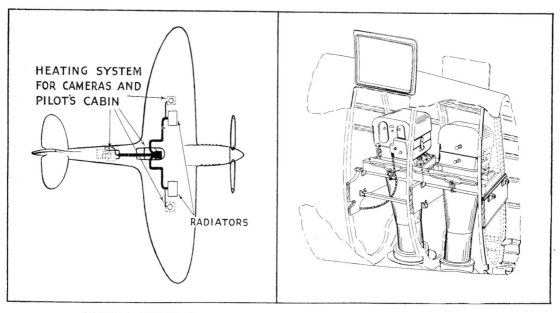

CAMERA HEATING
Diagram of camera heating in Spitfire which is produced by hot air from the cooling system.

CAMERA INSTALLATION
Installation of the F.52-36" split vertical camera with 36" lenses in a Spitfire fuselage.

high altitude to survive alone over Luftwaffe patrolled airspace, so the small cameras and lenses they mounted returned small-scale coverage—making it hard to see small objects or detail. Douglas Kendall wrote, "We were covering much of Germany on each flight, but the detail was so small that it was almost impossible to see the roads, let alone the traffic on them" (Kendall, Spring 2008 Medmenham Club Newsletter, p. 21).

By 1941, the obvious need for a better look at enemy territory resulted in Spitfires mounting four cameras. The short focal length original cameras provided area coverage and the addition of a 24" or 36" lens vertical camera mounted behind the pilot brought back a larger look at specific objectives directly below the aircraft. Longer focal lengths compensated for higher taking altitudes, returning film with larger scale and therefore more detail for PIs to work with. A 36" lens from 35,000' yielded a scale of around 1:11,750. (1/4" on the photo = 250' on the ground.) The length of film carried in each camera was doubled and 7" wide film came into use. However, the larger scale greatly reduced the area covered, so Spits and Mossies soon mounted a pair of large-lens cameras (24" or 36") angled slightly to each side, nearly doubling the area covered but still provide stereo ("Evidence In Camera", ACIU magazine, March 1945, p. 10). Split-Verts became a staple of aerial photo collection for the rest of the war (and far beyond).

RAF de Havilland "Mosquito", note circular camera windows. (NASM)

"Cottonized" photoreconnaissance was so successful and considered so important to the war effort that, in July 1941, the RAF's first Mosquito was flown to Benson by Geoffrey de Havilland himself (*Air Spy*, p. 92). It was quickly decided to send the first "Mossies" to Scotland to range over Scandinavia, the Baltic ports and northern Germany. A Navigator providing another set of hands on long missions improved success on long missions. Faster than most fighters above 40,000 feet, the Mossie could go anywhere within range and was almost immune to interception until the advent of the Me 262 jet fighter. I consider the Mosquito the best photo reconnaissance aircraft of the war.

The incredible twin-engined de Havilland DH 98 Mosquito, stripped for recon work, routinely carried four to six cameras and could fly higher, farther and faster than a Mark I Spitfire—more important, it could outpace Luftwaffe interceptors at high altitude.

While most photo recce was done from high altitude, some targets required low passes called "dicing" after the First World War saying that flying "on the deck" in enemy territory was "dicing with the devil". Low altitude photo collection relied upon cameras shooting out to the side or mounted to look forward. The Damage Assessment (DA) function was also supported by cameras mounted in some of the strike aircraft. That imagery was used to tell where the bombs fell, but it too was forwarded to Medmenham for exploitation. Particularly early in the war the DA work by PIs (what we now call Bomb Damage Assessment or BDA) could be very unpopular since they often had to report that the target was completely missed, or the bombs went onto a decoy (See *Air Spy*, p. 63-77). I can sympathize, having first-hand experience in Vietnam seeing unwanted answers from PIs on post-strike recce met with rejection and anger by "operators"— some things don't change. Occasionally the bombing photos also showed something new and different of intelligence value beyond the falling and exploding ordnance.

Several examples of each of these types of imagery collection are included in this book.

As soon as an aircraft recovered the film was downloaded and processed. Speed was the name of the game and the work was quite manpower intensive. The RAF used highly flammable Cellulose Nitrate-base film throughout the war because of its resolution and because it allowed them to process on machines that were essentially large version of movie film processors. Safety Film was used by the USAAF and that necessitated a much slower process of cutting a roll of unprocessed film into 100' lengths and winding it back and forth in a series of tanks containing developer, wash, fix and final wash, then printing one exposure at a time. USAAF reconnaissance and mapping missions

Long focal-length cameras heading for a PR Mosquito. Probably Mt. Farm in 1944.

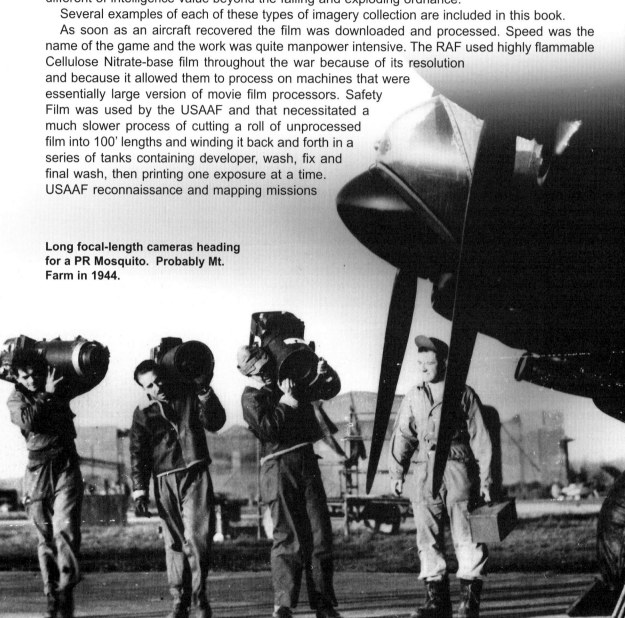

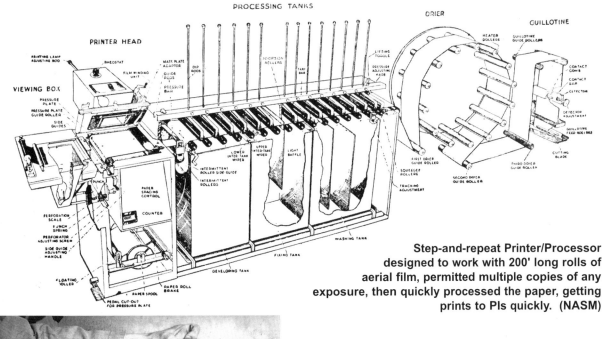

Step-and-repeat Printer/Processor designed to work with 200' long rolls of aerial film, permitted multiple copies of any exposure, then quickly processed the paper, getting prints to PIs quickly. (NASM)

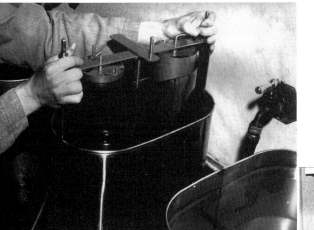

USAAF processing of Safety Film and roll paper was done in dark-room tanks. Initially wound through developer, fix and washes by hand, later a motor drive was provided.

Third Phase PI doing a detailed analysis of every building and machine at a target. In this case the Port of Hamburg.

This could be First or Second Phase PI writing a report using stereoscope, grease pencil, tube magnifiers and target lists.

stopped using the dangerous Nitrate-base film in early 1942 in favour of Acetate-base Safety Film despite its lower resolution and light sensitivity.

Once the negatives were processed, paper print positives of the critical points were quickly produced and delivered, often still wet, to First Phase PIs who were stationed at or near the airfield. Those PIs were responsible for determining two things: were mission objectives covered, and what was their status? The interpretation focus, like the recce mission itself, tended to jump from objective to objective with only a cursory scan of any intervening frames. Typical questions to resolve were: had warships moved, what type and how many aircraft were on an enemy field; how many invasion barges were in the Channel Ports; or, what was the damage done to a recently bombed target? Of course First Phase PIs would also report anything new and different they happened to notice during the "quick and dirty" first look at the take but, unless their collectors covered a target repeatedly, they were unlikely to recognize minor changes at anything beyond their mission objectives, nor did they have the enlargement options available at Medmenham. With a dozen or more aircraft at each recce base, the few collocated PIs were kept very busy on clear-weather days, commonly working through the night. Following exploitation, the original negative was sent to Medmenham to clear the decks for the next day of Ops. At Medmenham, the next phase of interpretation began.

This is a good place to explain PI. It is the job of the aerial photo interpreter to translate images into words—to extract every scrap of information from the film that some pilot risked his life to gather. Anyone can look at an aerial photograph and see things like a battleship, runway or bridge, but look through partial cloud cover, or camouflage the target, and it gets harder. Anyone can see an airplane on the ground, but what type is it? What threat does it pose? Does it have any modifications indicating new technology? What is the plane when you can't see the whole thing? Like any skill, it takes training and practice, to "read out" the imagery, to explain what is seen, to translate its nuances from an image into written intelligence that a layman can understand. Over the years I have observed that the best photo analysts have four traits in common: excellent spatial recognition and memory; patience (to get through the often tedious, methodical aspects of scanning every millimetre of each exposure); motivation, and experience. Starting from scratch, the British academy and certain professions were drawn upon to provide people with the first two attributes, and usually the third. Motivation came from the German Navy threatening Britain's lifelines, the Luftwaffe bombing its cities, and the Wehrmacht massing in Channel Ports to invade the island. In 1940-42, experience and skill came rapidly because there was a lot of film coming (and extremely high motivation) in so the "learning curve" was very steep.

Third Phase PI often resulted in Detailed Reports used by threat and target analysts.

At Medmenham, the negs would be printed again, usually in multiple copies. Processed negatives were loaded on Multiprinters that accepted 100 feet of roll negative and held up to 1,000 feet of roll paper. An operator could quickly make one or more copies of each exposure. The prints were processed, dried and came off the far end of the machine ready for PI and distribution to customers such as Bomber Command and the Air Staff. To keep them sorted out, all the prints of an individual mission were kept together in a box or boxes identified by date, taking organization, mission number and area covered. Plots of the imagery, or a pilot's trace, were also included in each box.

In Second Phase the mission was looked at as a whole, not as a collection of objectives, with every frame carefully scanned. Douglas Kendall was in charge of this small but growing phase in 1941 (*Air Spy*, p. 79). At Medmenham each mission was plotted, that is the "footprint" of the images on the ground was transferred to a 1:250,000 scale map so any PI could see exactly where the mission went and how far to each side of track the imagery reached. Plots of the imagery were necessary to tell other PIs if any targets or functions they were following might be covered (*Eye*, p. 42). Kendall mentions that by the end of the war sixty WAAF were working in the plotting and library sections. A single Spitfire could bring back 500 seven-inch square frames that would take an average of five hours to plot. Sometimes the exposures would run in a string of dozens of frames, sometimes it would be only five or six then camera-off and on to another objective. For a straight run, at least the first and last exposure would be plotted (the outline of coverage drawn on the map). Plotting was particularly useful for subsequent use of oblique coverage (looking right or left from vertical). The plots were even more important in the next

The Second World War Allied PI's main tool, a simple Stereoscope, showing how photo prints are overlapped so eyes focus on the same point to give depth perception. I believe the photo is Calais, 22 April 1944 (DAVA)

phase because they let analysts specializing in specific types of activity look at a mission (or research old missions) for the photos they needed.

Second Phase interpreters were of necessity "Jacks-of-All-Trades" and each mission was given a thorough scrub to extract every bit of intelligence possible. Second Phase PIs worked around-the-clock on rotating shifts as the missions rolled in and consolidated reports were issued every twelve hours, telling everything learned since the last report. Interpreters in this phase got to dig deeper on missions when weather denied or limited new input. The prints and negs on file in the CIU were also used to satisfy requests for copies by other activities, thus keeping the First Phase assets free for their high-pressure work closer to the aircraft.

Third Phase PIs may have had experience in either of the earlier phases of photo interpretation, but at Medmenham they were narrowly focused specialists, concentrating on topics such as industry and industrial decoys, camouflage, airfields, railroads and canals, merchant and naval assets, or finding German radar sites. There were about thirty of these sections concentrating on specific topics. Many of the Third Phase PIs had pre-war experience in their "specialty", i.e., engineers, architects, Army or Navy personnel. In this phase, interpreters needed an excellent memory and infinite patience. Manpower shortages resulted in women being recruited as PIs. It was quickly evident that women had the necessary patience and were particularly well suited for the meticulous, often tedious work, in all aspects of Third Phase exploitation. All Third Phase PIs got to know their subjects like the back of their hands and were able to recognize places and equipment at a glance. They could also quickly spot changes in those installations.

Where PIs in the first two phases worked against the clock, Third Phase PIs were researchers, a bit like bookworms using imagery, meticulous in their millimetre by millimetre examination of their subject. This did not mean they weren't often under extremes of pressure. It meant they took "shortcuts" or skimmed the prints at their peril. One of the most dangerous shortcomings of photo interpretation was that they tended to report on their assigned objectives; on things they knew and understood. If they didn't understand a technology, or didn't know what to look for, the interpretation could suffer. Another PI weakness was the difficulty in mentally rotating a vertical image of something new and unknown to visualize it in a more familiar horizontal plane to tell what the object was.[6] One example was "really an oversight on the part of the interpreters, in the failure to pick up the method of firing (referring to the V-2). For perhaps a year after we were aware that the enemy had a rocket we still believed that complex equipment, including guide rails, would be needed to launch it. It came as a complete surprise to us when we eventually found out that the rocket could be fired simply by standing it upright on any level ground. Unfortunately all the evidence was there on the photographs of Peenemünde and the interpreters overlooked it. The interpreter may miss important facts or may incorrectly interpret what he sees. Naturally the better the interpreter and the sounder his judgment the less the error" (Kendall, p. 161).

The oversight cited above occurred on Kendall's watch, so the comments above demonstrate his post-war honesty, however, "overlooked it" seems a bit of an overstatement, as the reader will see in the next chapter. This particular incident demonstrates how PIs are steered or hindered by what they understand, and well into 1944 there was no consensus or understanding of rocket size or launch method among Allied scientists, much less among PIs who knew little about the technology.

It was the task of Third Phase PIs to perform a forensic dissection of an enemy activity or installation. They not only identified new structures and equipment, but followed their charges mission-by-mission, noting minute changes that might further illuminate what was going on, be indications of intent or signal a new capability. Their job was to know everything knowable from imagery about enemy industries, installations, lines-of-communications, weapons or defenses and the narrow focus of each team allowed them to develop expertise in depth. This phase at Medmenham had a Section that made use of imagery from all missions covering an objective to make scale models and photo mosaics for use by decision-makers, targeteers and aircrew. The Medmenham map library eventually held a quarter of a million map sheets in various scales and the print library held some seven million prints and eighty thousand sorties covering vast areas of the world (*Eye*, p. 44).

Wing Commander Douglas Kendall and his deputy, USAAF Lt. Col. W J O'Connor, in the Medmenham Tech Control office.

It didn't do much good to have a library containing hundreds, eventually thousands, of boxes of aerial photo prints if you couldn't quickly locate coverage of a given place. Medmenham invented a system of transparent traces of each mission that could be laid over the appropriate map to quickly determine which mission(s) covered the area or target of PI interest.[7] This capability was never more useful than in the battle against the V-weapons when new discoveries triggered a look at earlier coverage to learn when an activity or structure was begun. Use of "comparative coverage" was another of the greatest legacies of Medmenham photo interpretation.

Many Third Phase PIs were by background, or of necessity quickly became, experts on their assigned specialties. They worked with paper prints and one of the most valuable tools they used was the simple little stereoscope with minimal magnification (2x or 3x). Perhaps because the first PI work at Wembley was using commercial mapping equipment designed to use stereo to get precise measurements from very small scale imagery, or perhaps because experience proved its advantage, almost all Allied PI was done using prints and stereo. Stereoscopic viewing facilitated identification and measurement, penetrated most camouflage and speeded interpretation. It also disclosed small objects not readily apparent to the naked eye. Throughout the war the skill and success of PI at Medmenham steadily increased—German PIs were less effective because they used film (often negs) and seldom used stereo. Not taking the time to make positive prints made the Germans faster in First Phase (See *World War II Photo Intelligence*). After the war we captured examples of German stereo-pairs and excellent Detailed Reports, particularly on Soviet Industry, but they apparently didn't have a highly developed Third Phase system like Medmenham.

"It might well be asked why the enemy had less information on our activities than we had on his. An examination of his sources quickly shows that neither the Germans nor the Japanese had developed the PR/PI source to anything like the same extent as the Allies, in spite of the fact that they appreciated its importance long before the Allies. They treated it purely in a tactical role"

(Kendall, p. 160. quote edited).

The need for intelligence and expanding volume of PR also expanded rapidly through the war and with all that film, all those objectives to report, all those customers to satisfy, it is easy to see why working at Medmenham was a highly demanding treadmill.

"Looking back on the whole affair we were certainly lucky to have had a highly interesting task, particularly since the main curse of so many war jobs is the utter boredom. Even so, it was not an experience which any of us would wish to repeat. The pressures and urgencies, with long hours seven days a week, were inevitably the forerunners of nervous disorders and the physical strain was considerably greater than would appear at first sight" (Kendall, p. 81). He added, "My US opposite number in the unit, Lt. Col. WJ O'Connor, was finally a victim of this. For almost three years of war we shared an office and were jointly responsible for the internal operations of the interpretation unit. Throughout this time we never had a major disagreement and Bill was a tower of strength, never flustered and perpetually calm under all conditions. He survived the war, but once it was over the strain had been too much and he had a serious nervous breakdown. Fortunately he recovered in due course."

Using what we now call "all source intelligence" was a serious problem in the 1940s as each source established tight controls to protect their methods and capabilities. "Ultra" was a highly restricted security compartment above "Most Secret", requiring special permission for access. "The fact that Douglas Kendall was the only officer in ACIU with 'Ultra' clearance must have severely limited the use of that source and the HUMINT material available to R V Jones was, I believe, only made available to ACIU on a very selective basis" (Chris Halshall, Medmenham Collection Curator).

Douglas Kendall pointed out that "in combating the V weapon program, it would only be proper to emphasize once more the vital part played in an investigation of this type by the other sources of information. These, in effect, directed the PR effort. They gave hints, as in the case of Peenemünde, of where we should obtain photographs and when. Perhaps 95 per cent of the time they were wrong or contained only half truths but without their direction, PI would be half blind. PI provided the answers, correctly and in great detail, but other sources provided the inspiration. PI in turn played a great part in checking the sources. With PI, reports which came in from elsewhere could be checked by simply examining the photographs, allowing us to test the reliability of a particular source. This is very important as reports need to be graded according to probability. ...successful intelligence is always a matter of checking one source against another" (Kendall, p. 162, quote edited).

The WW II Allied PI's main tool, a simple Stereoscope, showing how photo prints are overlapped so eyes focus on the same point to give depth perception. I believe the photo is Calais, 22 April 1944 (DAVA)

By 1944 there were 1,400 Royal Air Force and WAAF Officers and other ranks at ACIU with a grand total of 1,715 officers and other ranks. This latter figure includes Army, Navy, Canadians and USAAF personnel. Kendall wrote that "the unit consisted of some 550 officers and 3,000 other ranks of whom about half were American" (Spring 2008 Medmenham Newsletter, p. 23). By the end of the war Medmenham had produced just under twenty thousand photographic prints (roughly half of them in 1944 because of the V-weapons hunt and D-Day), duplicated 2,323 aerial recon sorties and constructed 5,489 Mosaics. The negative library held more than 35,000 images from RAF and USAAF sorties.

OTHER SOURCES

Other means of intelligence collection used in combination with photo to get a more complete picture of enemy activity were what we now call HUMINT and SIGINT.

Human source Intel can come from agents, sympathizers behind enemy lines, prisoners of war, pre-war tourists, third country Attaches, defectors and escapees. It is often information from deep in the warp and weft of the land and can provide details not apparent from any other source because it can be the product of tens of thousands of eyes and ears. People inside Nazi-controlled Europe risked torture and death to pass along things they heard and saw. Agents slipped behind enemy lines did the same. The disadvantages of human source intelligence are: often slow passage to someone who can use the information; something misunderstood by an untrained observer; uncertainty as to where what is being reported occurred; difficulty recognizing when you are getting the same thing reported from multiple sources and not multiple events; and, sorting out planted information. HUMINT, particularly from agents (spies), must be carefully disguised and narrowly disseminated to protect the life of the source. That too limits its utility.

Signals Intelligence is the "stealing" of electronic emissions out of the air. They might be radar, telemetry, aerial navigation beams, clear or encrypted radio transmissions. Of course the most valuable material was in the codes and ciphers unlocked at Bletchley Park under the codename ULTRA (this subset of SIGINT is called COMINT, or Communications Intelligence). The "captured" communications were things the enemy did not want the Allies to read but had to put out on the air because of time or geographic distance. SIGINT can expose enemy intent and capability and can give indications of things photo and human source should look for. It is weakest in providing locations (though Radio Direction Finding is generally reliable), and can only vacuum up what the enemy inadvertently puts into the air. The value of ULTRA was considered so precious that it was extremely "close hold" during the war (and long after) to protect the fact of interception, interception methods, and how good the Allies became at delving deep into what the Germans believed hidden and safe. Another disadvantage of SIGINT was that there could be a delay, sometimes quite long, between collection and decryption. If the delay was too long, the intelligence could be overtaken by events.

While both human and electronic collection were covert, operating in secret and depending upon picking up what the enemy inadvertently offered, aerial photography was overt: the enemy knew the planes were there, if not necessarily when the cameras were actually operating. Photo Recce was the only intelligence source that could go where something was needed and see what was happening, returning to base quickly with the information. The disadvantages of this source were its limited coverage and the problem of knowing where to look. PIs were often given carefully "sanitized" information gathered by agents on the Continent, but they were never told who the agents were. Nor, with the exception of Kendall, were the PIs ever told where the COMINT tips came from. Even so, other sources "tipping" where to photograph proved increasingly profitable as the war progressed. A few SIGINT tips were particularly important in hunting down the V-weapons.

Using the three Intelligences sources in conjunction to confirm or deny each other eventually proved highly successful. In the words of one of the primary players in this intelligence war, Wing Commander Douglas Kendall, "How efficient air reconnaissance can be was effectively proved during the war. This may perhaps be illustrated by the story of a battle which covered three years, the battle for information on the V-weapons which were the secret means devised by Hitler to win the war. These could have played a very major part in winning the war for the Germans if we had not had full information to enable counter measures to be taken" (Kendall, p. 84). A pre-war PI, Kendall's greatest triumphs may have occurred when he headed Third Phase Interpretation at Medmenham during the V-weapons threat.

He also wrote, "Without PR/PI, we would have had only rumours of V-weapon developments in the Peenemünde area. We would still have been subjected to the propaganda of Dr Goebbels but would have had the added uncertainty of not knowing the nature of the weapons with which we were being threatened. We would certainly not have been able to start planning any counter measures, such as the attack on Peenemunde itself."

"We would undoubtedly have received reports that sites of a type such as Bois Carre (the first identified V-1 launch site in France) were being constructed in North France. It is highly unlikely that our agents could have given us exact positions; they would probably have reported a site as being near such-and-such a village. It is also unlikely that our agents would have reported all ninety-six sites and, due to the great difficulty of checking the report of one agent with another, we would have had on our maps several hundred sites rather than the ninety-six which existed. Agents actually put the number of sites at 400" (Kendall, p. 157).

---

1   Target is used in two senses: for operations, an objective for destruction; for intelligence, something to be noted and watched, possibly for nomination as a bombing target at some later date.

2   I have a vertical print from what I believe was a covert Cotton Lockheed 12A mission covering the Soviet oil port of Baku on the Caspian from high altitude on 30 March 1940. The camera had a 12" lens and film is simply labelled XEA/002.

3   The Allied Photo Wing in North Africa included three USAAF Photo Squadrons (5th, 12th and 15th) and three Allied (SAAF 60th, RAF 682nd, and the 683rd, commanded by the legendary recce pilot Wing Commander Adrian Warburton).

4   In the USAAF, the hierarchy was Flight-Squadron-Group-Wing. The 7th PG at Mount Farm was renamed the 7th PR and Mapping Group then became the 7th Photographic Group (Reconnaissance) on 13 November 1943.

5   Imagery taken when the aircraft wings or fuselage were not level gave inaccurate measurements and was hard to match into multi-exposure mosaics. A rectifying enlarger tilted the copy table to "crank out" tip or tilt to make a true vertical.

6   I know an "old hand" CIA PI who used to deflate dilettante interpreters with a small-scale 1950s vertical of a little Carousel in a German town. "So...you're a PI too, great; maybe you can help me tell what this is?" I never heard him tell that any of the amateurs ever got it right, and my friend got a good private chuckle each time.

7   With minor variations the effective plot-trace system and the three phases of interpretation evolved at Medmenham were still in use in the USAAF units I served with from 1959 through the mid-1980s.

A photo mosaic I made from German imagery captured after the war. The airfield, rocket and flying bomb test sites have yet to be built.

Chapter III

THE HOME OF WONDER WEAPONS

PEENEMÜNDE

German scientists had been experimenting with rockets for years, but to do anything other than small-scale experiments they needed a lot of funding and support, and the only way to get it in Hitler's Germany was to apply their efforts to a weapon. They weren't alone. Other military developers had ideas of their own for unusual and "cutting-edge" weapons. Land for a secret joint Army/Air Force research and test facility was procured in the spring of 1936. Construction began in August and Peenemünde opened for work in May 1937. The great race to field unstoppable long-range weapons began on the north tip of isolated Usedom Island on the Baltic coast almost due north of Berlin. The German Army was to develop a series of large "artillery-type" rockets and the Luftwaffe would work on a rocket fighter, a flying-bomb and long range air-to-surface devices.

Aside from obvious secrecy advantages, the Peenemünde location had 250 miles of clear water to the east-north-east for a firing range. With the Army and Air Ministry sharing costs, the facility would truly be an omni-faceted weapons development centre. The synergy that might have resulted from a multiplicity of weapons underway at the same time could have resulted in accelerated results as technologies complimented each other, but this apparently did not occur. Even so, rocket planes, a number of more mainstream aircraft variants and usages, pilotless glide bombs of several types, anti-aircraft rockets and the huge V-2 ballistic rocket, were all designed, built and tested under heavy security at Peenemünde on the north end of the island.

The first rocket launches here occurred in December 1937 using the A3 rocket, the precursor of the A4 that became the V-2. The earliest aerial photos of Peenemünde I can find were taken by the Germans themselves, probably in 1937-38. The coverage appears to be part of a routine mapping programme, not documentation of the secret facility.

Snuggled in the pines are well-built housing for families and dorms for single workers as well as labs, measurement houses, workshops and test stands. The Army programmes obviously had priority. Many of the buildings in the Experimental Area were already built and rail lines ran to the sites of the power plant and port slip. The coast road ends at the location that will become the main rocket launch station. There is some construction on airfield facilities in the area and a short cleared area serving as a grass light-plane landing strip is available, but the site on the coast for

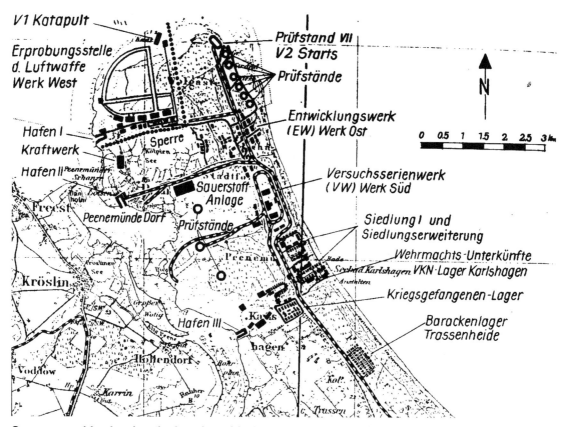

German graphic showing the location of facilities is helpful in viewing subsequent aerial photos.

flying bomb launching was not yet in existence; in fact, there is not even a road crossing the swampy land to that location. Nor is there evidence of dredging to expand the airfield into something able to handle larger aircraft. The land reclamation work and airfield expansion resulted in a twin-engine capable landing ground by 1940.

Mixing Army rocket development with Luftwaffe R&D resulted in a series of scrambled advantages and disadvantages for both services. Ironically, the developing airfield guaranteed RAF photo cover, once it was located. There is no category of target Air Intelligence follows more closely than airfields. Surely the Germans understood that the airfield would mean a lot more exposure than General Dornberger would have liked for the rocket programme. On the other hand, the "normal" developments at the airfield undoubtedly took some Allied attention away from the more arcane developments in the Army compound, made them harder to separate out and understand.

PEENEMÜNDE: 1942

First mentioned in an anonymous package secretly slipped to the British Embassy in Oslo, Norway on 4 November 1939, Peenemünde, on the northern tip of the Baltic coastal island of Usedom, was identified as one of two test locations for several weapons including several

46

different rockets, homing torpedoes and precision bombing systems (*British Intelligence in the Second World War*, vol. 3, p. 360. Hereafter noted as *Brit Intel.*). After the Second World War, Professor R V Jones learned that the author of the Oslo Report was Hans F Mayer, an Electronic Engineer for Siemens in Germany. Mayer died in 1980 but Jones kept his secret until after Frau Mayer died (*Intelligence in War*, p. 261). Jones' identification of Mayer is questioned by other authors.

Despite surprisingly technical outlines of eleven different advanced weapons mentioned, and the inclusion of a sample anti-aircraft proximity fuse, many in British Intelligence thought the Oslo Report was a German plant; a hoax. The report languished in Intel files as the onset of war diverted interest to more pressing matters such as German radar, submarines, surface raiders, invasion preparations and selecting targets for RAF bombing.

On 13 June 1942 an A4 rocket (later to be better known as the V-2) had been launched from Peenemünde on a one-mile flight. By 3 October 1942 the range was up to 120 miles. There were three more good shots that year, giving a high degree of confidence to Nazi decision-makers. Serious plans were laid to build the weapon in large numbers and how, and where, to establish launching facilities, but the Allies had heard only rumors.

The Baltic Coastal site came up again in a December 1942 message from a Danish chemical engineer who referred to a German rocket (*Wizard War*, p. 332). There were also agent reports from the Continent telling of "secret weapon trials" (*Air Spy*, p. 147). Some of these referenced large, long-range rockets capable of destroying large areas (up to 200km range and 10km square destruction radius) (*Brit Intel*, vol. 3, p. 360). Unfortunately these reports sent PIs on a long "wild goose chase" based upon estimates that a rocket with the stated range would require a sharply inclined ramp about 100 yards long (*Air Spy*, p. 148).

British Intelligence was convinced there was a threat out there, but didn't know enough about it to assess its capability or devise a way to impede or stop it. However, it was increasingly apparent that Peenemünde was at or near the heart of the matter.

Initial RAF aerial coverage of the installation occurred by chance on 15 May 1942—some ten weeks prior to the first successful V-2 launch. The airfield and three large circular structures standing stark against the forest and field patterns caught the eye of a PRU Spitfire pilot on his way to photograph the German Naval Base at Swinemunde, farther south-east along the coast. This was the first instance of having the Luftwaffe share the installation working against protecting the secrecy of the German Army special weapons programmes. The mysterious earthworks, huge cement cisterns and other unusual large constructions related to the rocket, piqued curiosity in England. However, Peenemünde might have escaped attention for a considerable time if not for the rocket motor test stands and the airfield.

The recce pilot diverted slightly to overfly Peenemünde and expose a few of his precious frames of film on the unusual structures and airfield expansion. The story is told in detail in *Air Spy* (p. 147). Those photos were small-scale, so little detail was observable and nothing unusual was noted by British Intelligence. The airfield didn't show any fighter Air Order of Battle that would menace RAF Bomber Command sorties and no one knew the meaning of the large "bathtubs". Medmenham PIs knew nothing about the Oslo Report so they weren't looking for rockets or flying bombs—in any case, image scale and quality would have precluded seeing them on this imagery. The number of aircraft types on this cover, and on subsequent missions, helped identify Peenemünde as a test and research facility. Reclamation of land for a landing field was well under way. In fact, the dredges and runway improvements were a continuing activity at Peenemünde right up to 1945.

First Allied coverage, 15 May 42. Huge rocket test stands attracted attention but weren't understood at the time.

Just like the Oslo Report, the Peenemünde imagery was shelved as other more urgent targets and situations absorbed the attention of photo analysts. However, the 1942 mission provided a baseline to measure facility changes over time.

PEENEMÜNDE: 1943

The first time that RAF photo interpreters knew anything about Germany's secret weapons threat was in January (*Eye*, p. 188). "Early in January 1943, we got the first hint of developments taking place in the Peenemünde area on the Baltic coast. At first there was no particular indication that these developments were tied in with long range rockets or V-weapons of any type. All we had was the report, from a Swedish traveller I believe, that the Peenemünde area was closed usually to prevent discovery of what is actually taking place there - from the ground at least - to the public and that secret developments were taking place there. It is the sort of rumour which is bound to surround any military area which is not open to the public. The existence of such military areas is impossible to hide although security regulations can usually prevent discovery of what is actually taking place there - from the ground at least" (*Kendall*, p. 84).

Radio Intercept capabilities (Y Service) and Bletchley Park code-breakers were already on alert to watch for any evidence of long-range firings along the Baltic coast (*Wizard War*, p. 336). "In February, Major Norman Falcon, the officer in charge of this section (Army PIs at Medmenham), was warned by the War Office that the enemy was planning to operate 'some form of long-range projectors, capable of firing on this country from the French coast'" (*Air Spy*, p. 148).

During this same period agents were reporting that "a new factory had been built at Peenemünde where a new weapon was being manufactured. It was a rocket which had been fired from a testing ground" (*Brit Intel*, vol. 3, p. 360). We now know that the rockets had been produced and fired for many months. Of course this good information was almost buried in the flood of less valuable and/or less reliable information, such as the rocket had already been tested in Latin America. There was also the problem of agents seeing things they didn't understand, such as a rocket fired vertically and disappearing horizontally (*Brit Intel*, vol. 3, p.360-361). There were also reports of long-range rocket guns to be fired from the Continental side of the English Channel.

While trying to sift the truth from a continuing flow of reports on new weapons, Allied photo intelligence was concentrating on higher priorities, and recce flights only occasionally looked at places like Peenemünde.[1] After all, Medmenham analysts still didn't know what to look for, or how many different weapons were under development and the place didn't present an imminent threat. Of course the PIs would methodically scan every inch of every frame of imagery, but finding something is immeasurably aided by knowing what one is looking for. At this stage it was impossible for Allied Intelligence to discriminate among reports of rockets, rocket planes, rocket anti-aircraft weapons and air-to-ground weapons—including the very real possibility of "planted" information (*Brit Intel*, vol. 3, p. 361-362). Agent and POW reports told of rockets "as big as a motor" car, others of one weighing 120 tons with 60 to 80 tons of warhead. This "fanciful" information tended to reinforce the doubters and legitimate intelligence being developed on Peenemünde.

What little information was available, and the best estimates by Allied scientists, warned that the new weapons would have a range of about 130 miles, so PIs were tasked to review all imagery collected in 1943 within that range of London and Southampton. Almost immediately they began finding unexplained construction in France (see Chapter IV). Agent reports seemed to relate the new construction to weapons thought to be under development at Peenemünde. Though well outside the threat radius itself, Peenemünde had become enough of a question mark to attract more attention. When the Peenemünde imagery was reviewed again, the large concrete circles we now know were rocket engine test stands, were still not understood, but obvious enough to the naked eye, even on small-scale photos, to warrant a better look. A lot of effort went into making those huge bathtubs and expanding the airfield. If the place meant that much to the Germans, Medmenham needed a new look to see if changes would permit a better understanding of what was going on. That alone insured Peenemünde would be covered again,

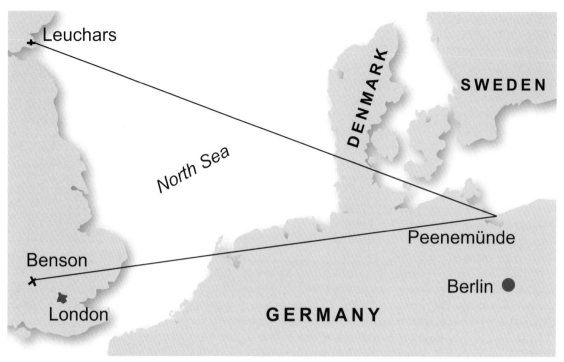

Baltic coast photo recce flights were shifted from Benson to Leuchars in Scotland to avoid overflying areas heavily defended by fighters and flak.

and this time it would be coverage of the whole complex. Who knew what else might be discovered?

The weapons search was still, of necessity a groping, plodding, methodical approach to a poorly defined problem, but it was the best that could be done at the time. Intelligence was convinced that Peenemünde was involved in experimental weapons development so Photo Interpreters were given guidance from "one of the MI branches of the War Office.

1. There have recently been indications that the Germans may be developing some form of long range projectors capable of firing on this country from the French coast.
2. There is unfortunately little concrete evidence on the subject available, except that the projector may be similar in form to a section of railway track.
3. It is obviously of great importance to obtain the earliest possible warning of the existence of any such device, and we should therefore be grateful if you could keep a close watch for any suspicious erections of rails or scaffolding, and consult M.I.10, through us, on any doubtful cases.
4. ...." (Kendall, p. 84-85. Edited for brevity).

Peenemünde was covered by high altitude photo reconnaissance on 19 January 1943, and again on 1 March (*Brit Intel*, vol. 3, p. 363). Kendall says the missions were on 9 February and 1 March but he sometimes mixes date flown and date arriving in Third Phase. Apparently three weeks was par for the course between coverage and a Third Phase PI Report. New construction was noted but not necessarily understood and the existence of the rocket weapon could neither be confirmed nor negated. The PI report on the latest coverage, submitted to the War Office on 27 March, called particular attention to the three large circular earth and concrete works. They were seen to have centre scaffoldings, but their use was still unknown (*Eye*, p. 188. Kendall, p. 86). This initiated another "wild goose chase" since the "rocket" specs were more than twice the length and half the diameter of the actual weapon. The War Office provided additional guidance on 19 March.

"The following approximate characteristics have been supplied by M.I.10 for a two stage compound rocket with a maximum range of 130 miles. The total weight approximately 9? tons. Total length 95 feet. Total diameter 30 inches. Approximate weight of rocket head 1? tons. Length of projector 100 yards" (Kendall, p. 85). It was easily deduced that the target of such a weapon would be London, and the launching sites would be in northern France, but the weapon was reportedly being developed at Peenemünde. At least that gave the PIs something to look for— long tubular objects and a steeply angling ramp, but the status of Peenemünde was still "watch and see if anything turns up". Photo Interpreters are not scientists. They are eyes and memories. They will identify known objects and activities, spot changes, even highlight the unusual, but they can't do much with something they don't understand. Meanwhile, on 20 April, "arrangements were made for all areas within 130 miles of London and Southampton to be photographed. This work, as with all photographic reconnaissance work required in the European Theatre, was shared by both the RAF and the USAAF Photographic Reconnaissance Squadrons"(Kendall, p. 87).

The methodical search for some unknown new weapon kicked into high-gear after British intelligence "bugged" a cell holding German generals von Thoma and Cruewell.[2] On 22 March 1943, General von Thoma, newly arrived in the North African desert prior to his capture, told his cellmate things he had seen and knew about experiments on rockets that were claimed to "go 15km into the atmosphere then plunge into a targeted area". The general apparently had some first-hand knowledge, "Wait until next year and then the fun will start...."

This new information from such high-ranking officers spurred action from the Prime Minister down. Very quickly THE ROCKET became a major focus of British Intelligence. "On April 24th, a group of engineers and scientists from the Ministry of Supply visited the PI unit and detailed technical discussions on the possible nature of the weapon were held. It is fair to say that at this stage of the investigation the whole emphasis was on Peenemünde and any suggestion that the weapon could be anything except a rocket was discounted" (Kendall, p. 87). Unfortunately, British Intelligence seemed to visualize the German rocket as an evolution of the nineteenth century Congreve rockets, or a ten ton version of the Soviet "Katyusha" artillery rockets, assuming solid propellant.[3] Other estimates suggested an even larger rocket of 60 to 100 tons (*Mare's Nest*, p. 70). That didn't give PIs much to work with, but in early April, Medmenham analysts concluded that the Peenemünde earthworks might be related to rocket motor testing. Indeed, later cover caught flame and smoke on one frame and none on the next frame, proving firing of a rocket motor mounted horizontally (*Eye*, p. 191).

On 29 April, Mr Sandys' office concluded that Peenemünde was probably an experimental station, not yet in full use, and probably an explosive works. They thought the circular and elliptical constructions were for the testing of explosives and projectiles and opined, "It is clear that a heavy long range rocket is not yet an immediate menace" (Kendall, p. 87).

At Medmenham, "Fight Lieutenant Andre Kenny and three other PIs were assigned to search for clues of experimental work and production, especially at Peenemünde. At the same time,

Norman Falcon, and two of his Army interpreters were to concentrate on the military side of the investigation, which meant primarily watching potential launching areas on the French coast. Meantime, a special flying program was laid on—shared by Benson (RAF) and the Americans at Mount Farm—to insure that every square mile of the French coastal area from Cherbourg to the Belgian frontier had been photographed since the beginning of the year" (*Air Spy*, p. 149). Interpreter Constance Babington Smith[†] wrote that, "No one really quite knew what they were looking for, although the Air Ministry did suggest that the interpreters should be on the lookout for three things: a long-range gun, a remotely controlled rocket aircraft, and 'some sort of tube located in a disused mine out of which a rocket could be squirted'" (*Air Spy*, p. 149).

The F-5s (higher performance version of the F-4, Lockheed Lightning photo aircraft) and large-format multiple camera installations of US 13th Photo Squadron were particularly well suited to collect the broad area coverage of France while RAF Mosquitoes of 540 Squadron at Leuchars, Scotland, had the range, altitude and speed needed to cover Peenemünde.

A major participant in the hunt for Germany's secret weapons was the Assistant Director of Intelligence (Science), Professor R V Jones. He made some marvellous, even spectacular, contributions to Allied Intelligence, but he could also be a thorn-in-the-side to those at

---

† Hereafter sometimes referred to as C B S.

Under construction when first photographed in 1942, a large rail-served power plant (upper left corner), and port facilities needed to support the Peenemünde complex, were rapidly replacing a little village.

Medmenham and some of his widely read assertions on what happened, when and how, were either incorrect or heavily slanted.

For example, Professor Jones wrote that the "first sortie" over Peenemünde was 22 April 1943. Actually that was the fourth coverage. He also wrote, "A special section was set up at Medmenham, the Photographic Interpretation Unit, to undertake the interpretation for Duncan Sandys. In this he was unlucky because the principal interpreter assigned to the task supplemented his powers of observation by a remarkably fertile imagination" (*Wizard War*, p. 339). Presumably he is referring to Andre Kenny, though Jones doesn't name him. Jones then tells the well-known and oft-repeated "sludge pump" story claiming Medmenham PIs missed the V-1 test launch ramps, or misidentified them as part of the land reclamation effort to expand the airfield (see below).

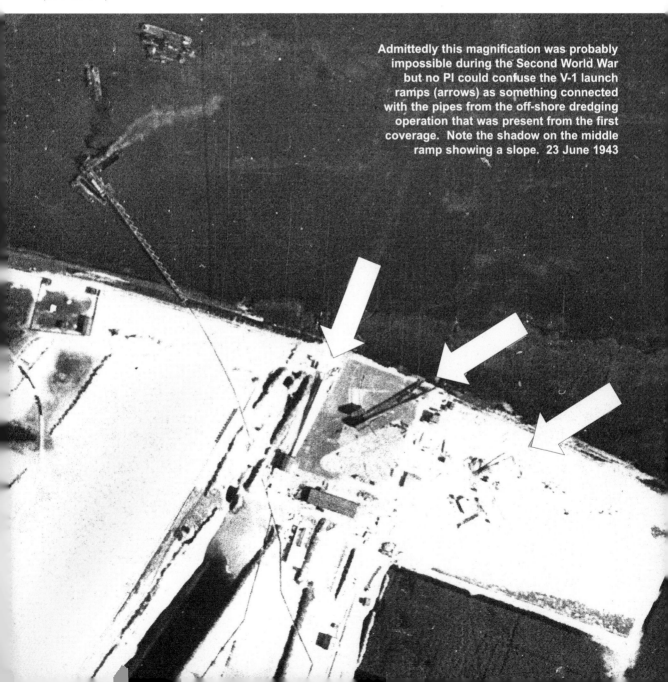

Admittedly this magnification was probably impossible during the Second World War but no PI could confuse the V-1 launch ramps (arrows) as something connected with the pipes from the off-shore dredging operation that was present from the first coverage. Note the shadow on the middle ramp showing a slope. 23 June 1943

In my experience, everyone who ever seen an aerial photograph fancies himself a photo interpreter. Dilettantes seldom realize that there is a lot more to it than just looking at the imagery and considerable training and experience are needed to master the nuances and become proficient in the craft. Apparently Professor Jones was no exception. The nature of his work necessarily brought him close to the work at Medmenham on many occasions and, it seems to me, the above quote from his book indicates the generally collegial relationship between Medmenham PIs and the ADI (Sc) could also be fraught with friction, at least with some of the PIs.[4]

Despite the inaccuracies in estimates of the size of the rocket, the information provided at least gave Allied photo interpreters something specific to look for and the search for a German "long-range-rocket-weapon" began in earnest. This search also resulted in creation of an organization later code-named "*Bodyline*", with ministerial powers, to pull together what was known, and what to do about the German long-range rocket threat, the only new weapon known at the time. As other new threats were discovered, the code-name search effort came to apply to all of the V-weapons. On 20 April, Duncan Sandys, Minister of Supply and Winston Churchill's son-in-law, was appointed to head the new organization to examine the existence of a long-range rocket. One of his first acts was to look at Medmenham's forensic dissection of Peenemünde.

The nearby electric power plant was much larger than needed for the little town and airfield. What was being built in those large "industrial" buildings? Active reclamation work was continuing to expand the airfield but had no apparent relationship with any sort of rocket. At least that airfield activity was understandable and familiar to PIs, but why was a larger landing area needed?

The PI giving the briefing, Flight Lieutenant Andre Kenny, was in charge of the Medmenham sub-section responsible for Peenemünde (*Eye*, p. 189. *Air Spy*, p. 149). He walked Sandys through his reasoning for concluding that the new weapons everyone sought would be found at this place.

By April 1943, Flt Lt Kenny had correctly deduced that the huge earthworks "might have something to do with rocket launching pads" (*Eye*, p. 190-191). "A later sortie confirmed the opinion" when it showed flame and smoke on one of the test beds. We now know that rocket engines were tested there and rockets themselves were not launched from those concrete bathtubs.

"This was the first time that Mr Sandys had come into touch with a photographic interpreter, and he was much surprised and impressed by the amount of detailed information the photographs could yield" (*Air Spy*, p. 149-150). Mr Sandys asked for more photo recce over Peenemünde, which was becoming firmly tied to the new weapons development effort by a combination of aerial photos, communications intercepts and agent reports (*Air Spy*, p. 149-150).

A well-developed housing area was present on 14 May 1943, but no unusual or new weapons were observed.

At last, Allied intelligence had something, or things, to look for, and a place to look. RAF PRU aircraft were running regular long-range photo reconnaissance along the Baltic Coast to Swinemunde, Gdyna in Poland and Konigsberg in East Prussia, watching the German Navy, which was still a major threat to Allied convoys.[5]

On deep penetration missions the recce planes stayed near the coast to be able to slip north into neutral airspace if the Luftwaffe set up an intercept for their way home. This northern route

Good imagery from a 36" lens showed a variety of aircraft on the field, but nothing unusual. 20 May 1943

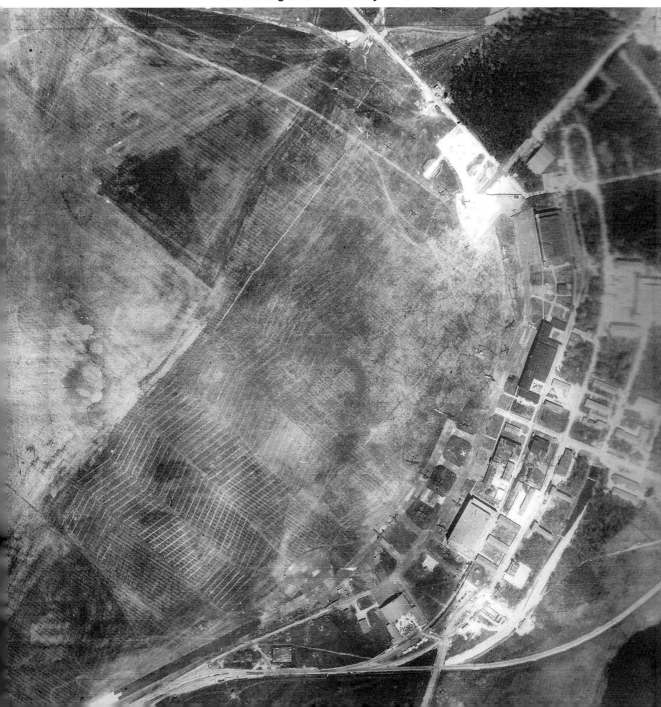

regularly took the British recce aircraft over Usedom Island and interpreters began to get a stream of Peenemünde coverage—four times in June 1943 alone according to *Air Spy*, but all the other covers were small-scale and of little use for finding small/new objects. Quite naturally, the most obvious and best understood part of the target, the expanding airfield, got most of the attention from PIs. As an aircraft/airfield analyst, this is where and how C B S came into the game, eventually leading to her remarkable discoveries later in the year.

The 22 April mission disclosed continuing construction to expand the landing ground and the "industrial area". Coverage of 14 May ran right up the coast, disclosing well-developed and elaborate housing facilities near the factory buildings. "The general appearance of the factory suggested that it might be for the manufacture of explosives because it had extensive steam piping: some of its buildings had been there since May 1942, some were new, and clearances indicated that more were to be erected. Two buildings, whose construction had been in an early stage in May, were unusually large, one 670 feet by 318, and the other 810 feet by 400; they too, were thought to be concerned with production of explosives" (*Brit Intel*, vol. 3, p. 366).

A mission on 20 May (above) had good contrast and complete coverage. The collection aircraft was clearly at high altitude and despite the 14" lenses the resolution limits of the film made detail what PI Babington Smith called "woolly". Those photos showed two dredges working hard just off

The first sighting of a V-2 was on imagery of 12 June 1943. Understanding vertical launching came months later. The first rocket reported was horizontal on a rail car in front of the large building. Both rockets were minus nose cones, confusing length measurement for future PI. (Medmenham Club)

shore, a wide band of swamp land filled in from the Baltic to the airfield, and many other "fill ponds" lined out toward the airfield road and the area that would eventually be recognized as the flying bomb launch area. The long black bands show water-filled settling ponds that would be turned into dry land by drainage and evaporation. The landing ground had a cross-section of Dornier, Junkers, and Heinkel twin-engine aircraft, along with smaller types, sailplanes, and one example of the unusual asymmetrical Blohm and Voss BV.141 in front of the second large hangar. There are at least seven types of twin-engine aircraft (mostly He 111), four different single-engine types and two sailplanes. Though one shows well, near-noon shadows didn't make the flying bomb launch ramps stand out so they didn't attract special attention. There was no activity noted in the mysterious 670 foot by 470 foot earthen ellipse with its internal towers and travelling cranes (*Brit Intel*, vol. 3, p. 369). The reference says imagery of 20 May "also revealed a cylindrical object, 40 feet by eight, on a transverser carriage". I haven't been able to locate that object on the imagery I have. Recent road and cable-scars ran to near the centre of a fan-shaped area on the foreshore just beyond the earthen ellipse, but no functional significance could be attached to them. The small port area was operational as was a large power plant that displaced the small village seen on 1938 imagery.

The first sighting of a V-2 was on imagery of 12 June 1943. Understanding vertical launching came months later. The first rocket reported was horizontal on a rail car in front of the large building. Both rockets were minus nose cones, confusing length measurement for future PI. (Medmenham Club)

Imagery of 2 June captured a four-foot diameter, 40-foot high column standing vertically on a large paved triangle between the conspicuous elliptical earthwork and the sea. The only way to get that measurement information from the prints was use of stereo viewing and attention to the shadow of the object—things experienced interpreters did almost instinctively. Medmenham PIs had just seen, and accurately measured, a rocket erected and ready for launch, but they couldn't call it that. Fortunately, Flight Officer[6] Ursula Powys-Lybbe[††], a PI who knew all the Medmenham players in these dramatic events and participated from early in the war, set the record straight by interviewing Andre Kenny for her wonderful book (published five years after Jones' book). She wrote, "It must be stressed once again that interpretation officers were not permitted to make definitive statements about any object they might have seen on photographs until it had been established by the authorities for what it was in actual terms, no matter what the PIs might have deduced personally.

Andre Kenny, who had the misfortune to describe the mysterious things he saw at Peenemünde as either an object or a vertical column according to the rules laid down by his superior officers, has been pilloried by almost every writer on the subject for not spelling out the word 'rocket'."[8]

Imagery from 12 June 1943 showed the first "official" sighting of a V-2, horizontal on a railway car. Vertical launching was not yet understood. For some reason, both rockets had blunt tips (were minus nose cones), confusing length measurement for future photo interpretation. At left is a contemporary graphic made from the 12 June imagery noting the "rocket" and a "vertical object".

It must also be remembered that, at the time, powerful factions in London disagreed on the rocket as a weapon, and, if there was indeed such a weapon, it was expected to be much larger

---

†† Hereafter sometimes referred to as U P-L.

than 40 feet, because solid fuel was still incorrectly assumed. Also, a substantial launch-ramp was thought necessary. Churchill's personal scientific adviser, Professor Frederick Lindemann, (Lord Cherwell after 1941), led a group that thought technical problems made a rocket with the necessary range and payload infeasible. Cherwell maintained that what was being found at Peenemünde was an elaborate German hoax to distract Allied Intelligence. The opposite view was held by those agreeing with ADI (Sc) Jones, who maintained that rockets were real and could, and would, be launched against England. This disagreement actually continued until the first V-2 hit London in September 1944.

Medmenham's work through May 1943 convinced Mr Sandys that "the whole Peenemünde site was an experimental station...for the testing of explosives and projectiles" (*Brit Intel*, vol. 3, p. 367). It was the work of Intelligence to find the weapons and prove the point, one way or the other. Signals Intelligence could retrieve clues. Human Source Intelligence could supply hints on where to look and rumors of capabilities and intents, but only Photo Intelligence could prove the case by actually seeing the weapon, and everyone knew that was as much a matter of luck as interpretation skill. The elusive object had to be caught in the open. In the meanwhile, the scientists reserved the right to decide what was and wasn't THE ROCKET.

"Since 11 June, when a reconnaissance programme had been agreed between Sandys and the Air Ministry, the PRU, in addition to Peenemünde, had photographed (a list of targets east along the Baltic Coast) but without producing any firm intelligence on weapons or their testing" (*Brit Intel*, vol. 3, p. 369).

For years, books parroting the story have criticized Flight Lieutenant Kenny's team for "missing the rocket" several times on the missions of early June 1943. A variation of the tale is "The photographic interpreters might be forgiven; what they had first described as 'objects' were only 1 ? millimeters long on the film" (*Intelligence in War*, p. 265). While true that they apparently missed more than one example of an erected rocket, so did everyone else because the shape, size and vertical orientation didn't fit the template of how a rocket would be launched. It must also be noted that stereoscopic viewing would disclose the "column" was tall but couldn't tell the length and shape. In many of the coverages the shadows (the only way to tell length and shape) were quite short and therefore much harder to measure. The erected rockets are apparent to our eyes today because we know what to look for. Apparently, the large towers in the earthen ellipse and elsewhere at Peenemünde convinced Allied scientists that the rocket needed a large launch apparatus and stabilization of some sort early in flight (*Brit Intel*, vol. 3, p. 451), and that guidance was passed on to Medmenham.

The "they missed it" story was apparently begun by R V Jones who took credit for being the first to find the rocket when he looked at prints of 12 June imagery some six days after the mission—two days after the Medmenham report on the mission had been issued (*Wizard War*, p. 340). This was the first of several interpretation V-weapons related disagreements between Jones and Medmenham. Experienced PIs do not jump to conclusions, nor do they miss much, even when going "full tilt" in First Phase Interpretation. In detailed interpretation phases, the pace and atmosphere are almost librarial and detail is the name of the game. I can't imagine the Medmenham Third Phase PIs missing the "horizontal object" as Jones maintains and Powys-Lybbe refutes.

Of course objects on a rail line just naturally attract a look. Once again Powys-Lybbe sets the record straight. Andre Kenny told her neither he nor his team doubted that they had found a long-range rocket resting horizontal on the 12 June coverage. It was on a rail car in front of the large building near the elliptical earthwork (*Eye*, p. 191). This would have to have been on the same 12 June imagery that Jones used to stake his claim to "finding the rocket". Within a few weeks Medmenham produced a model showing the object (see below). Apparently everyone DID miss the erected rocket until months later.

Rail tracks naturally attract attention by PIs, so it was not surprising that those cars got a good look. Stereo coverage gave a good idea of the shape of the unusual object on the flat, even though the length and tail fins were not what was expected of the rocket—it was blunt ended. Those were the same tracks where characteristic liquid oxygen/hydrogen peroxide rail cars had previously been seen and that association suggested liquid fuel for the new weapon—a major subject still in dispute in London.

The 12 June imagery convinced both the ADI (Sc) and Duncan Sandys that the rocket was real and they'd finally seen it. "'This object is 35 feet long and appears to have a blunt point. For 25 feet of its length the diameter is about 8 feet. The appearance…is not incompatible with it being a cylinder tapered at one end and provided with 3 radial fins at the other.' The CIU also said that the object had a definite resemblance to those revealed in earlier photographs" (*Brit Intel*, vol. 3, p. 369). This information was from a June CIU report Addendum. The shorter length measurement may also be explained by: "We now know the warhead had not been fitted" (*Intelligence in War*, p. 273). Post-war books and recent internet sources have a consensus that the A4/V-2 rocket was just over 46 feet long and 5.5 feet in diameter, with 11.8 feet width at the fins. Douglas Kendall remembered: "A vertical column 40 feet in height was also noted on the fore shore but not identified at that time" (*Kendall*, p. 88). He noted that, if possible, Peenemünde was being photographed twice a week and his memoirs noted the date of that discovery as 16 June, but I suspect that is the date of the PI work and not the date of the imagery. If from the 12 June imagery, it demonstrates how a special PI team at Medmenham, and emphasis on Peenemünde, had reduced Third Phase PI output to four days after collection, and two days before Professor Jones saw the prints. Kendall also noted that this imagery proved the cranes in the circular and elliptical pits moved location. It was expected that movable cranes would be needed to handle the bulk and weight of the rocket, so that further focused the PIs on the area near the ellipse to find the weapon.

It is interesting that each instance where Professor Jones claimed a rocket discovery coup over Medmenham involved a horizontal object (12 June 1943 at Peenemünde and 5 May 1944 at Blizna, Poland). Apparently he wasn't any better at figuring out the vertical objects than the photo interpreters. No one in England expected to see a rocket standing alone like that and the only way to understand them was by their shadow; something an amateur PI might not notice—but a professional should have. The "vertical columns" just didn't make sense.

While Medmenham interpreters were still searching for more information on rocket-weapons at Peenemünde, agents in France and signals intercepts were providing indications that there was more to be found (*Wizard War*, p. 337-338). For example, a Luxembourger the Germans sent to Peenemünde as a labourer wrote to his father about the noise of a large rocket and a doctor smuggled out a sketch of Peenemünde mentioning a rocket ten metres long. In June a source inside German High Command mentioned weapons, launched by catapults, intended for London. It wasn't yet clear that these were two different weapons. Because of security the CIU PIs were not told the details or sources, just asked to scrub Peenemünde imagery again for "anything queer" (*Air Spy*, p.151). Coverage improved with Mosquitoes carrying larger cameras and film loads. Interpreter Babington Smith wrote that Peenemünde had been covered eleven times before 23 June 1943, but on that date a 540 Squadron Mosquito carrying long-focal length cameras got excellent, large-scale cover of Peenemünde. It was unquestionably the best coverage yet (I only know of nine prior missions), and certainly one of the most significant PR missions of the war.

The sky was clear and the sun bright, the shadows were strong and resolution on the film particularly good, so it stood up well to magnification, giving photo interpreters their best look they'd ever had at the place (*Eye*, p. 191). Kendall (p. 88), possibly using U P-L's book as a memory aid, says this mission was flown 28 June 1943, but I have copies of the titled film and 23 June is correct.

Medmenham interpreters were confronted with a treasure trove of objects to analyze and the quality of the imagery permitted more detailed analysis, but, at that time, they didn't understand everything captured on the film.

If the airfield was part of the Luftwaffe defense against Allied bombers or a training base there would have been many aircraft of the same type. Instead, the number and variety of aircraft present on the landing area reinforced the judgment that this was some sort of test or experimental facility. Third Phase analysis at Medmenham resulted in the head of the Aircraft Section, PI Flight Officer Babington Smith, noting "jet marks" on the airfield sod, the first of their kind ever seen on aerial photos, showing burning of the ground characteristic of the rocket plane take-off. The enlargement above shows a P30 rocket fighter ready for flight. This was almost invisible on the original prints.

At least five distinct "jet trails" can be seen; three running straight out from a small hangar and two from its larger

Four P30 (Me 163), first seen on 23 June imagery. One is ready for flight. Note burn marks.

First photo pass on 23 June 1943 caught all four P30s at rest.

A white dot to the naked eye on the original imagery, maximum enlargement shows the tailless P30 being readied for a test flight.

neighbour to the south. The grass repaired itself over time, but if coverage was frequent enough, the burn-marks could be compared and new ones counted to show the number of test flights. The burned trails certainly identified the nature of activity at the small hangar. On the first pass over the airfield two small bat-wing, tailless aircraft were photographed parked in front of the small hangar (a place a PI would naturally look at closely) and two more could be seen less distinctly in the shadow of the adjacent larger hangar.

On the second pass of the Mosquito over Peenemünde, about a half hour later, one of the little planes in front of the small hangar was missing and Constance Babington Smith spotted it on the field, clearly prepping for flight (Kendall, p. 88). He says the new plane was identified on 2 July, nine days after the imagery was collected. There were no burn marks on the grass from that location so it was plainly a new take-off axis. To the naked eye on the original print the new plane was just a tiny white dot, but white paint or bare metal finish was halating strongly and was well contrasted against the grass so it stood out better than its fellows (on reflective concrete backgrounds). The 23 June imagery held up under magnification and the plane could be accurately measured. She dubbed her find the Peenemünde 30 (P30)—newly identified aircraft were initially named for discovery location and wingspan in feet. We now know the plane she found as the Me 163 rocket-propelled fighter (*Air Spy*, p. 151). The new aircraft was found by good, meticulous PI work, not a tip-off from other intelligence sources.

Using past coverage for comparison is the PIs equivalent of acquiring hindsight and it is amazing what you can see when you know what to look for and the "jet marks" were not present a month earlier, indicating the P30 was a new programme at Peenemünde. Though earlier coverage disclosed the plane present, but too indistinct for recognition, this was the first time that non-propeller aircraft had been identified in Germany and, while a matter of great significance, it was decided that these were not associated with the secret weapon being sought.

Discovery of yet another new and technologically advanced weapon further heightened concern about what was going on at Peenemünde, and the 23 June mission would eventually yield up even more treasures, but it seems at the time no one noted a probable rocket launch exercise in progress on the foreshore beyond the ellipse.

Not a "pair" of anything. Note "hook" tail shadow at left and distinct fins on right.

There were vehicles in positions eventually associated with a V-2 firing, but if the rocket itself is present the shadows are too short to show it. During this exploitation of the mission, the major excitement was identification of what has often since been referred to as two ballistic rockets horizontal on transporters inside the elliptical earthwork on the coast north of what was understood to be the development area. PIs called them "torpedo-like objects" because of the ongoing prohibition on calling them rockets until the detailed analysts and scientists had decided that was what they were (*Air Spy*, p. 150; and *Eye*, p. 191).

Among other problems, this restraint caused the Scientific Advisor, ADI (Sc), Professor R V Jones, to write that the PIs had "missed" the horizontal rockets (see *Wizard War* for his version of events). Noted military author, John Keegan, wrote, "These photographs proved critical in advancing the debate about what Peenemünde threatened" (*Intelligence in War*, p. 273).

At left, two photo passes over the rocket test area about half an hour apart on 23 June disclosed movement of vehicles in the ellipse, particularly two transporters near the entrance and the addition of something alongside the "rocket".

The new objects were measured as "38 feet long, 6 feet in diameter, with a tail of three fins which started 25 feet from the nose and was 12 feet wide. This evidence of the activities at Peenemünde proved to be a critical point in the investigation" (*Brit Intel*, vol. 3, p. 369, quoting from a CIU

Above—German movie of failed launch in the ellipse found post-war. Note hook-like "tail fins". (NASM)

Report of 28 June 1943). The measurement was still short, probably influenced by earlier reports of the "column" and the one seen horizontal on a railcar just a few weeks earlier. The rocket was already solidly associated with moveable cranes needed for off-loading and this sighting also firmly associated the rocket with specialized railroad tank cars probably carrying their fuel (Kendall, p. 88). Most important for subsequent PI of the rocket was an understanding that it tapered to a tip.

The activity and erected rocket on the foreshore were apparently missed and at least one of the "rockets" in the ellipse misidentified. Even so, these photos of the horizontal objects inside the earth ellipse were some of the most significant in the war, certainly having a far reaching impact. On one photo run the two objects are joined by another, probably a transporter.

In every book on the subject the horizontal objects are annotated as rockets or V-2s (including books by my favorite PIs, C B S and U P-L, neither of whom actually worked on the rocket problem). The magic of hindsight and modern magnification techniques make it easy to see what was photographed on the 23 June imagery was not a pair of German rockets.

The unusual "hook-like" shadow of the tail from the object nearest the earthen wall shows it to be very different from its fellow which has quite discernable tail fins. I believe the shape near the wall was some sort of training module or safety device. Just such a device can be seen on frames of a German film of a failed rocket launch inside the elliptical enclosure—which of course Medmenham PIs wouldn't have seen until after the war ended.

The most obvious horizontal object had the right size and shape but was probably not an actual rocket. The solid white "rocket" played a trick on the silver-halide emulsion of the black-and-white film, reflecting so much light that the object seems larger than it really was. Experienced PIs understand this halation or "blooming" of something highly reflective (white paint, glass or bare metal for example) and compensate for it, thus allowing a reasonably accurate measurement of the object. The PI measurements were too short by eight feet and too thick by six inches. Measurements of the "columns" (based upon shadows) came closer on height but were farther off the mark in diameter.

Again with the benefit of post-war information, the all-white paint job doesn't match any other photos I have seen of the V-2, making the object in the ellipse more suspicious. Test rockets were usually painted in patterns of black and white to make the missile easier to track optically and tell if it was rotating on its axis. All the later operational crew firings seemed to be with camouflage painted rockets. More than three decades after these events, Professor Jones wrote that in a storage cave in France, in the summer of 1944, "...we actually found a great white wooden dummy rocket, which had clearly been used to give the troops experience in handling the missile..." (Wizard War, p. 446). Measurements of the dummy rocket found in France permitted further refinements of the estimated V-2 capability a few weeks before the first ones landed in England.

Of course, no one in England in June 1943 knew any of this "ground truth" about the rocket so they did the best they could with what they had. Fortunately the size and shape of the "rocket" were near-correct so PIs now knew what they were looking for.

Lord Cherwell thought the Peenemünde "torpedoes" were dummies designed to fool Allied Intelligence, but then he was ever a skeptic when it came to the rocket.

"The PI source, having established the dimensions of the rocket for the scientists of the Ministry of Supply, had no means of establishing the tonnage and performance of the rocket. The scientists had to work entirely from theoretical figures and were bound to take the most pessimistic view possible in order not to be caught unprepared; they produced a figure of 45 tons for the rocket with an explosive charge of 10 tons. Had the explosive charge indeed been that large, the menace from the V-2 rocket would have been far more severe than in fact actually developed. As it was, the one-ton heads caused a great deal of damage whenever they made a direct hit on any building. The PI source has the obvious limitation that it can only report performance by inference under most conditions, whereas, for instance, a prisoner who had worked with a weapon can be much more specific on certain points. An even better source, of course is actual enemy equipment" and eventually the Allies did get their hands on pieces of actual V-2s from Sweden and Poland (Kendall, p. 161).

Professor Jones thought what was seen on the 23 June imagery was indeed the rocket they'd been seeking and accepted the measurements, from which he made surprisingly accurate calculations about payload and range. So, perhaps Cherwell and Jones were each right in their own way, but ADI (Sc) assumptions, based upon the June photos, validated the existence of the rocket, sharpened understanding of the threat and, fortunately, moved the *Bodyline* hunt forward. "The next day the Prime Minister directed that the maximum possible contribution to the investigation was to be made by the PI unit who were to be given all necessary facilities and manpower required. Fortunately we already had the resources needed" (Kendall, p. 88).

Actually, having nine women nine months pregnant doesn't get you a baby tomorrow and there was a lot of hard flying and PI-ing yet to do—and a lot of good weather and good luck were needed.

Seeing the rockets and new aircraft on good quality and scale imagery allowed interpreters to go back to earlier, poorer quality imagery to find the same things present. It also allowed the PIs to identify associated objects: transporters, fuel vehicles and rail cars. Associated objects and ground patterns are called "signatures", and they help a PI identify something. From this mission forward actually seeing a rocket wasn't necessary. If the support equipment was present, the *Bodyline* relationship of a site was settled. Now that they knew what to look for based on that wonderful June coverage, the rocket fighter and what seemed to be a ballistic rocket were both verified as present on earlier imagery. It didn't change anything, but the two rocket weapons were mistakenly thought to be related because Allied Intelligence didn't understand that Peenemünde hosted distinctly separate Wehrmacht and Luftwaffe programmes. It did however reinforce the concept that liquid fuel was being used and that made for a smaller, lighter rocket—and made hydrogen-peroxide manufacture a target.

The V-1 was also on the 23 June imagery, but it wasn't on the airfield proper where a flying

Another important sighting was high pressure rail tank-cars for V-weapons fuel (the large building nearby made hydrogen peroxide). Sighting these anywere in Europe initiated a search for the rocket. 4 July 1944

vehicle would be expected and wasn't spotted during initial exploitation of the mission. At two-thirds the wingspan of the P30, the little plane was close to the minimum size the film could resolve. In addition, the small diameter fuselage and narrow wing cord didn't provide much of a surface to reflect light back to the film 35,000 feet above. Even so, two new weapons positively identified had already made the 23 June mission a landmark among Second World War photoreconnaissance successes. Medmenham PIs were also starting to learn "signatures" of the rocket weapons. One of the most important was the unusual, high-pressure railroad tank cars that transported alcohol, oxygen and hydrogen peroxide that fuelled the rocket motors. Immediately south of the launching ellipse was a plant making hydrogen peroxide. A sighting of those tank cars anyplace in Europe initiated a search for V-weapons and strengthened the idea that the weapons had to be rail-served.

Considering what had just been found, the information in the Oslo Report was looking better and better and there was more than enough evidence to run Peenemünde up on the target list. Meanwhile, mysterious massive concrete structures were discovered being built in the Pas de Calais suggesting nearing deployment of "something", and, at Peenemünde, "a railway flat wagon had been loaded with a cylindrical object projecting over the end of the following flat, approximately 38 feet by six feet. Another of these objects was seen on a second sortie,"(*Eye*, p. 190)[9] leading Sandys to conclude that the rocket not only existed, but might be in limited production.

The Lisbon Report, probably originating from a member of the Schwarze Kapelle,[10] handed to an MI6 agent in Lisbon, set 20 October 1943 as Zero Day for rocket attacks (*Bodyguard of Lies*, p. 364).

Actually, the V-1 was farther along toward operational status than the rocket, and a larger potential threat because of the numbers of the relatively simple and inexpensive bombs that might be delivered, but the Allies didn't yet understand that danger at all. Stopping or slowing the rocket was still the priority. Meanwhile, ULTRA intercepted a German Air Ministry message putting Peenemünde at the top of the list for applying for petrol coupons. That proved to Professor Jones that Peenemünde was significant. He alerted Bletchley to look for any signals indicating German radar units being moved to the Baltic coast and got a hit. Tracking codes from that unit were soon intercepted, allowing location of launch sites and giving info on missile performance (*Bodyguard of Lies*, p. 363-364).

Imagery of 27 June showed the frequency of coverage was stepping up, but added little new to understanding Peenemünde. The P30 was still present, though only two can be seen and only one new burn-mark (*Brit Intel*, vol. 3, p. 350). The P30 was not seen anywhere else until one was photographed at Bad Zwischenahn in March 1944. No rockets are visible on the late June imagery. One of the dredges had shifted (photo below) and one of the nearby "ramps" showed particularly well. The V-1 launch ramps were certainly no secret, three can be seen on the film, but apparently no one in Allied Intelligence had yet associated them with any weapons system

Based upon the excellent June coverage, Duncan Sandys reported his reasons for believing in the existence of the rocket to the Defence Committee and recommended bombing of Peenemünde.

In her book Flight Officer Ursula Powys-Lybbe wrote about several scale models of Peenemünde being completed by 11 July (*Eye*, p. 191-192). Medmenham often made models to facilitate planning for RAF bombing. Several were made for selection of aiming points for the forthcoming air attack on Peenemünde. A model of the rocket-associated area (Medmenham Club photo below) also shows the horizontal rocket on the rail car in front of the large building, indicating

More land reclaimed for airfield expansion. Clearly visible V-1 launch ramps were still not understood. Note web of dredger pipes passing the ramps and extending along the "fill ponds". 27 June 43

that the ACIU model was based quite precisely upon 2 and 12 June imagery, but didn't use coverage of the 23rd or anything collected later (since the horizontal "torpedoes" were not shown inside the earthen ellipse). We know the model was finished, in early July and the 12 June photos were still undergoing Third Phase PI into the latter part of the month (18th or 20th at least), suggesting the meticulous measuring and fabricating required for the model was a process taking several weeks.

The "vertical column" with a blunt tip and no tail fins was modelled standing on the foreshore beyond the earthen ellipse, just as it was imaged on 12 June.

Below, my arrows point to an erected rocket and heavy liquid rail car on the 12 June imagery.

The blunt tip on the modelled "column", and a measurement short by six feet, tells me that the PIs saw an erected missile without a nose cone. I see nothing to indicate whether the Germans erected a rocket without a nose cone, or if it was temporarily removed for some reason, but the Medmenham PIs and model makers got it right based upon what they could see. If, as it seemed, PIs understood in July 1943 that the 'column' was a rocket, it is hard to imagine making a model showing the vertical object without assuming vertical launching, so this story would seem to be at odds with Babington Smith's rendition that Kendall's understanding of vertical rocket launching came during a May 1944 revisit of the June 1943 imagery—see below. The shadow on the 12 June imagery is quite distinct and the "vertical column" doesn't have a pointed tip. The length of that shadow would have been used to determine the height of the "column". Knowing the day and time the image was taken, the latitude of the target establishes sun angle. A precise measurement of shadow length on level ground allows a PI to grind through a formula to tell the height of an object, but minute differences in shadow measurement can result in large differences in calculated height. The larger the shadow angle and longer the shadow, the better the measurement will be.

The same Peenemünde model also showed what PIs had identified as the first sighting of a "rocket" horizontal on a railroad flatcar in front of the large building adjacent to the test oval. This

68

model either disproves Professor Jones claim that Medmenham PIs had missed that object found by him—or that the model and its fellows were made in less than three weeks and incorporated his interpretation of the images. The model rocket on the rail car had three tail fins, which was what Medmenham PIs believed until June 1944 when they saw the rocket better on 5 May 1944 imagery from Blizna, Poland (see Chapter IV). That model rocket on the rail car also had the same length and a blunt tip as the "column", suggesting the Medmenham model-makers knew the vertical and horizontal objects were the same, therefore both rockets. Clearly the model-makers simply created faithful replicas of what they saw without any assumptions, decisions or judgments as to function or identity of any of the objects miniaturized. If they had modelled fins on the vertical column the argument of what Medmenham PIs knew in July 1943 would be completely settled.

Sandys summarized for the Cabinet the current state of the investigation on 26 July. He believed the rocket existed and was being developed at Peenemünde. He accepted the PI measurements and gave the range "in the order of 140 miles", driven by "some new fuel of very high calorific value". Having finally got the fuel right, his minute goes astray by concluding, "Having regard to the size of the projectile, it should be taken as certain that the projector sites will be rail served. Certain unexplained installations, rail served, have been observed in north France notably at Wissent, Marquise and Watten. Intelligence indicates that the rocket is directed by radio" (Kendall, p. 89).

The size and construction of the transport allowed analysts to make better estimates of the empty weight of the rocket thus refining their probable range (*Brit Intel*, vol. 3, p. 405). The debate in London began to shift from "was the rocket real" to "when would it be operational" (*Brit Intel*, vol. 3, p. 398-400). Lord Cherwell still led the group of doubters still skeptical of the rocket and believing

Meillerwagern—rocket transporter/erector. It also served as a ladder to work on an erected V-2. (NASM)

that there would be a long time or development before deployment. June and July imagery made it apparent that the rocket was not only being tested at Peenemünde, it was being produced there. That was enough. Destroying the production facilities and the people making the weapon was an obvious way to upset its deployment.

As an aside, it is amazing to me that the officials at Peenemünde would have so many secret weapons in the open when RAF photoreconnaissance planes were in the area. Either the German Air Defence network wasn't telling Peenemünde when single aircraft (obviously recon) was coming their way or the Nazis didn't realize how good the Allied cameras (and PIs) were. The double pass cover of Peenemünde on 23 June is an outstanding example of handing Allied Intelligence a windfall.

Aerial reconnaissance of Peenemünde was limited to 22 and 26 July to keep from alerting the Germans that something bigger was coming (*Brit Intel*, vol. 3, p. 376). The 26 July film was clear, sharp, and large scale, yielding the best coverage yet of the ramps. It looked like something new was being built in the still not understood "ramp area". Handling vehicles but no rockets were in the earth ellipse; however, a long shadow disclosed a beautiful example of a rocket erected on the asphalt fan just beyond. This time the true length and pointed tip were in evidence. The weapon was standing at the terminus of the new cable scar seen on 30 May imagery and was surrounded by servicing vehicles preparing it for a vertical launch. Once again, no one noticed or understood—or were not permitted to say. The July imagery let the PIs better understand the function of what they identified as cradles or transporters for the rocket. Though no "torpedoes" were seen, seven of the cradles were spotted, including one in the factory area, telling more about what was going on there (*Brit Intel*, vol. 3, p. 377). Identifying the characteristic shape of the Meillerwagen transporter (Miller wagon) allowed PIs to look for them in earlier imagery, and more pieces of the puzzle were falling into place. Once again, all the analysis was based upon horizontal objects. The only thing to be learned from the vertical objects was the all-important method of launch, and apparently no one had yet picked up on that.

Opening the *Bodyline* bombing campaign, Operation *Hydra*, the RAF strike on Peenemünde, occurred the night of 17/18 August 1943, the first suitable night for this operation based upon a clear sky and good moon, but not so good that night-fighters could easily see the bombers streaming toward their objective (*Schweinfurt-Regensburg Mission*, p. 271). Churchill wrote that a good

Photo taken during the Operation *Hydra* attack of 17/18 Aug 43. Circles show RAF Lancaster heavy bombers. Streaking lights are fires seeming to be moving as the bomber goes forward during the long exposure time needed at night. This was the same area covered on 14 May.

Key personnel housing was untouched, probably not on purpose.

moon was vital for target identification since Peenemünde was beyond the range of the "blind bombing" beams that were often used for closer targets. He also noted, "The weather was worse than expected and landmarks were difficult to find, but it cleared towards Rugen Island and many crews punctually started their time and distance runs. There was more cloud over the target and the smoke-screen was working" (*Closing the Ring*, p. 232-233). Time-On-Target was 1:10 am, a typical attack time for RAF Bomber Command.[11] "The crews were sobered to be told at the briefing that this was a visual 'radio-location laboratory and aircraft testing site', and that if they failed to destroy it, they would be sent back again and again until they did" (*Bomber Command*, p. 238).

The target was 600 miles away, slightly farther than Berlin. The mission went close to Antwerp, and would require passing near other heavily defended areas. Daylight operations to Regensburg and Schweinfurt by USAAF "heavies" helped *Hydra* by drawing much of the Luftwaffe's strength down to the south. In some of the most intense air battles of the war many Messerschmitt 110 night fighters, that would otherwise have been at Peenemünde, were shot down during the day by the B-17s and P-47s (*Schweinfurt-Regensburg Mission*, p. 271). Other unique aspects of the *Hydra* raid were the low release altitude and the highly effective deception feints at Berlin and Stettin to draw German night-fighters away from the bomber-stream.

Luftwaffe cryptanalysts reading Bomber Command ciphers had warned German coastal defences of bombers leaving and entering the defence zones, so the Luftwaffe knew the RAF was coming to northern Germany but the RAF tactics were excellent. Agents in Holland cut a cable from General Kammhuber's air defence signals HQ to command posts, disrupting radars and night-fighters all over northern Germany. The main attack force crossed Jutland below radar, then climbed to 7K for bombing. Peenemünde was caught completely off guard. Confusion reigned (or an estimated 200 bombers could have been shot down on such a clear night with a bright moon). Even so, forty aircraft, and some 400 airmen, were lost in the raid. German day-fighters sent to Berlin began to attack German night-fighters. Flak sent up 12,000 rounds.

Left—The foreign workers camp was hit worst when some bomb runs went long on the target. Most deaths occurred here.

Below—The main rocket engine test facility was understood in London, and bombed accordingly.

Fighters began to run low on fuel. Suddenly they could see fires at Peenemünde 100 miles away. Luftwaffe defences began to recover during the RAF second wave but many intercepts were missed because German night-fighters expected the RAF at an altitude of 18,000 ft (*Bodyguard of Lies*, p. 366).

A flight of Mosquito bombers drew as many as 200 German night-fighters away to the south with feints toward Berlin, as 597 British heavy bombers in three waves attacked at half their normal bombing altitude to lay 281 tons of incendiary bombs and 1593 tons of high explosive on the target.

Aiming points were in the built-up areas, going for housing and production/research buildings. The attack was a straightforward north-to-south run down the coast, with aircraft in train; bomb then a pull off (probably left, out over the Baltic) and head for home.

First Wave targeted sleeping and living quarters. The Second Wave targeted factory workshops. Third Wave target was the Experimental Station but some aircraft dropped long and their bombs went into the concentration camp beyond the target area. When it was over, 730 people on the ground (most of them foreign workers) were dead, including two major scientists and "several" British agents who had slipped into Peenemünde as "workers" from Luxembourg. The housing, offices and fabrication areas of Peenemünde were heavily damaged, delaying development on both the V-1 and V-2 programmes.

Albeit not delaying the V-1 and V-2 programmes to the same extent, the raid was still a shock and embarrassment to the Nazis. The next morning, Hitler and Goring raged at the Luftwaffe chief for failing to protect Peenemünde. Generaloberst Hans Jeschonnek, Chief of Staff of the Luftwaffe, returned to his office and put a pistol to his head. Delayed fuses had bombs going off for days, hindering German rescue and salvage work.

Of course a photoreconnaissance sortie was sent to Peenemünde the next day and with the Germans expecting the mission, the sortie ran as fast and high as possible, yielding smaller scale imagery than optimum. Despite coverage limitations, damage seemed extensive in the housing and factory areas, though several of the large industrial buildings were untouched. Shadows suggest the imagery was collected soon after noon. U P-L says the BDA msn was flown 19 August but 18 August is the date on the

Workers housing and several factory buildings were hit. Imagery of 28 November 1943

prints I have. Initial PI suggested that the damage was so severe that a scheduled follow-up daylight raid by the USAAF was deferred (*Brit Intel*, vol. 3, p. 382). Bomber Command thought they'd done quite well, and a lot of buildings were destroyed, however, the damage was not as severe as the Allies estimated from post-strike imagery. A recent German book states that "more than 80 percent of all the bombs had fallen into open country, especially into the surrounding woods. At least half of the remaining bombs had hit non-military or non-industrial areas, or targets such as streets, which could be repaired easily. These results revealed that the Royal Air Force did not know of the vital installations at Peenemünde. If the total bomb load had been directed properly, the entire experimental station would have been destroyed, together with irreplaceable drawings" (*V-Missiles of the Third Reich the V-1 and V-2*, p. 90. Hereafter noted as *V-Missiles*). According to General Dornberger, in preparation for possible air attack, copies of all the drawings had been deposited elsewhere (*V-2*, p. 147). The claim that the "RAF didn't know" where things were also smacks of revisionism since the official intelligence history (*Brit Intel*, vol. 3, p. 366), references a Detailed PI Report on Peenemünde issued 29 April, followed by a large annotated map of the installation published in July 1943—though Allied Intel clearly didn't know the specific purpose of every building in the "experimental area". A more likely explanation of the bombscatter in the woods is "creep" of bombers releasing in train and the notoriously poor accuracy of night bombing. Author Hölsken goes on, "The entirely unexpected English attack against Peenemünde on August 17-18, 1943, must have been a shock, because it proved that in spite of very strict secrecy regulations, the enemy obviously was informed about the development of the long-range weapons. Hitler reacted to that situation by turning to an entirely new long-range weapon design, the HochDruckPumpe, which he immediately ordered to be produced without waiting for test results" (*V-Missiles*, p. 168. More on the High Pressure Pump gun in Chapter V below).

Not a single bomb landed on the airfield or its facilities. The day after the air raid the aircraft present (mostly He 111 and Do 17/217) were a little more widely dispersed but flight operations didn't seem to be hindered. No P30s were visible, but two scorch marks ran out from the apron near the second large hangar, indicating fairly recent flights. The V-1 launch area was also untouched, underlining that its function as part of a weapons programme was still undiscovered.

Operation *Hydra* bombing proved that Peenemünde had been "discovered" by the Allies. With the steadily increasing capability of Allied heavy bombers to strike anywhere within range the test and development location could well be attacked again. That caused some rocket production to be moved underground and some testing to be moved west, out of range. Estimates of delay to rocket operational status caused by *Hydra* range from a few weeks to a few months. Even discounting other bombing interruptions of V-2 transport, fabrication and launch sites, *Hydra* alone probably set the rocket back far enough to keep it from having any influence on the Allied Normandy Invasion or subsequent breakout from the initial lodgement.

Diplomatic decrypts involving messages from Embassies in Berlin and Rome to Tokyo suggested that bombing of Peenemünde and other places of production had delayed the V-2 but Germany still hoped to have the rocket operational by the autumn of 1943 (*Brit Intel*, vol. 3, p. 395). There was a growing consensus on the size and capability of the rocket but the warhead was thought to be "carrying unspecified materials or gas of 'bacteriological germs'" (*Brit Intel*, vol. 3, p. 396).

The Allies were now even more sensitive to new weapons that might be coming into use from Peenemünde. "Until the end of August the scattered hints in the intelligence about pilotless aircraft had done more to confuse the attempt to establish the characteristics of the long-range

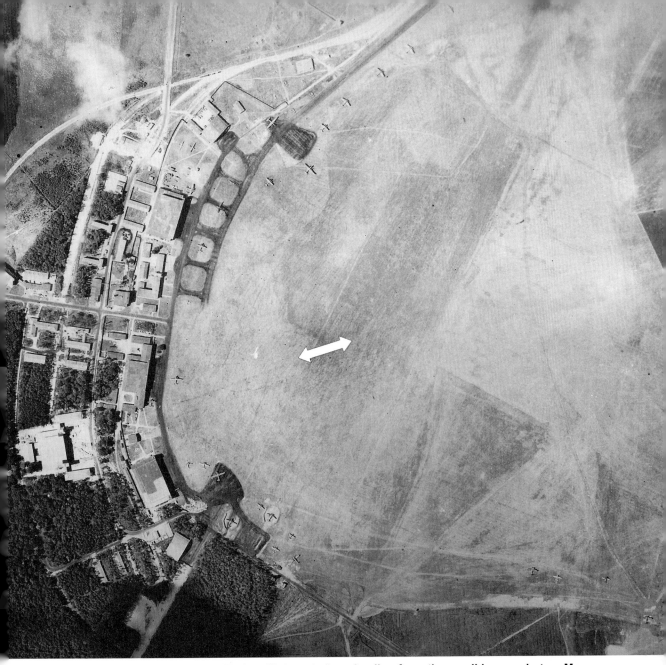

The airfield was untouched by *Hydra*. "Jet marks" are leading from the small hangar, but no Me 163s (P30s) are in sight. Other aircraft don't seem to be in dispersal positions. 18 August 1943

rocket than to prompt the conclusion that the Germans were developing two separate weapons for the bombardment of England" (*Brit Intel*, vol. 3, p. 390-391). Polish Intelligence had reported a flying bomb in April and "a bomb with wings" had been seen on Bornholm Island, coming from the direction of Peenemünde.

In August, SIS sources reported an aerial torpedo that was launched by a catapult. The

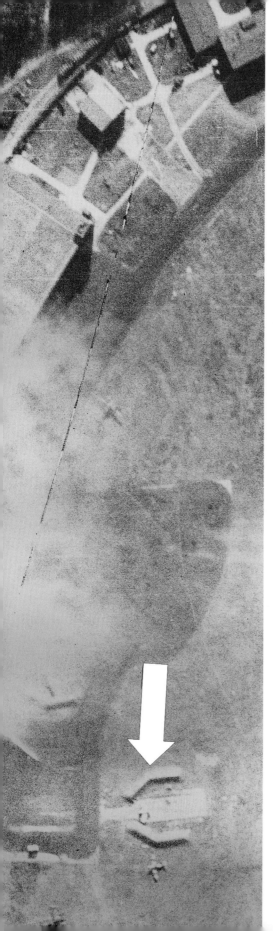

Germans seemed able to field new weapons technology that the Allies weren't even working on or couldn't get out of testing. In the summer and fall of 1943, German technology put spurs to the "weapons hunt" when rocket-driven, radio-controlled "smart bombs" were used to sink ships in the Mediterranean and Bay of Biscay.[12]

No one in England knew what the next surprise might be and no one wanted to find out the hard way. The Oslo Report was once again right on those weapons—and there were several other new weapons mentioned in the 1939 warning that had yet to be seen by Allied Intelligence. The long-range rocket still seemed the most ominous so emphasis remained on identifying and understanding that threat. This resulted in a series of *Bodyline* attacks, later in the year, on large unexplained bunkers being built in France that were assumed to be "rocket related". (See Chapter V)

Prior to September 1943, Flight Lieutenant Kenny was responsible for Peenemünde and Army Major Falcon worked the threat area in France. Now that the two areas were thought to be related, Wing Commander Douglas Kendall,[13] head of Medmenham's Technical Control Office and responsible for in-depth analysis and special imagery searches, was given overall responsibility for secret weapons activity and the two groups worked even closer together as the hunt intensified (*Air Spy*, p. 153).

This remarkable officer proved to be an excellent example of the right man at the right time in the right place. He shepherded the steadily expanding and improving PI effort, adroitly balanced application of limited resources against nearly unlimited demands, and gently steered PIs to find things with hints based upon other information only he had access to (*Eye*, p. 35).

In addition to Enigma and other SIGINT, Kendall also received selected reports from MI6 (mainly human source information). He also insured a constant flow of intelligence between Medmenham and Bletchley Park, where the communications intelligence work was going on, so each could benefit from using the product of the other's sources.

There was no activity in the V-2 areas but the P30 seen in a revetment ready for flight, proved weapons testing was continuing. 30 September 1943.

5304 V 540 N RAF 0860 23JUN43 PEENEMUNDE AIRFIELD 11937/03 RESTRICTED

Near original scale on the same 23 June 1943 imagery viewed by PI Babington Smith to find the P30—and, five months later, the P20. The rocket fighter is just visible on the airfield but the first sighting of the flying bomb was in an unusual location and invisible without extreme magnification (right). (Medmenham Club photo, my annotations)

In the fall of 1943 British radio and radar tracking intercepts suggested tests of a small airborne platform launched from Peenemünde and flying low to the southeast over the Baltic (See *Wizard War*, p. 360-370. Also, *Air Spy*, p. 164). There was no question that this could be the rocket. The low trajectory made that impossible. In November, decrypts of Luftwaffe messages established the speed (216 to 300 mph) and rate of fall of 2,000 meters in 40 seconds, "implying that the missile had wings, and that the maximum range might be 120 miles" (*Brit Intel*, vol. 3, p. 402). Meanwhile, agents in occupied France were reporting strange new construction at several locations not far from the Channel coast (see Chapter V and VI). Photo interpreters at Medmenham strongly suspected the rocket was not related to the strange "ski-sites" that were being found in France, but the new suspected flying bomb weapon had not yet been seen.

A Peenemünde mission of 30 September 1943 added little to understanding of the problem. The imagery was dark and grainy, the shadows long. There was no apparent activity in the ellipse where the rocket had been seen on earlier missions but a P30 was spotted in a revetment readying for flight. (The rocket fuel was extremely dangerous to the pilot and handling crews.)

"Up until now (late Nov), no one had seen this secret weapon (the V-1). However, we reached the firm conclusion that the weapon facing us was a flying bomb with a wing span of less than 20 feet (based upon measurements of the buildings in France). From the energy put into building the ninety-six sites and from Dr Goebbels' propaganda campaign, we also concluded that the Germans were in an advanced stage. It became essential to find out where the experimental work was taking place and, if possible, the source of manufacture.

"We had at the PI unit a section which focused on the German aircraft industry and its products. We instructed them to re-examine all likely areas in Germany to locate the missing flying bomb. It was a measure of their capability that they were successful in finding what we wanted within 48 hours" (Kendall, p. 100. Parenthetical comments are mine).

About 13 November 1943, based on the intercepted messages and radar tracking, Douglas Kendall asked interpreter Flight Officer Babington Smith to take another look at Peenemünde imagery for "a very small plane, smaller than a fighter" (*Air Spy*, p. 160). At this point she hadn't been told anything about ski-sites or rockets and knew little about *Bodyline*.[14] She trusted Kendall and knew he had access to several sources of "special Intelligence" so it was likely the little plane existed, and it was her job to find it. No one knew for certain, but the implication was that it would be even smaller than the P30. Something that small would only show up on good quality imagery so she began with the best coverage, the prints of the 23 June mission, methodically going over every millimeter of every print making full use of magnification and stereo viewing to ferret out detail. Her search surely worked outward from the logical places to find an aircraft: the hangars, then on the airfield itself. It was slow work and in late November she was still minutely going over the same prints of the double run over the airfield. Her patience won out and C B S finally found a little "plane". The building where the object was seen attracted her attention because similar buildings had been recently seen at several German aero-engine factories. She wrote, "It was sitting in a corner of a small enclosure some way behind the hangars, immediately adjoining a building which I suspected, from its design, was used for testing jet engines" (*Air Spy*, p. 160-162). She doesn't specify the actual date of the discovery. We only know it had to be before she saw the 28 November imagery, i.e. probably in early December (Craven and Cate wrongly say it happened in May, vol. III, p. 84 & 89). The tiny object was less than a millimeter across and not visible to the naked eye so she was undoubtedly using stereo for her scan. She must have noticed the tiny cruciform from its shadow, but couldn't tell anything other than its shape. Had the Argus pulse jet been tested on a wingless airframe, it would likely have been missed. But this one had the wings installed. The new aircraft was dubbed "Peenemünde 20". We now know it as the Fiesler 103 (Fi 103) or V-1 "buzz bomb".

Re-examination of imagery from 22 July and 30 September 1943 "disclosed a similar object.... The size was judged to be suitable for an expendable pilotless aircraft..." (*Brit Intel*, vol. 3, p. 402-40). One of the great gifts Medmenham photo interpreters gave later PIs was an understanding of how valuable it was to go back over "comparative cover".

The scale was very small and there was little contrast to break the object out from the concrete beneath, but the resolution potential of the imagery was excellent. My guess is that she switched to her jeweller's loupe for a better look at higher magnification and to measure the wingspan again, again probably using the shadow since the actual wingtips were less distinct. C B S was known to use a pre-war jeweller's Leitz magnifier for close in work (*Air Spy*, p. 108), but I have never seen anything that told the magnification she used. The 23 June imagery was excellent, but Second World War print resolution probably wouldn't normally have stood up well to more than 8x or 10x.

Babington Smith later wrote, "There was precious little I could say about it. The midget aircraft had the aggravating cotton-wool look that all light-colored or shiny objects acquire on aerial photographs, owing to the 'light spread' that blots out shadow and prevents detailed interpretation, and also makes things look deceptively larger than they are" (*Air Spy*, p. 160-161).

Over the years I have obtained several copies of the 23 June 1943 Peenemünde airfield imagery, albeit at least three generations removed from what C B S used, and without a stereo pair. Using her word picture of the location, I was pretty sure I knew where to look, but was never able to see the "little plane" on the coverage she cited until I got a better generation film positive from friends at the Medmenham Club. Suddenly, under maximum magnification, there it was! After such a long search, my thrill of discovery must have been close to the elation C B S felt—many PIs go for an entire career without a triumph like hers. I felt better about those months of failure after reading Ursula Powys-Lybbe explaining, "However definition was so poor that the evidence was not sufficient for confirmation" (*Eye*, p. 202). During my own look at subsequent coverage of Peenemünde from 1944, I found several V-1s, so I know how hard they are to spot—and I knew what they looked like.

To my eyes the narrow, straight wing made the tiny plane look much like a Bf 109, a shape every Medmenham PI would have been very familiar with, but C B S would have been careful to scale it and distinguish between the new object and the fighter which had a 12' 6" longer wingspan. Knowing PIs as I do, I'm sure Babington Smith quickly called to another Aircraft Section interpreter whose skill she respected, "Come have a look at this." As the word spread, the first chance they got, every PI in the shop would find an excuse to drop by and take a look at the new find—that's just the way it works in photo intelligence. So, if others had trouble seeing the little plane....

Other books on the subject include the well-known photo of the P20 caught on its launch ramp a few days later, treating it as though it were the first sighting, but that late November first sighting of the flying bomb ranks as one of the great PI achievements of the war. From that moment on, Medmenham PIs knew they were looking for a tiny "plane" and, thanks to C B S, they knew its size and shape. A wing required lift and that required a way to get up to speed. The "plane" was so small it was unlikely it had much range, which fit with the estimated 140 mile threat zone from London. It was equally unlikely that it would take off from a landing strip then proceed to a target. The result was a rapid cascade of discovery at Peenemünde and in France that laid bare an entire V-weapons programme. Consider the location of the find; not a place one would expect a "plane", then consider the size of the object. Look at the original scale image showing the P30 and recognize that the V-1 was just 2/3 of that span and with a much narrower wing. The fact that she could get a measurement accurate to within 15 inches (less than the width of a sharp pencil line at the scale she was working) has to elicit admiration of Flight Officer Babington Smith's interpretation skills.

A consensus at Medmenham quickly agreed that the flying bomb of the Oslo Report, and subsequent SIGINT and HUMINT indications, had finally been seen. Checking earlier coverage, the tiny airplane was also identified on imagery of 22 July and 30 September 1943 (*Brit Intel*, vol. 3, p. 403). For the first time interpreters were certain that they were searching for two completely different un-manned weapons. It also meant that finding other examples of the P20 were now more a matter of the luck of coverage, thorough scanning and recognition—not having to visualize something new and different.

PIs immediately understood that a small pilotless aircraft would require a shallow ramp/catapult to build up lift for flight. The pieces were falling into place. Concrete pads and studs seen in France suggested a shallow ramp would be erected. Medmenham PIs quickly guessed that the mysterious "ski-sites" being found were probably not rocket-related, but rather were for the newly discovered flying bomb. That was confirmed when interpretation of the "ski-sites" in France suggested that the weapons were stored in the "skis" and assembled in a small square building near the launch ramp. The width of that door, 22 feet, would allow passage of an assembled Peenemünde 20. Identical orientation of the assembly building and ramp on London completed a basic understanding of this threat—the flying bomb was guided by a compass that would be aligned in the assembly building. It was still assumed that the rocket would need a steep (high angle) ramp.

The requirement for some sort of launching system for the P20 kicked off another search of other prior Peenemünde imagery and resulted in suspicion that those "unidentified rails" on the coast beyond the airfield might indeed be the launching devices for the pilotless plane. As mentioned earlier, for years since the war, authors discussing discovery of the V-1 have erroneously reported that those ramps on the Baltic Coast were previously noted by Intelligence Analysts but ignored as being associated with the nearby pipes and equipment dredging offshore, used to fill in swamp land with earth pulled up from the Baltic bottom to expand the airfield.

The dredging activity had been present at Peenemünde from the very first coverage in 1942. The land reclamation was completely understood and certainly wasn't threatening. Work was steadily expanding the dry area and progress could be measured between successive coverages. The truth is that Medmenham PIs didn't mistake the launch ramps for sludge pumps—they simply didn't know what they were for. Early in their training, PIs learn to rely upon shadows, and shadows of the ramps on many sets of Peenemünde imagery clearly show the initially unidentified structures sloping upward from the ground and ending in air nearest the shore. Industry Section PIs knew what the ramps weren't; even a dilettante can look at the photos and see that the ramps had nothing to do with the dredging. The sludge distribution pipes, easily seen nearby, are all horizontal and clearly not connected to the ramps in any way, so the ramps didn't interest interpreters working on industrial developments.

The ramps were far enough from the airfield that they weren't associated with it except by the access road, but there were other access roads leading to the port and power plant and those weren't the province of the Airfield Section either. Since nothing tied the ramps to a threat, Third Phase PIs concerned with weapons hadn't looked at them. The Medmenham system of rapidly and thoroughly going over new coverage culminated with a high degree of compartmentalization in Third Phase and in this instance it worked against them. The system passed imagery from initial search and overview to detailed view to highly specialized analysis, dividing the prints of a mission to make sure they were seen by the proper analysts. Experts on aircraft and airfields got copies of those prints; transportation experts got prints covering roads, rail, bridges, tunnels and such. People who knew industry inside and out got factories, refineries and other commercial interests. Army PIs looked at land warfare defences, tanks and artillery. Air experts, like Babington Smith, got everything related to aviation. Other PIs got naval and merchant shipping. That system worked well for known targets, weapons, objects and activities but risked stumbling on the unknown—unless fate or curiosity intervened. But if the right analyst didn't see the right prints....

Until late November 1943, Medmenham knew nothing about the flying bomb itself so its launch ramps didn't fit into a known category. They didn't belong to anything going on at the airfield, the

Industrial Section didn't want them, no one could see how they might be rocket associated, so the flying bomb simply "fell through the crack".

The falsity of the "they thought they were sludge pumps" story was confirmed by Ursula Powys-Lybbe, who knew and worked with all the Medmenham players in this saga. Once again, her discussions with Andre Kenny while researching for her own book were invaluable in righting the misunderstanding. "To put the record straight I contacted Andre Kenny who assured me that the allegation was incorrect. In his capacity as a land-drainage expert (before the war), a much earlier sortie covering the area was brought to him for his comments, and he was able to identify suction dredgers but did not apply this term to what later turned out to be the launching ramp. These findings were supported by his senior officer Squadron Leader Hamshaw-Thomas, and had nothing in common with a ramp seen on the later sortie" (*Eye*, p. 202).

Unfortunately, the "they thought the ramp was a sludge pump" story is still being circulated.[15] A European author recently cited Irving's 1964 book as his authority then went on to conclude that early PI mis-interpretation led to a lack of attention for the Luftwaffe test centre (known as Peenemünde-West), because it had no connection with the development of a rocket (*V-Missiles*, p. 270).

There are two glaring flaws in that conclusion. Aside from the misleading impression of the "sludge pump" story, I can assure readers from my own twenty-seven years experience in and around photo intelligence that no enemy airfield photographed ever escaped attention. Airfield coverage, and minute PI analysis thereof, is one of the most important and enduring legacies of Medmenham. The first and greatest threat to air-offense operations in the Second World War was to be found at an airfield, and aerial photoreconnaissance took great risks to cover them frequently. It was crucial for control of the air to know what, and how many, threat aircraft were stationed at various locations a bomber stream might have to pass on the way to targets, or bomber bases that could threaten one's own territory. Each airfield covered was (and is to this day) always carefully and thoroughly reviewed with the utmost suspicion in all three phases of interpretation, each phase with its own bias. The PIs might not understand everything observed, but nothing in proximity to an airfield (and within the resolution scope of the imagery) is missed by oversight; nothing escapes comment. I have no doubt that Medmenham practitioners of the craft carefully identified and noted the location and type of every aircraft present at Peenemünde each time it was covered.

Powys-Lybbe credits fellow PI Babington Smith with first becoming suspicious that the "ramps" were threat related. "Babs, being more flying-bomb-conscious than her colleagues in industry although she knew practically nothing about *Crossbow* at that stage, notified Wing Commander Kendall who, almost at once, recognized the mysterious shape for what it was; the missing launching ramp for fitting onto those concrete studs seen on the Bois Carre sites (in France)" (*Eye*, p. 202).

Tipped off by "ski-site" indications of ramp signatures in France, and her new-found Peenemünde 20, interpreter Babington Smith extended her search, looking beyond her realm of the airfield itself.[16] She was still checking other locations to find another P20, and it wouldn't hurt to find something to put the little plane into the air, though Peenemünde had plenty of twin-engine aircraft that could carry it for an air launch (and indeed that did happen). So, the new weapon opened up plenty of possibilities for photo interpretation. Her responsibility was "aircraft", but she had found the little airframe at an unusual location so why not look farther afield. "This first excursion beyond the official bounds of the airfield encouraged me to try my luck in the other direction, and I decided to follow the dead-straight road which led northward along the eastern boundary of the airfield toward the Baltic shore. I passed the limits of the airfield and went on toward the extreme edge of the island" (*Air Spy*, p. 162). She goes on to describe the land reclamation project, pointing out that she wasn't interested in it and it "belonged to other PIs", but she identified the "ramps" for what they were. She had been alert for a catapult of some kind since she'd identified the P20 a few days earlier (*Air Spy*, p. 162). Looking at the previously unidentified structures where the airfield road met the sea, it was plain they were not part of the airfield activity, but the exceptionally good 23 June imagery (which I assume she was still using) had strong shadows clearly showing the obvious upward angle of the structures as they neared the shore. There were three of them, and two showed particularly well. F/O Babington Smith correctly guessed they were the launching ramps for the flying bomb.[17]

Douglas Kendall returned from briefing the new *Crossbow* committee in London on recent discoveries in France (see Chapter VI) and C B S immediately told him of her suspicions. He agreed that the flying bomb launch system had been found and showed the imagery to the Army Section (which was working the problem on imagery of France), then he and F/O Babington Smith worked through the night going backward through Peenemünde imagery to learn the history of the ramps (blessed comparative coverage). They found one ramp present on the small-scale cover of 15 May 1942 (*Air Spy*, p. 164).

Kendall hurried back to London to argue his case for the flying bomb to the War Cabinet. While he was gone, Babington Smith went over all the old covers again and found what may have been P20 airframes (or fuselages and motors without wings) near "four rather fancy modern buildings set by themselves in the open here, which I was sure housed some sort of dynamometer test beds" (*Air Spy*, p. 162). I located the buildings she referred to, but I don't have stereo so my copies of the imagery don't let me see anything I can call the new airframe. If they were bare metal or painted a light colour, they would "bloom" (appear larger) because of the way silver-halide emulsion on film reacts to light, making them harder to see or measure against a concrete background.

While this flurry of flying bomb related activity and discovery was going on at Medmenham, another one of those fortunate coincidences of war was occurring in the skies over Peenemünde. On 28 November, a 540 Sq Mosquito from Leuchars carrying both 14" and 36" focal-length cameras had been weathered out of its primary collection objectives around Berlin. The crew shifted to alternate targets on the Baltic coast on the way home, covering Stettin, Swinemunde, airfields near the coast, and Zinnowitz (eight miles south-east of Peenemünde) where experimental German radar was undergoing tests.

With film left, the high-flying recon pilot decided to use it on Peenemünde's airfield, turning the cameras on again just in time to cover the mysterious ramps, but without a stereo pair (*Air Spy*, p. 161-64). This is a true statement for the 36" focal length cameras. Two consecutive exposures covering the same location are necessary for stereo. Actually the 14" F/L cameras caught the entire installation (a photo of the ruined living area from one of those cameras is included in this book). I doubt the scale of imagery from a 14" lens would have permitted seeing the P20 in launch position.

The imagery was hard for a PI to use. At 54 degrees North Latitude the November sun was low and the shadows long, contrast was poor, making the film appear grainy but this time the focus of attention for Third Phase interpreters was not the Peenemünde airfield of the ellipse, it was strange the ramps and a tiny cruciform shape.

Film had to come down from Scotland, be printed at the ACIU, and the prints distributed for

Extreme enlargement of 28 November 1943 imagery. Original Second World War annotation indicates the V-1 (the arrow was drawn on the negative with a fine-tip ink-pen). The oldest ramp (aiming straight up) has been disassembled but shadows show the other three.

Coverage of 28 November 1943 at near original scale for the 36" cameras. V-1 ramps are on the shore at upper left and the rocket launch area is lower right. Note, a foreshore V-2 exercise is visible to the naked eye.

Second Phase and plotting before Third Phase PI work could begin. In the meantime, PIs working Peenemünde were comparing notes with PIs following new discoveries in France and the synergy was obvious. Army Section PIs at Medmenham looked at the 28 November cover of Zinnowitz to satisfy an Air Ministry request for a report on the Luftwaffe radar British Signals Intelligence had indicated was tracking low-flying aircraft from this area. They quickly spotted an assembled ramp, reporting it on 1 December.

This part of the story is a "chicken-or-egg" situation that will probably never be completely unravelled. Douglas Kendall remembered: "We had never photographed Zinnowitz before, so you can imagine our satisfaction at finding a complete Bois Carre type site minus the skis there.

The importance of the Zinnowitz site was that it not only gave us a link back to the notorious Peenemünde area, but it revealed a site in a finished state. So far none of the other sites we had examined had their firing ramps installed. At Zinnowitz, everything was complete. We could see the firing ramp in detail. By using a stereoscope, we took three dimensional measurements to calculate the ramp incline at about 10 degrees and length at 125 feet. Everything fitted our theories" (Kendall, p. 100).

So Kendall's memory of the sequence was: understanding the flying bomb from sites in France; seeing a typical site at Zinnowitz; leading to the Peenemünde ramps and finally seeing and measuring the V-1 ready for launch. Perhaps because she published first, there is quite a consensus in print for the slightly different Babington Smith sequence of: finding the flying bomb; identifying the Peenemünde ramps; equating them to those in France; equating those to Zinnowitz; and seeing the V-1 in launch position.

To some, this parsing of events may seem like clerics debating how many Angels could dance on the head of a pin, but the late November 1943 PI work at Medmenham ranks as one of the great Intelligence triumphs of the war. Following this, the V-1 was laid bare and attacked from factory to launch site, delaying use of the weapon until after Allied armies were ashore in France and the weapon could do little to change events on the ground.

Elements of Kendall's rendition seem more likely since he was working with both C B S and the Army Section looking at France and saw the event from both standpoints. As a priority collection objective, Zinnowitz would have been looked at quite early in exploitation of the 28 November mission; perhaps even in First Phase because the radar was a mission objective, but certainly before Third Phase PI Babington Smith had access to a set of prints. That priority-PI would automatically result in the serendipitous identification of the Bois Carre look-alike (see Chapter VI).

Babington Smith knew that new cover of Peenemünde was flown on November 28, but she couldn't claim the photographs before various sections with higher priorities. Late in the afternoon she asked Ursula Kay to try and get copies of that new cover of Peenemünde (Air Spy, p. 164). Years later C B S said Ursula Kay was the first to spot the P20 on a ramp, presumably looking at the prints as she brought them to her Section Leader.

While she waited for the new prints, Douglas Kendall came in and they discussed the probability of the "ramps" being the launch system for the P20. Kendall left before the prints arrived, so C B S and Ursula Kay checked the plots. They were disappointed to see that the photo run started just at the ramps and there would be no large-scale stereo pair to aid interpretation, but they went right to the single 7" print showing the ramp area.

When PI Babington Smith got to see the 28 November mission, probably also about 1 December, after what Kendall characterized as "an exhaustive examination" (Kendall, p. 101), C B S wrote that she could see the V-1 with the naked eye (Air Spy, p. 164). I can't on any original scale imagery I've seen—only on extreme enlargements of the near-perfect 36" coverage. She recognized a tiny cruciform disturbance in the line of the launch rail at the bottom of one of ramps. This was a good example of the right PI working the right imagery. Having studied the ramps shortly before, she immediately recognized the shape was not just a normal part of the ramp. As one of the few people who'd seen the "little airplane" on aerial imagery she recognized it as her little P20 sitting ready for flight. It was so small another analyst might have easily missed it. In another fortunate coincidence, what were the chances of aerial photos being taken in the few minutes the flying bomb was on the ramp? Had it not been for the incredible patience of the interpreter and the perpendicular line of the tiny wings breaking the line of the ramp, the mere 19 foot wingspan of the flying bomb might not have been spotted or understood—but now the P20 and ramps were undeniably associated as the flying bomb launch system (an understanding that would be another six months in coming for the V-2).

Of course everyone wanted a piece of the PI triumph. Professor Jones wrote that he asked that the sortie be flown in a time frame matching when many of the V-1 test flights had been noted, but other sources document that the coverage was actually a fortunate accident. Authors, going back to Dornberger in 1954, have also incorrectly written that the P20 (V-1) was first seen ready to launch on the 28 November imagery. Even Powys-Lybbe (*Eye*, p. 203) mentions it in that light, but we know better.

As it was, the object seen on the ramp pressed the limits of image scale and the limits of the film's resolution. The enlargement shows that the imagery had to be magnified until the grain of the film emulsion was starting to show and may be understood by realizing that the white arrow annotation was probably drawn on a "second generation" negative with a very fine tip pen and black acetate ink. The small unsteadiness of hand would have been imperceptible on the original. The number of ramps, one going back to 1942, indicated a very active testing program.

Once again, when PIs knew what to look for, the meaning of the ski-sites cropping up all over coastal France was crystal clear (see Chapter VI). As late as 18 November, authorities in London were telling the Defence Committee that "there was no evidence that a pilotless aircraft was yet in production" (*Brit Intel*, vol. 3, p. 412) That opinion was completely reversed by early December, thanks to Medmenham's discovery of the P20 and its launch system. The proliferation of ski-sites within range of southern England convinced PIs that the flying bomb was not only a real weapon, but its threat was near-term.

The lucky late-November photo mission allowed Wing Commander Kendall to send London a report (about 3 December) on the ramp-flying bomb relationship, establishing the flying bomb as the most immediate threat to England (details of this story are exceptionally well told in *Air Spy*). Assuming the ski-shaped buildings were for storage of weapons, analysis of the sites in France indicated they could store approximately twenty of the weapons in each "ski". With three "skis" at each of nearly 100 sites, the maths suggested some 2,000 bombs launched every twenty-four hours (*Air Spy*, p. 165). In practice, the average was more like 100 launches in twenty-four hours because the ski-sites weren't used. The flying bomb threat resulted in *Bodyline* (the rocket) being superseded by *Crossbow* (the V-1) as the highest priority.

Meanwhile, every PI Medmenham could spare was working on a number of suspicious construction sites in France within the "threat range", the zone that had become known as the *Bodyline* Area and was now to be known as the *Crossbow* Area (see Chapters V and VI). Signals Intelligence Intercepts of German flying bomb tracking had given the Allies confidence that they knew the range of the new weapon.

The next order of business was to find out exactly how the bomb was to be launched and propelled. "About this time, the Germans started using some glider bombs which were launched from aircraft against ships. They were known as the Henschel 293. Some of them did not find their targets and the Royal Navy were able to recover them intact. What we found was a new fuel system based on mixing hydrogen peroxide and potassium permanganate. We felt that this fuel might also play a part in the new flying bombs. However, rocket propulsion, as used in the Henschel 293, seemed to be out of the question because of range. All the sites were about 140 miles from London. We assumed that the warhead would be between 2,000 and 4,000 lbs. This heavy weight would require a very powerful system to bring the flying bomb from a stationary position at the bottom of the ramp up a 10 degree incline at a speed high enough not to stall out. The ramp clearly was some form of catapult. We called in a number of experts. At the sites there was no sign of supporting machinery or hydraulics that normally went along with a catapult. On close examination, we were surprised to find two blast marks in a fan shape pointing out at about 45 degrees on each side of the forward end of the ramp. At first this made no sense at all. But after an evening of trying to invent a new type of catapult, we came up with a new theory. The firing ramp consisted of a simple hollow tube with a slit throughout its length on the top side. We believed it to be a piston of sorts. And this is how it worked. The piston was placed at the bottom of the ramp and had a small fin which stuck out through the slit. This hooked into a U-shaped collar in the bottom of the flying bomb. To send the bomb on its way a mixture of hydrogen peroxide and potassium permanganate was fed from two cylinders at the base of the ramp. During the launch, the flying bomb and the piston were released from the platform, the bomb flying towards London and the piston falling to the ground in front of the ramp. In fact, by counting the number of skid marks at the site, we were able to tell how many bombs had left the site" (Kendall, p. 101-102).

Of course Peenemünde pistons fell in the water so Kendall's observation about piston skid marks pertained to events in France after 13 June.

The same 28 November exposure that caught the V-1 ready for launch showed a number of vehicles on the fan just beyond the earthen ellipse. It looks like fuel trailers and at least three V-2 transporters, but I don't see a rocket either vertical or horizontal. Perhaps a launch has just completed, but I can find no record of a rocket test on that day.

Enlarged 28 November 1943 imagery.
Right—Foreshore exercise.
Below—New heavy AAA battery as a response to "Hydra."

In response to *Hydra*, a heavy anti-aircraft artillery battery had been emplaced on the shore near the airfield and V-1 ramps (circle of revetments). The site is occupied (dot in the centre of each position is the gun) and the centre revetment is the fire director.

PEENEMÜNDE: 1944

By January 1944, the ever-present threat of another "*Hydra*-style" bombing, and with regular surveillance overflights as a reminder, it was obvious to the German establishment that Peenemünde was becoming increasingly irrelevant as a secret facility. Development and production activity continued but a sense of vulnerability caused a search for alternatives. The airfield and both V-1 and V-2 launch areas had been untouched by the bombing but no one on the ground could count on being skipped the next time. Imagery of February disclosed a lowering of activity in the factory areas, indicating lowered interest even though there was still activity on the airfield, roads and rail lines. With much of the test firing effort shifted to Poland (see Chapter IV), the chances of Medmenham seeing a rocket at Peenemünde diminished.

A fly-by mission out over the Baltic collected oblique coverage on 4 January 1944 but the scale and quality from the high-oblique 14" lens precluded adding anything to what was going on at Peenemünde. The photo, included here, shows the relationship of the airfield, flying bomb ramps, rocket launch area, and the experimental buildings.

Fly-by from a Benson Spitfire, 4 January 1944. Left arrow is the V-2 launching foreshore. Right arrow is location of V-1 ramps. Airfield paving hasn't begun. Smoke streaming from near the power plant (far side of peninsula) and near coast is an ineffective passive defence measure.

Considerable activity was seen in the rocket test launch area on 19 February 1944, including construction. Trains were moving materials in and the level triangle on the foreshore showed strange markings along with trenching for a new cable. Another long cable-scar, with a fainter series of markings and four distinct nodes, ran parallel to the shore, both indicating that some new scheme was afoot. The import of that second cable was not understood until May (see Chateau du Molay below).

Naturally, anything new in the "rocket associated area" still attracted a lot of attention from photo interpreters.

The same imagery shows a large triangular area of land reclamation almost complete, but does not show activity in the adjacent V-1 launch area. It appeared that the original ramp had been disassembled. The fourth launch ramp was definitely completed and it appears that a fifth is under construction. The fifth ramp has blast walls and a simple long narrow rail similar to those being found in France.

The three newest launch ramps were aligned to fire closer to the German shore. Perhaps this was a defence against parts of stray vehicles falling into "neutral" or enemy hands and winding up in England, perhaps it was to facilitate following the flying bomb test shots on radar. For some time the British had

Several new foreshore cable scars were noted on 19 February 1944 imagery. The one going to the right had nodes that meant nothing until a similar pattern was seen in France three months later.

been "stealing" German radar plots of V-1 test flights. The ADI (Sc) wrote, "Watching his plots of the Baltic trials over the next few months (Dec 43 – May 44), we could see that the reliability and accuracy of the flying bombs were rapidly improving" (*Wizard War*, p. 414). This improvement suggested to Allied Intelligence that deployment of the flying bomb might be more imminent.

Peenemunde's unusual foreshore cable scaring was also seen at Chateau du Molay, France, on 27 May 1944. 10th PG photo. The site was being prepared for primitive launch of multiple rockets as tested in Poland. The sole French V-2 launch site was overrun by ground troops before it could fire.

New cable scars extend from flying bomb launch ramps 3 and 4—which were doing all the test-firing by this time. Ramp 5 (the lowest) is under construction and appears alined with ramp 3. 19 February 1944

Even so, the rocket was still considered the most serious threat.

"Our original investigation of the enemy's secret weapons focused on their rockets. Since all we ever saw were rockets lying in the open at Peenemünde, this seemed logical. It was only later that we found an actual flying bomb. Once the immediate threat of a flying bomb was identified, our day to day activity changed. However, we never really abandoned our investigation and research in rockets. Much of the evidence was in our hands but it took us a long time to assess its significance (Kendall, p. 120).

The 19 February imagery also showed the housing area seemingly abandoned, based upon un-repaired buildings, rubble and unfilled bomb craters. It is probable that some of that was a ruse similar to what was being done at German factories and airfields.

Surveillance of Peenemünde was picking up through the spring and

Partially erected rocket on a transporter beside the hydrogen-peroxide plant. 26 April 1944

photoreconnaissance of 26 April 1944 was flown by a Spitfire from Benson carrying 36" lens Split-Vert cameras. Earth excavated from the cable trenches had been spread around, making the cable-ways impossible to see, but the new quadruple-noded cable showed well.[18] If the previous cable lines led to firing points, this new pattern presumably meant multiple firing points. According to agent reports this pattern was the prototype for what would eventually be a multiple-launch location for rockets in Normandy.

This mission was large-scale, good quality imagery, and caught another prime example of a rocket horizontal just south of the large hangar-like building next to the ellipse. Its shadow clearly shows the narrowing tip slightly raised off its transporter.

I'm going to do some PI work here and deduce what was happening. Medmenham analysts were looking at the ellipse and area around it because they'd seen rockets there before. The shadow shows how tall the large building was. It was clearly associated with the ellipse because of a horizontal transfer table track running from the building to the wide opening of the ellipse. It is curious that no one seemed to question why. (The track looks like a wide road leading toward the lower left of the photo and was familiar to every PI because of common use on railroads.)

If the transfer table was to move rockets to the firing location then the large building was for assembly and check out (to understand the height, compare the shadow with other structures nearby). Why

German photo of a partially erected V-2.

would it have to be so tall—unless the rockets were to be stood vertically inside for inspection? In any case, the area around the ellipse and check-out building were a natural search area. The "nose-high" rocket between the assembly hall and the next (much lower) building was easily found by its unusual shadow. The shape was expected and the angle was a potent clue that the rocket was simply tilted up for launch.

The 26 April 1944 36" film collected by a 544 Sq Spitfire from Benson quickly proved to be as significant as the 23 June 1943 mission. From the description of the location of the V-2 that was identified, I'm convinced this was the imagery that resulted in the discovery related below.

By May "there were a number of (agents) reports of vertical launching" (*Air Spy*, p. 168).[19] As

Kendall and PI Captain Robert Rowell, a British Army Officer with several years of CIU experience, rescreened all the thousands of Peenemünde prints from thirty-five earlier missions, their attention "focused on the fan-shaped stretch of foreshore that lay to seaward. At the end of the short road from the elliptical earthwork, it looked almost as bleakly bare as a parade ground. He checked it patiently from cover to cover, and then at last sat back."

"'Yes, it's asphalt,' he (*Kendall*) said to Rowell. 'I've found when they started laying it. The Germans wouldn't lay all that asphalt without a good reason.' He returned to his stereoscope. Then after a minute or two he handed a pair of prints to Rowell."

"This is the 'column forty feet high' which was photographed last June. Have a look and see what you make of it."

"Rowell looked, and then gave an explosive laugh, 'A column forty feet high, my foot! It's a rocket sitting on its fins!'"

"Kendall smiled and nodded, 'That's why they needed the asphalt. The fan-shaped foreshore must be a practice site for operational launchings. The elliptical earthwork was for early experiments" (*Air Spy*, p. 169). This version of the story varies some from that told by U P-L.

Douglas Kendall remembered those events as: "I have already reported that at Peenemünde there were certain crane-like structures surrounded by earth and blast walls which we deduced were designed for static ground running. This was a correct deduction. In front of these structures on a reclaimed beach area near the water there was laid a fan-shaped piece of asphalt. Looking back on it I cannot think why we did not ask ourselves the reason for such a surface in the beach area. The Germans would certainly not do anything without good reason. Furthermore early in the investigation we reported the erection on the asphalt area of a tower approximately the same height as the rocket. This was in fact one of the rockets sitting in a vertical position on its fins ready for firing. Had we appreciated the full significance of this, it would immediately have been apparent that the rocket did not need any special sort of firing ramp, any special handling gear

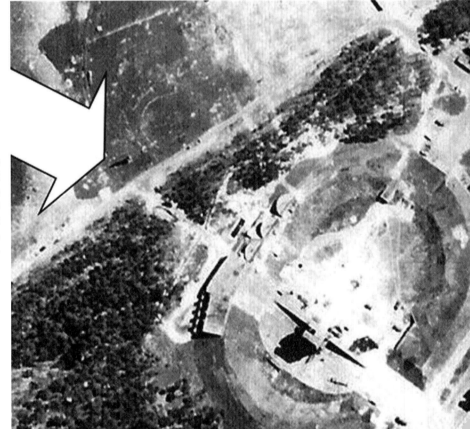

The near perfect shadow of a vertical rocket just beyond a road from the ellipse exactly matches Kendall's description in May (in text above). 26 April 1944 imagery.

of a fixed nature or the supposed guide rails for sending it on its way. This would have saved us a great deal of trouble in our subsequent investigations in Northern France. However I doubt whether the outcome would have been different, although we might have been saved a certain amount of bombing effort. I believe that we missed this important factor because the interpreters did not have a sufficiently open mind and were handicapped by the belief of our scientists that the rocket had to be guided by rails in a nearly vertical position during launch" (Kendall, p. 120-121).

They had indeed seen a rocket in launch position almost a year earlier and not recognized it. The vertical column standing alone wasn't what PIs had been told to expect—there was no ramp, no "projector". They had seen several examples since, but not recognized them. Gantry cranes in the ellipse indicated that heavy handling equipment was needed but obviously the rocket didn't need rail service or an elaborate launch site. Once they knew what to look for there was a scramble to scan earlier cover. It didn't take long to find other examples of erected rockets on the paved ellipse, confirming the hypothesis. The exact date of this incident is difficult to establish. If ADI (Sc) discovered vertical launching of the rocket in mid-July, the Kendall-Rowell anecdote is moot. If, as I suspect, Medmenham finally recognized vertical launching in mid-to late-May (as told above), the photo-search in France and identification of the du Molay site makes a lot more sense. Apparently "who figured it out first" was a huge brouhaha between the Intelligence and Scientific communities (See *Brit Intel*, vol. 3, p. 453-454, which follows the ADI (Sc) version and timing of vertical launching discovery).

The absence of recent burn or blast marks told Medmenham PIs that the elliptical earthwork was just for the early tests and all subsequent rocket firings had probably been made from the fan-shaped asphalt pad—where burn marks wouldn't show.

Meanwhile, USAAF Tactical units were using Tri-Metragon camera installations at medium altitude collecting horizon-to-horizon coverage of France in preparation for the Normandy Invasion. Imagery of 27 May 1944 confirmed the new Peenemünde multi-node cable-scar pattern duplicated at Chateau du Molay, near Bayeux, giving the Allies another proof that the V-2 could be field-launched from almost any flat surface with a modest clearing.[20] This caused another flurry of re-looking at earlier imagery of the threat area in France.

A cable temporarily laid on top of the Peenemünde asphalt would be invisible unless the shadow conditions were perfect but a cable trench is easy for a PI to see, at least until it weathers. As far as Medmenham could tell, the du Molay pattern was not repeated elsewhere in Germany, France or Poland. More worrisome, 26 April photography of Peenemünde disclosed a rocket apparently erected for firing (or training exercise) but not near the original cable scar or the du Molay cable pattern (or any other cable scar previously identified). This suggested an even more temporary field-launch control was possible.

Douglas Kendall wrote about another significant find at Peenemünde that had an impact on understanding what was going on in France. "During one of our photographic missions over Germany, we observed one of the firing ramps under construction. It appeared as a metal inclined ramp mounted on a concrete base. We could see that the ramp was assembled from sections about 6 metres (19 feet) in length."

"On June 6th, I issued a memorandum to the officer in charge of the *Crossbow* interpretation section. The memorandum is of interest since it shows our appreciation of the serious threat represented by the Belhamelin sites.

1. Following a meeting which I attended yesterday in London, would you please arrange for an investigation to be carried out within the next 48 hours into the firing ramps at

Belhamelin sites. The following information is required:

a) Whether they are the same length as Bois Carres. In this connection, we know that the firing ramps are manufactured in six metre sections so that if there is a difference between the two firing ramps, it is likely to be a multiple of six metres.

b) Apart from the Belhamelin sites, a number of Bois Carre sites are being sufficiently repaired to be used as Belhamelins. It therefore seems likely that, should attack develop, it might come from well over 100 sites. With priorities on bombing, it is obviously not a feasible proposition to attack these. The greatest importance therefore attaches to finding out whether the supply sites form an essential part of the system, and if attacked, would stop or seriously reduce the rate of fire. I have asked the *Crossbow* Committee to request twice weekly reconnaissance at a very large scale of all the supply sites and wish you to allot priority to the production within the next seven days of a special report on the supply sites. I should like to see this in draft please. The greatest importance of course attaches to being able to prove that some, if any of the supply sites are inactive.

2. Will you please convey the main results of the meeting in London yesterday to the *Crossbow* interpreters, i.e. that the main installations are probably prefabricated and might well be installed in a matter of days, once the foundations had been laid. This seems to account for the peculiar way in which they have developed so far, foundations only being laid and then the sites, as it were, abandoned. It is, therefore, of great importance that the *Crossbow* interpreters keep a watch for the first indication of a general attempt to put up the missing installations. The conclusions that at least one other building, a combined RI and R2, is necessary for the operation of the site should also be conveyed to the interpreters so that they will pay particular attention to the appearance of this or to the modification of nearby buildings. The latter system is being employed wherever possible (*Kendall*, p. 106-107).[21]

The entire area of Peenemünde showed well on small-scale imagery of 13 June 1944. The airfield and weapons launch sites had yet to be touched by bombing. The airfield was still being improved with extensions of the paved taxi-ways, and a paved runway under construction. It is clear that the RAF damage from *Hydra* was confined to the living and factory areas, but imagery of 4 July 1944 once again suggested that damage to those areas had indeed been heavy.

Peenemünde's runway paving work was proceeding rapidly on 4 July 1944. None of the Me 163 rocket planes were in evidence, nor were there any of their characteristic take-off scars on the grass. In fact, compared to earlier imagery, the field is rather empty.

The paved taxi-way heading toward the V-1 launch ramps leads to a hardstand and the buildings that would support the V-1 air-launch program, but there was no way that an Allied PI could know that one. It looks to me like two V-1s (arrow) in a revetment just off the new hard taxiway (though I can't find them mentioned in any contemporary source). This location could indicate air-launching experiments in progress. The 4 July imagery also shows a new heavy AAA site on the shore and a flying bomb standing alone on the road leading to the ramp area. Sixty seven exposures later, on a second pass over Peenemünde, the same V-1 in the same location appears being set up for a tow. If so, it will be towed away from the launch area tail-first.

Here "halation" worked in reverse with the light roadway reflecting so much light that the darker, but narrow, wings and fuselage of the Fi 103 almost disappear.

Peenemünde installation, 13 June 1944. Arrow shows runway paving in progress. Note how much land has been reclaimed.

7PG, 4 July 1944

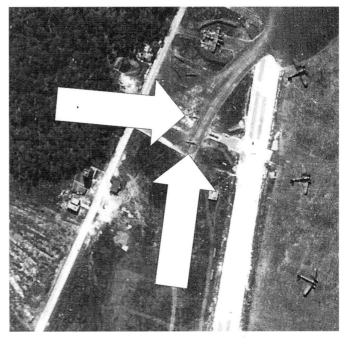

Enlargements of 36" lens imager, 4 July 1944.
Above—Two V-1s in an airfield revetment.
Top Left—V-1 on road to launch ramps (top of photo).
Newest ramp (lowest one) has blast walls similar to those
being seen in France.

Above—German photo of Peenemünde
launch failure (US National Archives).

Left—New foreshore crater (note blast
scatter of dirt) is evidence of a failed
V-2 launch. 4 July 1944

The 4 July imagery suggests a decline of activity in the V-1 launch area itself, and why not, the first flying bombs had been launched operationally from France three weeks earlier (see Chapter V). The original long V-1 launch ramp is at least partially disassembled, and the first of the short ramps looks abandoned, but a new ramp had been built. This simple rail is probably the prototype for the more austere "modified site" launch ramps.

There was also a lot for the PIs to see on the V-2 launch pad. Apparently a failed rocket landed dangerously short in the recent past. The crater showing blast marks radiating out in all directions indicates the exploding vehicle coming nearly straight down. The fact that the crater is alone, proves it doesn't represent damage from Allied bombing. Note that the Chateau du Molay cable line now only shows the four nodes that represented four firing positions. Douglas Kendall wrote that it was August 1944 before they "realized, from the Peenemünde evidence – which had been available to us for well over a year – that the whole firing mechanism for the rocket was mobile and that it could be fired from any relatively small flat area" (Kendall, p. 121).

Imagery of 4 July should have been enough for anyone. The number and type of vehicles present make it obvious that a major launch exercise was in progress. Special ground handling vehicles and fuel wagons are on the pad, and wonderfully clear shadows show three V-2 rockets erected (arrows), with at least one being fuelled for launch (the one with vehicles clustered

Shadows disclose a foreshore multiple-launch exercise, with three rockets erected (arrows), 4 July 1944.

Multiple launch exercise on the foreshore, date unknown. (NASM)

around its base). My identification of the rockets differs slightly from other annotated versions of the photo I've seen published. There are at least three, possibly four other rockets on transporters in an arc around the perimeter of the paved foreshore. It is impossible to tell if the "extra" rockets are for a subsequent exercise or to replace any of the initial rockets that fail to check-out for launch. In light of the new crater, it would seem risky to leave them so near with a triple launch exercise about to go.

Though the rocket hadn't yet been fired at England, the flying bomb had and activity seen on 4 July imagery proved that the V-2 was nearing operational status. That was enough to send another bombing mission to Peenemünde—this one in daylight.

Strike photography of 18 July 1944 documents some of the results of the first Eighth Air Force mission to Peenemünde.[23] The same raid also attacked the V-1 experimental site at Zinnowitz. Three hundred and seventy-seven B-17s put 995 tons of ordnance on the factory and launch areas, and, for the first time, the airfield was included. One of the major aiming points was to destroy the plant (between the experimental buildings and housing) thought to be producing hydrogen peroxide, production of which was under attack all over Germany at that time.

Other photos from one of the bombing aircraft show that the attack axis was almost due west, at right angles to that used by the RAF in *Hydra*, possibly so the bombers were on a heading home following release or because the airfield and rocket motor test stands were also to be struck.

Post-strike photoreconnaissance was flown at 28,000 feet by a Mount Farm-based F5 of 7th Photo Group—dangerously low for a lone recce plane this deep in Germany but guaranteeing good scale imagery.

Bombs from 8th AF B-17s on the way to the factory area. 18 July 1944

This time the rocket test sites and airfield got a share of the bombs. Strike photos, 18 July 1944

The 23 July 1944 PR mission shows bomb craters throughout the Peenemünde complex. Daylight bombing may not have been as "precision" as touted, but it clearly got the job done. Enlargements show the extent of damage to the airfield and rocket and flying bomb test areas. There were still plenty of aircraft on the untouched side of the field, but many were destroyed and the facilities west of the runway were hit hard. Heavy damage was also the rule in the rocket launching complex with at least twenty bomb craters inside the oval or on the asphalt pad. Ironically, the V-1 launch area didn't take a hit, but then the Allies were seeing all they wanted, and more, of the flying bomb in France.

Despite the damage, it looks like the V-2 launch programme resumed soon after the bombing. There are four V-2 handling vehicles on the asphalt pad (or three and a possible V-2 resting horizontal). The reason I guess that a launch is about to happen is the little blobs on the road (arrow). I read these as people gathered in a favourite spot to watch a launch. This little group of spectators was present on 26 April and 4 July, and each time the equipment present looks like a launch. They were not there on 19 February when no launch was apparent. Therefore, I assume a rocket launch must be in progress on 23 July.

Post-strike imagery of 23 July also showed extensive damage to the rocket engine test stands. The Allies still didn't know for certain what those things were for (but obviously up to no good) so

US 7 Photo Group post-strike recon. 23 July 1944

they were bombed. The shadows show that the main tower may be damaged but is still standing.

On 4 August 1944 8AF sent 221 B-17s with another 522 tons of bombs to Peenemünde, concentrating on the airfield and the V-weapons fabrication and test areas. Four days later 7th PG sent a pair of F-5s, escorted by sixteen P-51s to record the

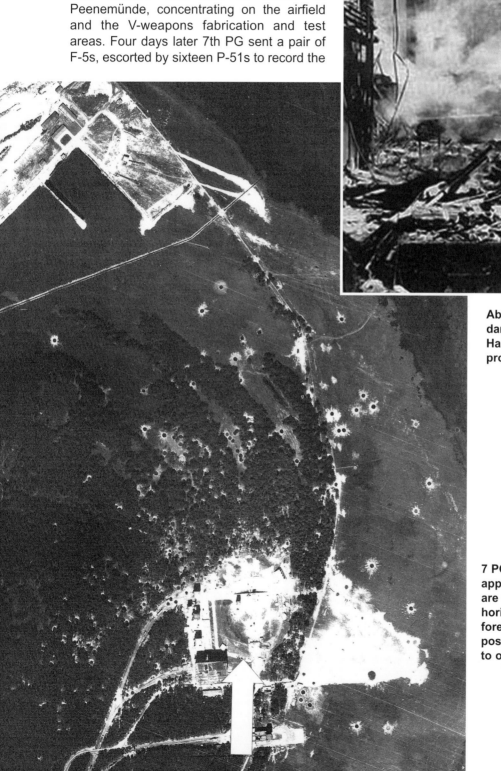

Above–German photo of damage in the "Rocket Hall," date unknown but probably about 18-29 July.

7 PG BDA 23 July 1944. It appears the rocket facilities are still active. Vehicles and horizontal V-2s are on the foreshore. The arrow shows possible workers gathered to observe a launch.

status of Peenemünde. More bombs had hit the airfield facilities, but there was activity on the field itself. The newly paved runway was untouched and operational. The V-1 and V-2 launch complexes still look relatively inactive. However, "*Crossbow*" policy at that time was to keep on striking targets until they were pounded into abandonment, so 146 B-17s took another 365 tons of bombs to Peenemünde on 25 August 1944.

In September the V-2 was in use and German experimental emphasis at Peenemünde shifted to other weapons that never went anywhere. Allied heavy bombing returned to targets that better supported ground forces in France and strategic objectives in Germany.

PEENEMÜNDE: 1945

Research ceased in January and February. All Peenemünde research personnel were evacuated to safer territory by March. Soviet ground troops occupied the installation on 5 May.

PEENEMÜNDE AERIAL PHOTO COVERAGE (* = imagery I know about but haven't seen)

1939 ?	German photos captured at the end of the war
1942 05 15	A762 according to C B S
1943 01 19	mentioned in *Brit Intel* *
1943 03 01	mentioned in *Brit Intel* *
1943 04 22	according to Professor Jones *
1943 05 14	N825 540Sq F/36 frame 5065
1943 05 20	N832 540Sq F/14 frame 2063, F/36 frame 1060
1943 06 02	**C B S says Kenny rpts 40' column** *
1943 06 12	N853 540Sq **horizontal V-2 identified by Jones?** * **Vert rocket on foreshore**
1943 06 16	Kendall, 40' vert column. Could be referring to PI date not msn date?
1943 06 23	N860 540Sq F/14 frame 1042 22-24K = **P30, P20, V-2 & 2 "torpedo-like objects" in elliptical earthwork**
1943 06 27	N867 540Sq
1943 06 28	reported msn poss confused with N867*
1943 07 22	
1943 07 26	N890 540Sq frames 5208, 5209, 5210
1943 08 18	N902 540Sq *Hydra* BDA
1943 08 20 *	
1943 09 30	N945 540Sq frame 3078 **V-1 seen at engine test stand in late Nov**
1943 10 03	N946 540Sq
1943 11 28	N980 540Sq F/14 frame 2021 **V-1 identified on ramp**
1944 01 04	oblique
1944 01 05	*Brit Intel**
1944 01 07	*Brit Intel**
1944 02 19	L/43 540Sq F36 frames 4129, 4130 **BDA, du Molay pattern seen**
1944 04 26	msn131 106W 544Sq F/36 frame 4094 **V-2 launch exercise, V-1 on road**
1944 06 13	**BDA**
1944 07 04	msn 1201 106G F/36 frames 3005, 4065, 4071, 4072 **BDA, V-1 on road**
1944 07 09	544 Sq 106 msn 1201 frame 3006 ??
1944 07 18	SAV-91-423 F12 24.8K, **8TH AF strike photos**
1944 07 23	msn2427 US7 F24 28K frames 3058, 3076, 4067, 4068 **BDA**
1944 08 08	frame 3056 **BDA**
1944 09 ?	From Benson – 544Sq

1   Finding targets for the heavy bombers, noting German air defences, performing BDA, watching German naval and air offensive capability, and supporting ground operations or planning were all demanding attention as "flames closer to the front door". There was never enough film, coverage, PIs or time. In 1968 I worked on a mission that brought back over a mile of aerial film and covered almost all of North Korea in three passes. Such things were impossible in 1943 when an aerial mission might return a maximum of 500-600 feet of useable film covering a swath a little over a mile wide.

2   Lt. Gen. Ludwig Cruewell, Commander Afrika Korps from August 1941 to June 1942, was captured when his light plane was shot down at Gazala. General Ritter von Thoma commanding Afrika Korps was captured at El Alamein in November 1942. See *Brit Intel*, vol. 3, p. 362-363 for details of this story.

3   Ironically ignoring American Robert Goddard's work on liquid fuelled rockets (which Wernher von Braun was following).

4   It is interesting that in his book, *Wizard War*, Jones mentions Douglas Kendall several times (not always favourably) but does not name another PI except for a note referencing Babington Smith finding the V-1. In her book, C B S mentions Jones twice but neither in the context of the V-weapons search. Powys-Lybbe mentions Jones three times, two in which she disputes or debunks his assertions. Kendall does not mention Jones at all in the context of the V-weapons hunt.

5   Major intelligence collection objectives in the Baltic were submarines, the unfinished aircraft carrier *Graf Zeppelin*, and the damaged battlecruiser *Gneisenau* at Gdynia (Gotenhafen).

6   Or F/O, a Women's Auxiliary Air Force rank equivalent to RAF Flight Lieutenant and USAAF Captain.

7   *Eye*, p. 191. Powys-Lybbe attended the same WAAF officer's class as fellow PI C B S. After a stint in Second Phase, they also worked together in the Airfield Section in Third Phase.

8   The actual missions were not noted, but they had to be those in early to mid-June. Once again the measurement indicates movement of the rocket without a nosecone.

9   The Black Orchestra. A group of disillusioned high ranking Nazis and German officers plotting to overthrow Hitler.

10   In *The Rocket and the Reich*, p. 197, the author states, "The RAF had quite consciously decided to try to catch the leading engineering personnel in their beds." Of course the highly specialized and perhaps irreplaceable personnel would be targets, but there was nothing particularly nefarious in the night bombing—it was the norm for the RAF.

11   The air-launched, radio controlled, rocket boosted HS 293 was used on 25 August 1943 and the air-launched glide bomb, Fritz X, sank the Italian battleship *Roma* and damaged sistership *Italia* on 9 September.

12   *Eye of Intelligence* is an excellent source for how this pioneering officer got into photo intelligence, and some of his accomplishments. He had been an RAF photo interpreter since 1939.

13   *Brit Intel*, vol. 3, p. 402-403, says CBS found the P20 on 13 November 1943, apparently confusing the date she was asked to look with the actual discovery several days later.

14   The story seems to have begun through a misunderstanding of what was written in *Air Spy* (p. 163) where C B S says the Industrial Section PIs had looked at the ramps "long ago, and interpreted them as something to do with the dredging equipment" – not mentioning that the PIs specializing on weapons hadn't come to that conclusion and hadn't weighed in yet. *Wizard War* and *Mare's Nest* have the same version of events. It is even repeated in the "official history". After a thorough look at the imagery, the Kenny/U P-L version rings more true to me.

15 The flying bomb/ramp or ramp/flying bomb discovery sequence was another of those chicken-and-egg situations with all the elements identified in France, Zinnowitz and Peenemünde during what must have been an exhilarating and bewildering three or four days of revelation and analysis at the end of November and the start of December 1943. For a PI the adrenaline rush of "finding" things more than makes up for those hundreds of hours of going over images of the known to confirm or deny minute changes. Those are times when PIs don't want to leave the work even for rest.

16 The Medmenham Club archive holds an undated annotated graphic attributing the discovery to Flt Lt G. B. Reynolds.

17 On 29 February, 540 Sq. Mosquitoes had moved south from Leuchars to Benson 10 miles SE of Oxford (and home of the PRU) so their film was available at Medmenham much sooner after a mission. This mission was from 544 Sq.

18 If correct, this launch understanding preceded the same revelation based upon 5 May cover of Blizna, Poland, which Medmenham PIs didn't see until late May (or early June according to some sources)—see Chapter IV below.

19 The Chateau du Molay site for multiple V-2 launching was never used and never bombed. It was overrun by the Allies in June, following the Normandy landings—and the rocket was not operationally ready until September. Professor Jones wrote that the site was found on the ground first, then equated by him to Peenemünde, not the other way around: *Wizard War*, p. 432-433. Unquestionably the site was hard to see and almost meaningless, but it clearly "doesn't belong" where it was found. Unless Medmenham PIs missed it completely, the May imagery suggests that the sequence related in my text is correct.

20 Elements of a V-1 launch site were given letter designations. The ramp was "P", launch control "K", launcher service "R2", cistern and pump station "C", water cooling reservoir "E", final check (the non-magnetic building) "Q", preliminary services "R1", "S" for storage and personnel shelters, "A" for storage or delivery building.

21 Titling on the imagery says the camera had a 12" lens and bombing was from 24,800 feet.

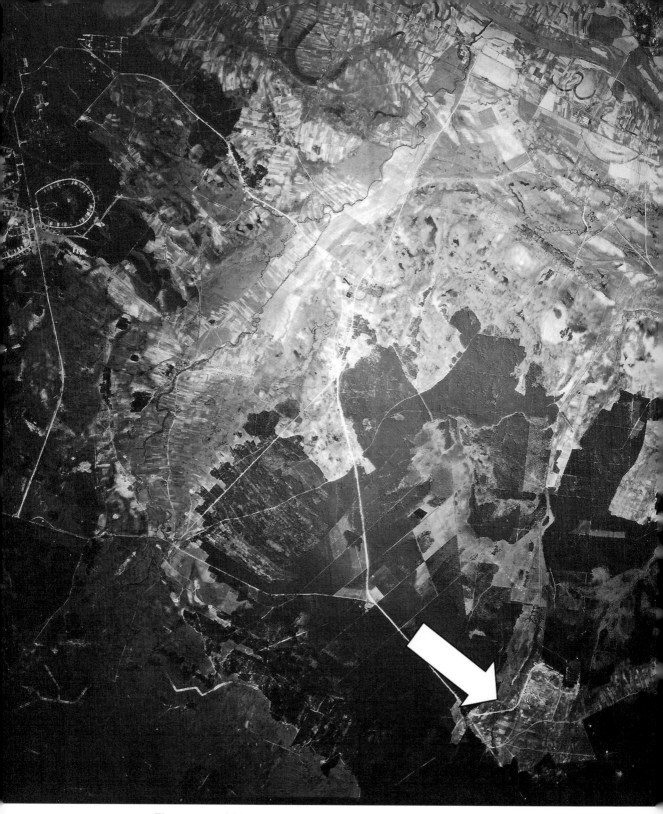

First cover of Blizna, Po, 19 April 1944. Note horseshoe housing area.
Arrow shows V-weapons test site.

Chapter IV
THE WILDS OF POLAND

DISCOVERY

When Operation *Hydra*, and worries of another air attack, made the comfortable and well equipped facilities at Peenemünde too dangerous, much of the Nazi rocket test-firing programme went to the relative safety of the remote, dense forests of south-eastern Poland. The place selected was Blizna, a former Polish Army artillery firing range between Krakow and Lvov. The first indication of V-weapons activity was Ultra traffic concerned with flying bomb tests over land (*Wizard War*, p. 430). Apparently another motivation for relocating to Poland was to get the still erratic unmanned missiles away from accidental landing on German citizens.

Daring members of the Polish underground were soon reporting unusual activity in a vast area where it was instant execution to be caught. The characteristic liquid oxygen/hydrogen peroxide rail cars were seen entering the secure area. An Ultra intercept referred to a crater 160 miles down range, beyond the assumed reach of the flying bomb, leading to the conclusion that the rocket was also being tested at Blizna (*Wizard War*, p. 430-431). An A-4 rocket was launched from Blizna in December 1943. It was a failure.

At great risk, the Polish underground managed to gather information and even parts of failed V-2 shots the Germans made in February and March 1944 to test the range of the rocket.

In a related intelligence coup, in May a

German chemical warfare expert was captured in Italy. He had attended a rocket course at Peenemünde in August 1943 and his interrogation revealed fuel, warhead weight, and range data on the V-2. He also revealed that the rocket was fired from a simple metal base or frame that was carried on the transporter with the missile. His description indicated that the rocket was fired vertically (*Brit Intel*, vol. 3, p. 442).

Intercepted communications referring to "apparatuses" being sent back and forth also tied Blizna to Peenemünde (*Wizard War*, p. 435). Indications were solid that both the flying bomb and rocket were being test fired from this location. In February and March 1944, code-breakers at Bletchley Park discovered Luftwaffe messages explaining that three different fuels were used at Blizna, providing the first firm indication that the flying bomb was not rocket driven (*Intelligence in War*, p. 280). From March through May the flying bomb had been seen in the air from Sweden and two examples had been dredged up by the Swedish Navy (*Intelligence in War*, p. 281).

British scientists were given access to the wreckage in late May and learned about the propulsion and guidance systems. This information was probably not available to PIs until after the first V-1s were landing in England in September. Clearly the Allies badly needed a look at Blizna.

Beyond effective range from England, the Blizna site was within reach of a Mosquito photoreconnaissance Squadron based at San Severo, Italy. Targets in south-central Poland were a thousand miles from England through the heart of Luftwaffe defences. The 900-mile round trip for RAF 680Sq, 683Sq or SAAF 60Sq from Italy was risky enough. Professor R V Jones requested cover of Blizna and wrote in *Wizard War* that it was flown on 5 May 1944. *Air Spy* and *Eye of Intelligence* say the first Blizna recce was actually flown on 15 April 1944. The print I have is dated 19 April and is probably the correct answer. Those 19 April 1944 photos left much to be desired. The collection aircraft was rather high, making for small scale imagery, and two of the three short focal-length camera exposures were "thin" or washed out because of a bad sun angle. If that mission collected imagery of Blizna using long focal-length cameras, I couldn't find the film. The April mission was adequate for recognition of the obvious, but not sharp enough for details or identification of something unexpected.

Near the target, a modern housing complex was covered. Though larger, its horseshoe pattern was reminiscent of the housing at Peenemünde. Imagery of the test facility itself was good enough to allow interpreters to positively identify the site as "V-weapons" related. Babington Smith wrote that no rocket was seen but the "place smelled of *Crossbow*" (*Air Spy*, p. 168). Medmenham PIs quickly recognized a flying bomb ramp (*Eye*, p. 192), and plotted a narrow-gauge railway leading into the woods to what were most likely dispersed storage buildings. The imagery was good enough to show that the light-rail line running into the woods disclosed no signs of construction (newly disturbed earth) so it probably pre-dated German occupation of the site. However, a new spur of the light-rail had been run to the centre of the open area, terminating at or near a large area of paved/disturbed ground, later identified as the probable launch pad for the rocket.

The April imagery shows three small clearings lined up in the nearby forest. At least two craters, appear to be from failed launches. The largest crater shows blast directionality that plots back closest to the V-1 ramp, but that evidence may not be conclusive. A high angle impact scatters spoil evenly. A low angle impact scatters most spoil in the direction the vehicle was going.

Blizna showed none of the large earthworks associated with the rocket at Peenemünde and

Allied Intelligence still expected to see some sort of ramp to launch the rocket. *Air Spy* and *Eye of Intelligence* relate this story identically. The quandary over how the rocket was launched was still unresolved in May 1944. A railroad train was unloading on the regular tracks and some of those cars were the unique hydrogen peroxide/liquid oxygen transports seen at Peenemünde. The most significant result of the April cover was to establish a bench mark against which to measure future changes to the site, including the location of craters that probably indicated failed launches.

The next coverage occurred on 5 May 1944. The recce plane was at about the same altitude as in April, but the time of day was better so the cover was quite good. The collection aircraft got a string of photos with a small-lens area-coverage camera but also used a pair of 36" lens Split-

Blizna, 5 May 1944 at near original scale for 36" lens cameras.

Blizna, Poland, 5 May 1944.

Vertical cameras, then flew off to expose about thirty frames from the small-scale camera on other targets. On the way home to Italy, the second photo pass (some 200 exposures later on the longer focal length cameras) showed the site even better. Shorter shadows suggest this overflight was closer to noon and at least a half an hour later than the first pass, perhaps more. The contrast was near perfect so detail was as good as it could get with the aerial cameras and film of the day and ability to enlarge was excellent (*Mare's Nest*, p. 264). Irving states that this coverage was not interpreted until 3 June. Surely that meant not finished in Third Phase (detailed) Interpretation, or, the report hadn't yet been issued. Even though the film had to be sent to Medmenham from San Severo in Italy I can't imagine that no one looked at it for nearly a month. There were PIs in Italy, and the film covered many other targets besides Blizna, most of them important to heavy bomber missions being flown from Italy.

The 5 May imagery was an excellent example of why comparative coverage is invaluable—in this case changes between passes being more important than between missions. This imagery also resulted in another "dust up" between Professor Jones and the PI establishment over things the pros had "missed". ADI (Sc) wrote that, going over the 5 May coverage on 17 July, he identified a rocket, believing he found something Medmenham PIs had overlooked (*Wizard War*, p. 436). The time delay presumably resulted from having to process and copy the film for use in Italy, fly the original negative to England, then make and distribute prints for Third Phase PI. In fact, Medmenham PIs had already noted the rocket and established that it had four fins, not the three that had first been assumed from poorer scale and quality coverage of Peenemünde a year earlier (*Eye*, p. 194).

I'm going to risk interjecting myself in the interpretations of both Professor R V Jones and Medmenham PIs again. There were enormous pressures on British intelligence to understand the V-2. Good PI is a matter of "what do you see, no more, no less". I know what it's like to search imagery for something specific—temptations are great. The people at Medmenham had lived through German bombings and anticipated worse if the new weapons couldn't be pre-empted. I had excellent enlargements and unlimited time. I also know what a V-2 looks like (hindsight is wonderful). The analysis given here is my opinion. It wouldn't bother me to be proven wrong by someone with access to better imagery or more skill as a PI.

Reading between the lines written by Professor Jones and several Medmenham PIs, I conclude that they were talking about different images of the rocket from the same mission, and each may have overlooked something the other found.

A large train had recently arrived at Blizna, and at least three of the big hydrogen peroxide/liquid oxygen rail cars often seen at Peenemünde can be positively identified where the rail spur curves (arrow). The dog-leg revetment, and what appears to be a launch rail closer to the top of the "U" of tracks (both thought to be V-1 sites) seem inactive (arrow). A triad of round objects have been relocated from right in front of the terminus of a narrow gauge rail line and concrete pad quickly believed to be the rocket firing site to a safer spot closer to the bottom of the "U" of the rail line (arrow). Most important, the 5 May imagery showed an object immediately beside the train and in proximity to two traveling gantry cranes, opposite the long building. Since its tail-fins are quite apparent in stereo, I conclude that this was what Medmenham PIs identified as a rocket lying horizontally, clearly just off-loaded from the train (*V-Missiles*, p. 217-219). Hölsken's excellent book has a series of German ground shots showing unloading a V-2 from a train. He doesn't identify them as from Blizna, but I will based upon correlation with the long building and trees in the background.

The 5 May coverage also proved that the rocket was shipped with fins attached. It also appears to have a nose cone. Prior to this mission, shipping method had been another unresolved question. The rocket (arrow) horizontal beside the train is longer than any nearby rail car, so it must have extended beyond its carrier over an "idler" car, but which is that car? The location of the rocket suggested that the gantry cranes were used for unloading. Similar cranes had been observed in the earthen oval at Peenemünde and it was something expected with the estimated weight of the weapon. The first time a rocket was seen it was on a rail car at Peenemünde and extending over the end of its flat-car, but there doesn't seem to be a flat-car and "idler" combination present anywhere in this train. The next closest rail cars to the off-loaded rocket are clearly hydrogen peroxide/liquid oxygen transports. An empty missile transporter is standing near the heavy liquid rail cars so there is probably another rocket somewhere else on the train.

On the second pass over the Blizna range, perhaps twenty or thirty minutes later, the empty Meillerwagen hasn't moved but the object (clearly a rocket) that had been alongside the train is at the far end of the unloading area on a turn-around loop for the narrow-gauge railway. There are vehicles apparently coming from the field to meet the train.

This stereo imagery was the best look the Allies had at the long-range rocket. Beyond doubt, it was present and there was ample multi-source evidence that was being fired, but there were no ramps or "projectors" anywhere to be seen. Based upon the Blizna coverage, though they'd yet to recognize an erected rocket, Professor Jones correctly deduced that the rocket was fired vertically, sitting on its fins (*Wizard War*, p. 436). But this time Jones didn't claim to "find" an erected rocket the PIs had missed. The official assumption of vertical firing of the rocket inspired Douglas Kendall to institute his monumental search of earlier imagery of Peenemünde, resulting in the identification of several examples of erected rockets and their associated servicing equipment erected for launch at the original rocket test location (*Allied Photo Reconnaissance of World War Two*, p. 107).

Powys-Lybbe tells of pieces of a Peenemünde rocket that dropped into Sweden on 13 June 1944 where they were examined by British officers. British Intelligence "bought" the rocket remains from Sweden for two squadrons of light tanks. Two Mosquitoes were sent to bring the parts to UK. This conclusively ended the debate over the existence of a more powerful weapon than the V-1 (*Bodyguard of Lies*, p. 726). At this point the threat was deemed so serious that the Allies considered use of gas or biological agents in retaliation for a rocket attack (but that wouldn't be possible before mid-1945, so the idea was dropped).

The ADI (Sc) report on analysis of rocket parts, and statements from a POW that the rocket was launched from a simple concrete platform, were not shared with Medmenham. So Kendall and his crew had to deduce the whole rocket mobility and firing system from imagery alone—and their interpretation was not confirmed on the ground until Allied troops over-ran a V-2 launch site on Walcheren Island, Netherlands, in November 1944 (*Eye*, p. 194).

In his book, Professor Jones quoted a memo he wrote the night of 16/17 July 1944 precisely noting the frame and location on the frame of an object he identified as a "rocket"—something he said Medmenham had missed in their look at Blizna.[1] Since the finned-object the PIs found beside the train was no longer in that position on the second-pass frame Jones cites, what ADI (Sc) noted was the same object moved farther back along the line and away from the train, and his measurement of the location is quite accurate. Though the rocket appears to be on the reversing loop of the narrow-gauge railway, it actually diagonals slightly across the track so it doesn't look like it could be on a rail transport. Therefore, it must be on a wheeled transport of some sort, probably a Meillerwagen. This essential piece of V-2 handling equipment was not understood until the Blizna missions. Its open framework made it difficult to see given the photo-scales and light conditions at Peenemünde.

Blizna imagery proved the rocket didn't require rail-service to its firing point, and that it was clearly much lighter than originally thought. But it is troubling that there was no tug or prime mover nearby. PIs could logically conclude the rocket was resting on one of those special V-2 related vehicles also seen at Peenemünde, but why would a rocket be moved into such a position and parked, even temporarily? And how? Was the transporter self propelled? This imagery doesn't provide answers to any of those questions. Three vehicles near the train moved between the two coverages: one seen near the first rail car on the first pass, the other two in the area between the tracks and the paved apron in front of the long building. One or more of these may have been tugs used to move the rockets on their carriages.

The road-carriage for the rocket could be expected to be a light and open framework, no more substantial than necessary to bear the weight of the rocket. It troubles me that in both coverages the "rocket" has no daylight between it and the shadow showing it to be raised up off the ground. Admittedly the shadows are not long in either coverage, but this indicated that the transport (Meillerwagen) carried the rocket very low to the ground.

The rocket tail-fins do not show well on the second pass photography used by Jones, which also suggests that the exposure he cited is not the one the PIs reported on, though the rocket in the return loop (the second pass) is so annotated on a Medmenham graphic reproduced in Professor Jones' book (*Wizard War*, Plate 26).

Medmenham PIs continued to dissect Blizna imagery for indications of a rocket launch system. During his interrogation, the prisoner referred to above told British Intelligence that the rocket had a "conical deflector" placed under it to deflect the hot gasses. Professor Jones relates that somewhere between the prisoner and Medmenham the rocket launching platform dimensions went from feet to metres, so PIs were looking for something 12 to 15 feet above the ground, and he says they thought they'd found such shapes at Blizna, naming them "Lemon Squeezers" after their characteristic appearance. Jones says that he "had spotted these same objects even before I found the rocket at Blizna, and had quickly dismissed them for what they were: bell tents" (*Wizard War*, p. 451-542).

Here was another Jones-Medmenham "dust up". There were at least three closely spaced bell tents present near one side of the "U" of the rail spur, but they don't look exactly like the objects in the centre of the open area. The close-spaced tents appear taller and smaller in diameter. The

A V-2 sat on a metal frame that held it above a deflector ("Lemon Squeezer") to keep debris from damaging the rocket on lift-off.

stereo I can get on this mission shows the central, more dispersed, objects having less height than 8-10 foot minimum expected for a tent, and the surrounding "walls" (probably sandbags) less high than would be needed to protect tents.[2] Nor do the shadows indicate objects with much height. We know from "ground truth", unavailable to the PIs at the time, that the rocket launch platforms were an open framework above the deflection surfaces, and those objects at Blizna have that appearance. On the other side of the debate, the "Lemon Squeezers" identified by PIs were twice the diameter of the fins on the rocket beside the train. One thing the PIs would have instinctively looked for were track patterns around the shapes. The "bell tents" had disturbed ground showing as light bands around them. Unless the "tents" were newly erected, or housed objects rather than people or working spaces, there should have been paths to the mess tent, the latrine and other places the men would go. Human activity makes tracks such as those visible in a matter of days and there are no such paths at Blizna on 5 May. Scale makes it difficult to verify the

112

presence of the Squeezer/tents in April, but compare their locations with the May coverage.

From what has been written by both sides, once again it is difficult to tell if Professor Jones and the PIs are referring to the same objects. The only frame of reference is the annotated print produced by Medmenham. In retrospect, based mainly upon the large diameter of the "Lemon Squeezers", this time Professor Jones may have been correct in his interpretation. However, comparison with April imagery shows three, possibly four, of the shapes in the same dispersed relationship but positioned astride the light-rail near the launch pad. Later coverage (not available to Medmenham or Jones until late July or early August) shows the three closely spaced conical objects (that are certainly tents) near the tracks and V-1 ramp were still in position and the four widely spaced objects the PIs identified as "Lemon Squeezers" are gone or moved again. In fact, only two similar objects remain inside the "U" of the rail spur and neither of those is in the same location as on 5 May. Why move a large bell tent a few feet every month? Why have troops living in such close proximity to something as dangerous as a rocket launch site? Questions like that can be raised by PI but not resolved by imagery. It looks like this topic needs some "ground truth" to explain what was going on.

The validity of the "Lemon Squeezer" identification was not just a matter of professional pride. It was crucial to understand how the rocket was launched. V-1s were landing around London and the rocket was expected soon. To do anything in defence against the rocket, the Allies had to understand the way the weapon was employed. By late spring, there was a growing consensus that the missile was fired vertically. In his book, Professor Jones cites his 17 July memo identifying a 35 feet square concrete platform in the centre of the open area at Blizna as the rocket launching surface (*Wizard War*, p. 437). His conclusion resulted from a re-look at the 5 May imagery of Blizna. Medmenham apparently agreed because a photo from a Third Phase report on the 5 May 1944 mission imagery is annotated "track possibly light railway leading from assembly hall to firing point". That photo is published as Plate 26 in Jones' book.

The ADI (Sc) concluded that once again the "professionals" had got it wrong with the "Lemon Squeezers". Apparently still nettled by Douglas Kendall's protesting to the Air Staff about the dangers of "amateur" photo interpretation, referring to Jones' earlier claims of "finding" rockets Medmenham missed at Peenemünde, Jones sent a tongue-in-cheek report to Kendall with a cartoon showing a rocket sitting vertically atop a tent.[3]

I note that if the Blizna "Squeezers" were tents, and the concrete platform was indeed the sole rocket launch pad, the people or equipment in those tents would have been in considerable danger from a failed launch and that doesn't seem too logical.

UNDERSTANDING THE ROCKET

By June 1944, the Allies still didn't know everything they wanted to about the rocket, but, though they hadn't seen many, photo interpreters in England were confident they knew what a German long-range rocket looked like. The tiny "flying bomb" was better understood, but it was even more difficult to catch on film. On small scale imagery, PIs must often rely upon measurement to support recognition and they were coming to realize that there were other shapes associated with the V-weapons programmes that closely matched the rocket in length and width. By mid-May it was finally understood that one didn't have to actually see the missiles themselves to positively identify sites associated with either of the V-weapons.

Meanwhile, a lot more was being learned about the rocket through access to an errant shot from Peenemünde that fell into Swedish territory and from pieces of Blizna launches snatched up by the Poles. In "Operation *Most III*", the night of 25/26 July 1944 the Polish Underground loaded 50 kg of parts and drawings into a RAF Dakota (C-47) at a secret landing ground near the Wisla River, deep in German occupied Poland (*Wizard War*, p. 432, *Brit Intel*, vol. 3, p. 442). The plane returned safely to Brindisi, Italy, and the parts were in England before the month ended. When the parts were analyzed in England in late July, the Allies finally understood the rocket warhead, guidance, propulsion and much of its capability.

An interesting observation at Blizna on the May imagery was additional damage or disruption to the forest just off of the large open area and to the left of previous craters. Two new craters down range, and two new clearings in the woods nearest the cleared area, probably indicate new launch sites or launch failures. "Craters seen on PR photographs of Peenemünde and Blizna indicated that the warhead (of the rocket) weighed between three and seven tons" (*Brit Intel*, vol. 3, p. 447). This serious overestimate continued until the rocket hit London in September.

In the large-scale photos from this series some of the holes in the tree cover could now be seen as intentionally created clearings in the woods. Several of the clearings show shadows of objects standing vertically. Were those rockets ready for test firing? In stereo, objects positioned off-centre in the nearest clearings look like the "Lemon Squeezers". Considerable track activity in the adjoining open area shows where many vehicles have turned around, suggesting (after vertical firing had been proven) that test shots were being made from these primitive locations in

Cover of 19 June 1944 showed a horizontal rocket (arrow), several transporters and possibly more V-2s to unload.

the woods. The most significant impact of the 5 May imagery was forcing British intelligence to conclude that, unlike the V-1, the German rocket could be launched from a very spartan location (*Brit Intel*, vol. 3, p. 449).

They also recognized that "…the rocket could be fired with a mobile mechanism from a simple concrete bed and did not need a bulky launching edifice."

Identification of a rocket on the sharp, large scale imagery of 5 May allowed more precise measurements to be made and the probable capability of the weapon to be better assessed. It gave Allied Intelligence confidence that they were finally understanding the German long-range rocket, though Lord Cherwell still denied its feasibility as a weapon (*Wizard War*, p. 433).

MORE ANALYSIS

Another significant coverage of Blizna was collected on 19 June (above). The small-scale camera shows the collection aircraft higher than on previous missions, and cumulus clouds in the area. It appears that the Mosquito flew over the installation, banked around, and hit Blizna again from

right angles to the original line, creating a situation that PIs dream of: different look-angles, good light and just enough time difference to make activity stand out (movement between exposures). The long train in the installation is moving past six hydrogen peroxide/liquid oxygen cars on another siding, probably empties waiting to return to Peenemünde. Earlier recce seems to have bothered the Blizna establishment because cars at the far end of the railroad track have been covered by netting. Since they show no movement from April to June, the cars at the end of the siding probably served as offices and billets for key or ranking personnel. The netting is so poor as camouflage, it may have been simply to provide shade.

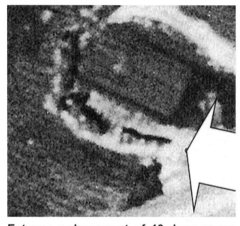

Extreme enlargement of 19 June cover. Camouflage-painted V-2 on light rail leading to storage areas suggests several to be unloaded and stored for later test firings.

The "Lemon Squeezers" are relocated or gone in the June coverage and there are new equipment positions in the cleared area, including a new road and revetment, but the overall count is more objects/buildings removed than added, particularly in the V-1 area, suggesting no more testing was needed. Moving the "Lemon Squeezer" shapes would be less likely if they were tents in

sandbagged revetments, but not unexpected if they were needed elsewhere to launch rockets—say, from those clearings in the forest. The three close-spaced tents near the railroad track and V-1 ramp are gone, though their revetments are intact. There are five

Possible erected V-2s in clearings. PIs didn't yet know of the vertical firing and so missed them.

such tents in a cluster in the centre of the open area, significantly in a direct line with the V-1 launch ramp, again suggesting it is no longer in use. Less V-1 activity is also understandable. By 19 June 1944, live operational firings of that weapon at London had been going on for five days.

There is a V-2 horizontal in the light-rail reversing loop. This time it is directly on the line of the tracks so it is probably on a rail transporter. I identify those other objects in the reversing loop as a brush-camouflaged narrow-gauge locomotive and two cars towing the camouflage painted rocket (arrow). Another camouflaged rocket and an empty Meillerwagen are in front of the long building paralleling the three tracks (arrow). Eight, possibly ten, cars on the train hold suspicious-looking objects that might be more rockets to offload (arrow heads).

Certainly, after mid-June 1944, Allied intelligence knew what the V-2 and its handling and support equipment looked like, and had ample evidence that the weapon was nearing operational status. This meant the hunt for the rocket could concentrate, like that for the V-1, on areas within range of England and the Normandy Invasion holdings. It was soon learned that the rockets were extremely hard to locate since, unlike the flying bombs, they had no discernable infrastructure.[4] Professor Jones used the available imagery and communications decrypts brilliantly to estimate

Blizna, Poland, 8 July 1944

the numbers of rockets the Nazis were producing and could produce (*Brit Intel*, vol. 3, p. 449). The most significant result of the Blizna coverage was the absence of an elaborate projector or ramp, and clear evidence from the ground of rocket firings, forced Allied Intelligence to accept the concept of vertical V-2 launching from pads or rudimentarily prepared flat surfaces. That understanding resulted in a re-look at earlier Peenemünde imagery and the recognition of several missiles erected and ready for launch from the asphalt fan beyond the earthen oval (See discussion, *Brit Intel*, vol. 3, p. 452-453). Ironically, no rockets so erected were observed on the Blizna coverage. If those objects in the forest clearings were vertical V-2s erected for test firing, they were indistinct and the trees destroyed any chance of seeing the characteristic shadows. Vehicles clustered in the open field just to the left of the trees indicate some sort of activity in progress.

Coverage of Blizna on 8 July 1944 (above) found the site in a state of draw-down, even abandonment. The office/billet rail cars were gone and the large and small conical shapes (tents/"Lemon Squeezers") are all gone. There is a new clearing in the near woods, but little other sign of activity. General Dornberger wrote after the war that by the end of July the Russian advance was making Blizna, or Heidelager as he called it, too hot for comfort and test firing was moved to Tuchel Heath, an even more primitive site south-west of Danzig (*V-2*, p. 211). Test work continued from the new site until January 1945, but, by September 1944 the Allies were getting more intelligence on the V-2 than they really wanted much closer to home.

Professor Jones wrote of sending a mission to the Soviets (in the summer of 1944), via Tehran, to go to newly captured Blizna and retrieve rocket parts. When the crates, which were held up by "Reds Red Tape", finally arrived in England, our "Ally" had switched out the critical parts for old airplane engine parts. In addition, cooperative Poles who had been interviewed and helped collect the parts from failed German launches were put on Soviet "pro-British sympathies" lists (*Wizard War*, p. 442).

---

1   *Wizard War*, p. 436, refers to frame 3240 of the 5 May mission. Frames from the long-lens split-vertical cameras were numbered 3xxx and 4xxx. Frame 3240 would be from the second pass over Blizna. The referenced object occurs on several adjacent frames as well. The rocket reported by Medmenham PIs can be seen on the first pass, on frame 3046 (194 exposures earlier in the mission).

2   The prints I used were made from the San Severo dupe neg. (since they were on American 9"-wide copy film), so mine were probably at least two generations beyond prints Medmenham PIs used made from the Original Negative. Some detail is lost in each generation of reproduction, and Second World War vintage copy film was quite grainy to start with.

3   *Mares Nest*, p. 275-276. Irving says Kendall had the cartoon framed for his office. Jones relates the anecdote in more detail in *Wizard War*, p. 451-452. Writing thirty-four years after the event Jones still maintained that the "Lemon Squeezers" seen at Blizna were bell tents, giving his rationale that surrounding sandbag walls proved that they were shelters protected against Polish snipers. Considering there was no similar protection for the presumably "high value" occupants of the train, the sniper story doesn't hold up.

4   The Allies had no better success interdicting the V-2 operationally than airmen forty-six years later had in stopping Iraqi Scuds during Operation Desert Storm I, and for the same reasons—a small, highly mobile target, able to hide, set up and fire quickly, is very difficult to find and attack. It is really only vulnerable at its manufacture and supply/ storage points.

**The huge Watten bunker under construction stood out from its background.
Pas de Calais, 3 November 1943.**

Chapter V

CONCRETE MONSTERS

LAUNCH FORTRESSES

With the Allied invasion of Europe obviously nearing, the flashy V-2 programme still had a way to go for operational status. The plodding, lower-tech, V-1, pilotless pulse-jet programme was closer to readiness and the Nazis badly needed a way to strike back at England which was sending bombers to punish the Continent night and day. Once the V-1 was given a "green light" Germany's Organization Todt, a military engineering group, began a flurry of design and construction intended to support putting warheads on targets as fast as possible in mass firings. Like tactical rockets, the inherent inaccuracy of the flying bomb was to be compensated for by sheer numbers of weapons fired. Workers and slave labourers were set to constructing a string of huge bomb-proof concrete works in north-west France. Some of these facilities were storage and supply depots for the V-1 or V-2; others were intended to be unsinkable aircraft carriers, capable of servicing and launching large numbers of rockets and flying bombs against England.[1] Meanwhile the Allies didn't know two very different weapons were involved.

While Lord Cherwell and others were going up a dead-end street assuming a solid fuel ballistic rocket of the size seen at Peenemünde, which would have a range or 40 miles, brilliant work by the ADI (Sc) suggested the rocket with liquid fuel would be lighter and have much greater range (see *Brit Intel*, vol. 3, p. 374). Those advising Medmenham had long guessed that the new weapons had to be fired from an area within 140 miles from England. Fortunately that same area was already the focus of intense intelligence collection as final planning continued on the Cross-Channel Invasion.

"The Army interpreters specializing in the northern France *Bodyline* area, found themselves in the same position as their colleagues working on the Peenemünde establishment in that they had no real idea for what they were supposed to be looking because of the vagueness of their brief. They had been told that the object to be fired (presumably a rocket) was so heavy that rail access was a prerequisite. On that account, not very much time was given to searching areas away from the main railway lines" (*Eye*, p. 195). Of course that didn't mean the "tween lines" spaces were ignored. Other photo interpreters were combing those same areas for defence positions, ammunition stores, anti-paratroop/anti-glider barriers, bunkers, command posts and all the other infrastructure of land warfare.

It didn't take long for the Allies to discover those large bunkers in early construction—they could hardly be hidden. Army PIs at Medmenham had seen the early site preparation at Watten,

119

near Calais, in April 1943, but the site hadn't been covered again until June, following agent reports of secret weapon activity (*Air Spy*, p. 152). Two other large sites were found near Cherbourg in May (*Brit Intel*, vol. 3, p. 375). New cover showed a flurry of activity and "suspicious-looking preliminaries were also going ahead at two other places in the rocket-range area" (*Air Spy*, p. 152). All sites were rail-served, at the time thought necessary for a rocket still estimated at 40-45 tons. PIs didn't yet realize they were looking for several different "Vengeance" weapons.

All of the new, massive construction projects were sited within a few miles of the coast, facing England but obviously too far inland to be coastal defences (*USSBS V-Weapons* (Crossbow) *Campaign*, p. 5. Hereafter noted as USSBS). When first discovered their purpose was only suspected and they were named "large sites". They were, however, squarely within the "threat zone" Medmenham was watching more closely.

"On July 9, Mr Sandys reported that, in addition to their plans for a rocket attack on London, there was also evidence that the Germans intended to use pilotless aircraft and very long-range guns. Two excavations of a suspicious character had been detected—at Watten, near St Omer, and at Bruneval, near Fecamp. Special instructions were therefore issued to the selected radar stations in South-east England to watch for rocket-firing. Plans were also made by the Home Office, not for any wholesale evacuation of London, but for the removal when the time came of a hundred thousand persons in priority classes, such as school-children and pregnant mothers, at the rate of ten thousand a day. Thirty thousand Morrison table shelters were moved into London, bringing the reserve in the Metropolis up to about fifty thousand.[2]

There was no proof that the newly identified large construction sites in France were rocket-related but the questions they raised only made them more vulnerable to discovery and underlined their probable hostile intent. At the time the first of the "large sites" were spotted, Allied Intelligence had yet to see either the rocket or flying bomb at Peenemünde so there was nothing apparent in the structures themselves that tied them to either of those weapons programmes. It

**Closer look at Watten
31 August 1943.**

was far too early in the construction for sightings of characteristic ancillary equipment related to weapons. Each new site appeared unique and there were no signature shapes, but new sites were being found on imagery, and agents in occupied Europe continued to report that the massive works were related to secret weapons. They were well inside the estimated range of the new weapons. Freshly turned earth showed up beautifully on aerial photos and made the new rail spurs pointers leading to the sites.

It was apparent early on that the heavy construction of the new bunkers anticipated a lot of bombing. It was conceivable that they might be command posts or something related to the defence of the Atlantic Wall, but they were not strung along the coast. Their locations only in the Pas de Calais and near Cherbourg suggested other functions. Flak defences also underlined the importance of these structures to the Nazis. Winston Churchill noted, "On 14 Dec, Air Marshal Bottomley, the Deputy Chief of the Air Staff, reported: The 'Large Sites' in Northern France (including three which have been attacked) are suspected to be connected with long-range rocket attack. One of these sites is protected by as many as fifty-six heavy and seventy-six light anti-aircraft guns" (*Closing the Ring*, p. 239).

Uncertainty in London was becoming anxiety (*Brit Intel*, vol. 3, p. 375-6). Worse yet, some of the enemy's new construction was actually in the area slated for Allied invasion in the spring of 1944. It was decided to delay bombing of the large constructions in the hopes that the specific purpose of the works would eventually emerge (*Brit Intel*, vol. 3, p. 374).

Though the Allies had no way of knowing exactly what each new structure was intended for, the massive scale of effort and the urgency of construction were sufficient proof of the threat they posed. It was determined that the "large sites" would not be allowed go operational. As far as I know, these were the only targets in the Second World War to which scarce bombing resources were extensively committed without a confirmed understanding of their specific purpose. Allied apprehension of the unknown power in a V-weapons assault was so great that as fast as intelligence identified one of these installations, it was bombed, and bombed repeatedly until it was totally destroyed or work abandoned.

In spite of an enormous effort by the Germans, and an enormous use of scarce construction materials, not a single V-weapon was ever fired from any of these massive "bomb-proof" bunkers.

WATTEN: After the war the Allies learned that there was a major difference of opinion inside the German V-weapons programmes on using "bomb-proof" bunkers. Some of the developers of the rocket and flying bomb wanted to use field launch positions with minimal site preparation. Others in Germany wanted storage and launch sites built to withstand the anticipated air attack. Hitler was finally convinced to go ahead with the bunkers when he understood that they would be built to the same "bomb proof" standards used for the submarine pens built in France which had already withstood several major attacks (*V-Missiles*, p. 174). Hölsken writes that Hitler decided on launch bunkers in November 1942, even before he decided on mass production of the rocket. Apparently the Germans did not foresee that the Allies would create larger, more penetrating bombs.

The first rocket launch bunker was to be Watten, near St Omer in the Pas de Calais. It was intended for completion in October to begin the V-2 offensive on London. Actual construction began in mid-May 1943 and the site was photographed almost immediately (*Eye*, p. 209). Hölsken (p. 174) says work began in August. First PR was on 16 May 1943.

"As the Watten structure could not be attributed to any conventional military purpose, it was

Watten had been extensively bombed by 30 June 1944.

naturally highly suspect as being associated with rocket firing. As a result on June 12th, Mr Duncan Sandys felt compelled to report to the Cabinet that in his opinion a long range rocket probably existed and might already be in limited production. Re-examination of all areas within 130 miles of London was once more ordered (Kendall, p. 88).

The outline of the Watten structure was apparent in mid-July. It was seen as a deep excavation, 460 feet by 330 foot long. Agents reported 6,000 men were working on the site (*Brit Intel*, vol. 3, p. 376). The bunker would quickly grow to a 100-foot high mass of reinforced concrete. It was not only easily seen by reconnaissance pilots but by bomber crews on their way to or from missions in occupied France. Ground intelligence linked the site to "secret weapons" and it was rail-served, suggesting a rocket relationship. By mid-August the photo coverage of the several buildings under construction showed they were far from complete, but "could throw no light on their purpose" (*Brit Intel*, vol. 3, p. 376).

At that point the Allies were still groping for something definite on what the site was for. A classic intelligence problem is too much information and much of it conflicting. How to separate the wheat from the chaff? Imagery said Watten was of major importance but couldn't provide evidence of why. Agents were reporting sites for long-range guns or rockets in the vicinity. Was this one? All the Allies knew for certain was that, whatever it was, Watten was too much effort, too large, and too close to England for comfort—so it got a lot of attention. It was so close to PR bases, and so close to the Channel coast, that recon involved short missions. The site was photographed on 14, 15, 17, and 26 July (*Brit Intel*, vol. 3, p. 376) so PIs watched it grow and understood something of its design and interior configuration.

Built in a former gravel quarry, the rail-served Watten bunker was intended to store, service and launch rockets. The facility was apparently designed to handle any type of warhead. Some room segregation even suggests anticipation of special warheads, though none were ever developed. Some room arrangement was apparent on aerial photos as the structure was built. Other information was learned after the site was overrun by Allied troops and post-war examination. Rail access and large rooms for long/tall objects and liquid storage suggested the bunker was being built for the rocket (*Brit Intel*, vol. 3, p. 384). German engineering figures indicate 20 thousand tons of steel and 200 thousand tons of concrete went into Watten. It has been reported that some of its tunnels were 250 feet underground. Watten was built largely by 35,000 slave labourers from France, Czechoslovakia, Belgium, the Netherlands, Poland, and the Soviet Union. The site is still maintained as a monument to them and the terrible conditions they suffered. By way of comparison, the Pentagon, for years the world's largest office building, was completed about the same time as Watten was under construction and used 870,000 tons of concrete. As the massive bunker took shape, it was reminiscent of a huge concrete command post and anti-aircraft artillery installation in Berlin. Human source intelligence was suggesting the Germans intended an October 1943 start for the "rocket offensive", and the rockets had to be launched from somewhere (*Brit Intel*, vol. 3, p. 386-387). The presumed threat presented by Watten resulted in emergency planning for shelters and evacuations of London, Southampton, Portsmouth and Gosport, and possibly of moving the government from London.

Analysis indicated Watten was to be completed in September-October time frame. Coincidence or not, that alone was enough to get Watten bombed.

First struck on 27 August 1943, just ten days after Peenemünde was initially attacked, heavy bombers from Eighth Air Force put 375 tons of bombs on Watten from lower than normal altitudes to improve accuracy. Damage Assessment imagery of 30 August showed "heavy concentrations of bombs had burst directly on the target" (*Brit Intel*, vol. 3, p. 385). Photos show remarkably accurate bombing, with only a few "wild" ones in the surrounding fields and woods. A lot of dirt was moved

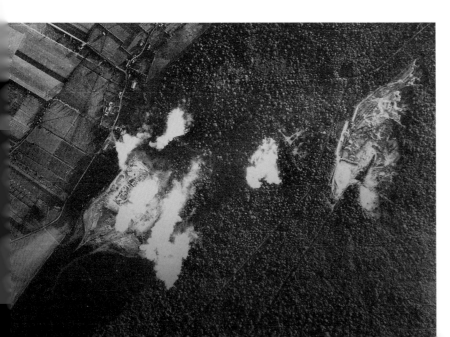

Photos of detonations in first bombing of Watten, 27 August 1943.

but little real destruction was achieved. However, in one of those accidents of war, a large amount of concrete had recently been poured and was still curing. Thrown about by the bombing, it hardened on the twisted mess of other destruction (*Air Spy*, p. 153). Imagery of 2 September showed that "the attack had been most successful and construction set back at least three months. A few days later the German Air force brought in large quantities of anti-aircraft batteries (flak) to protect the Watten site. This could be observed on the photographs and was so reported" (Kendall, p. 90).

Continuing activity at Watten and additional AAA batteries defending it, indicating that the target had not been destroyed. The site was struck again on 7 September with even heavier bombs and concentrations. This time British engineers estimated the raids had so disrupted the site that it would be more efficient to start again elsewhere (*Mare's Nest*, p. 124). The Germans seem to come to the same conclusion and subsequent recce showed a decided reduction of activity. "During the last week of September, 1943, a number of new construction activities in north France were reported. As they were still in a very early stage of construction, little could be said about their ultimate purpose. It was noted at this time that construction work at Watten, following the USAAF raid, was still at a standstill although the flak defences were being reinforced, but by early October, the enemy had started to withdraw their flak batteries from Watten and the site appeared to have been abandoned. Accordingly we reduced the photographic sorties over Watten from twice weekly to once a month" (Kendall, p. 90).

In June 1944, agents in France reported that the Watten bunker was not related to the flying bomb and it should be attacked again and the PM directed a daylight raid using the new, 12,000lb. "Tallboy" bombs (*Brit Intel*, vol. 3, p. 440). The site was struck on 19 June and 27 July, when one of the Tallboys actually hit the structure (*Hitler's Rocket Sites*, p. 59) but Watten was a really "hard" target. Henshall writes that after the site was captured an attempt was made to destroy it using the even larger, 22,000lb Grandslam bomb, which did penetrate the reinforced concrete roof. Bombs detonating in the earth all around the bunker overturned equipment, halting construction.

The five metre thick roof of one part of the structure was penetrated at least once, but apparently the bomb did not detonate. The twenty-three foot thick roof of the main hall was hit several times. Though not penetrated, the shock effect inside must have been terrible The 28 August and 7 September strikes by Eighth AF were cited as "causing great damage" (*Brit Intel*, vol. 3, p. 593). The collapse of the north end of the roof was presumably the major reason the Germans elected to give up on Watten and build another bunker nearby. While probably not damaged beyond all recovery, frequent Allied bombings effectively stalled construction at Watten by eliminating the possibility of outside work and storage of materials, and disrupting delivery of supplies. Though heavy bombing forced the Germans to abandon the work, the very existence of that massive installation still standing worried the Allies and they kept after it—just in case.

Since the USAAF bombers couldn't lift the RAF Tallboy or Grandslam bombs, war-weary bombers loaded with high explosives were to be used as drones to crash into the "hardest" targets. Under the codename APHRODITE the four-engine aircraft were stripped and equipped with radio control. They were loaded with ten tons of high explosive or napalm and remotely steered into the reinforced concrete "large sites" that didn't show signs of sufficient damage from normal bombing: Watten, Mimoyecques, Siracourt and Wizernes. APHRODITE attacks against all four targets occurred on 4 August and against Watten again on the 6th. None of the targets were hit. The technique was tried once more on 12 August 1944. The Navy PB4Y drone (B-24) exploded over England near Blythburgh apparently as the pilots armed the system prior to bailing out. One of the men lost was Lt. Joseph P Kennedy, Jr, USN (oldest son of former US Ambassador to England, Joseph P Kennedy, and brother of JFK). Some sources say their intended target was Watten, others say it was Mimoyecques.

The APHRODITE drone attack concept was an utter failure and soon abandoned.

Several authors have observed that Hitler wanted activity continued at Watten to draw bombing sorties away from German cities. If so, he succeeded. Construction at Watten was begun again in early December 1943, with rapid progress being made by the end of the month. Strong anti-aircraft artillery deployments defended Watten, convincing the Allies that the site was still important to the Nazis. That was just another reason to bomb it to a standstill and Watten was struck by heavy or medium bombers on 27 August and 7 September 1943; 2, 8 and 13 February, 19, 21, 26, and 29 March, 6, 18, 19 and 27 April, 1 and 30 May, 18, 19 and 25 June, 6 and 25 July, and 25 August 1944 (*Combat Chronology*). In spite of the heavy bombing, there was some activity at Watten right up to a few days before Allied ground forces overran the site on 6 September 1944, though one author reports that construction activity ceased at Watten after a direct hit (by a Tallboy) in the 6 July bombing (*Mare's Nest*, p. 246). The Watten bunker was never completed.

WIZERNES: Stalled at Watten, Hitler's engineers shifted emphasis to Wizernes, about ten miles away and closer to a railhead at St Omer. This site was begun shortly after Watten, and originally intended to be a rocket storage facility (*Brit Intel*, vol. 3, p. 593). "Activity was first noticed on 15 August." After redesign as a launch bunker Wizernes was slated to launch some fifty rockets per day with impunity. Like Watten this installation was constructed in a rail-served quarry and was intended to be a complete self-contained servicing and launch facility. Building the railway and creating stockpiles of materials attracted photoreconnaissance to Wizernes in mid-August 1943.

Heavy tunnelling began in early December and within a month work on the dome had begun. Right off an existing rail yard and in an established excavation, the only clues to new work were the short extensions of rail service to the dome and its support buildings and the unusual large round shape of the dome itself. On imagery of 21 January 1944 it looks like the 45,000 ton concrete dome was just being poured. With the Watten damage in mind, the massive twenty-three foot thick dome at Wizernes was poured at ground level then slowly jacked up to eventually provide sixty to eighty feet of clear space inside the growing excavation. Construction of the launch facility would take place under its protection. Unable to look inside because of this construction technique, the Allies were denied both an intelligence understanding of the site and a good way to attack it.

By 28 February 1944 the dome appeared complete. Eighth AF sent 129 B-17s to Wizernes and Watten with 500lb and 1000lb general purpose bombs on 19 March 1944.

Below is a contemporary BDA graphic using imagery from a 379th Bomb Group strike aircraft showing results. The target area is outlined. Bombing altitude was 24,000' and ordnance is all over the place—a few are in the fields to the north (down) and village to the south. Small smoke puffs are bombs from the unit taking the photo just going off. Most are on line but "short" of the target. Larger smoke shows an earlier Bomb Group was more on target but so far no one has hit the dome.

Photos from a 542 Sq Spitfire on 6 July confirmed bombs blanketing the target area but no damage to the dome.

Wizernes dome was hard to spot nestled at the upper end of a clay pit. 21 January 1944.

Enlargement of 21 January imagery shows shape and progress on the huge dome.

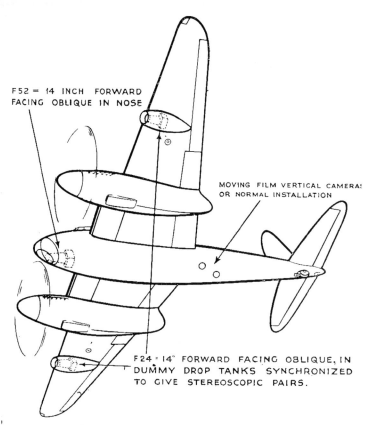

F52 = 14 INCH FORWARD
FACING OBLIQUE IN NOSE

MOVING FILM VERTICAL CAMERAS
OR NORMAL INSTALLATION

F24 = 14" FORWARD FACING OBLIQUE, IN
DUMMY DROP TANKS SYNCHRONIZED
TO GIVE STEREOSCOPIC PAIRS.

In an attempt to get a better look at the construction in hopes of understanding the purpose of the bunker, a 540 Sq Mosquito was fitted with cameras pointing straight ahead, to get stereo coverage. A daring ultra low-altitude mission was flown straight up the valley of the quarry and right over the concrete dome on 10 July 1944. Several lower entrances, at least one rail served, could be seen closer to the floor of the quarry. There was damage to construction equipment and scaffolding around the concrete dome showed damage but the dome was intact.

Imagery of late August or early September gave proof of regular and heavy bombing destroying everything near-by but not doing much to the dome which was now darkened for camouflage. Apparently work was still going on underground because the track was repaired to at least one ground level entrance and a large rail car is near the adit.

Because of its proximity to England, Wizernes got regular attention from recce and bombing aircraft until the site was overrun by ground troops in September 1944 Eighth AF bombed Wizernes four times between 11 March and 3 May 1944 (*Combat Chronology*).

The dome is at A; B and E are entrances; C and D are piles of spoil from the excavations. Note narrow gauge engine and cranes for construction.

WIZERNES
PRINT 4   K 87(E)

Wizernes was never completed.

Ground investigation of the site disclosed that the German plan was to erect rockets inside, wheel them out onto launch platforms, fuel and fire, exposing them to Allied attack for only a few minutes. However, as at Watten, the weight and persistence of Allied bombing, while doing little actual structural damage to the main facility, stripped away its capability to function.

The enormous concrete dome protected work underneath but it is unlikely that delicate servicing and guidance equipment for the rocket (and

ACIU drawing of Wizernes based on the 10 July RAF dicing mission (Medmenham Club)

Below and Inset–Intense bombing kept the dome-protected bunker from completion. RAF 52Sq. 6 July 1944.

August 1944, the dome was "darkened" to make it harder for Allied bomb-aiming.

probably the personnel inside) could have withstood the shock of the huge "Grandslam" bombs (which were not in existence when the facility was engineered and 23-foot roof thickness determined sufficient for "bomb proofing").

At right is a German graphic, captured at the end of the war, showing the interior plan for the Wizernes bunker and launch facility. By the spring of 1944 it was naïve of the Nazis to not understand that, even if the bunker had managed to go operational, streams of Allied bombers escorted by clouds of fighters based just a few minutes flying time away would be attacking Wizernes so often, day and night, that almost any firing would be impossible.

130

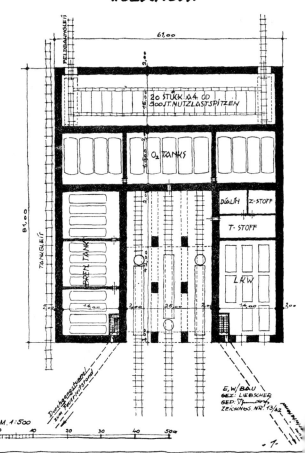

Der Plan eines Stockwerkes für den riesigen A 4-Einsatzbunker bei Wizernes. Die H̶ zum Klarmachen der Raketen reichte durch mehrere Geschosse hindurch

SOTTEVAST: This V-2 support site lies near Valognes in the Cherbourg Peninsula, roughly twelve miles from the city on the main rail line to the south. It was intended as the primary bunker for rocket bombardment of the south coast of England. Designed as an artificial cave made of concrete, one side of its "L" configuration is 591 feet long and nearly 30 feet wide, the other is 188 feet by a little over 30 wide. First seen on 20 October 1943 (*Brit Intel*, vol. 3, p. 593), Allied photo interpreters were easily led to the site by a new rail line and "turning wye" as well as the new excavation breaking the pattern of surrounding fields. They immediately noted that the long axis was perpendicular to Bristol. Though built on a more modest scale than Watten and Wizernes,

Sottevast had the obligatory 23-foot concrete roof thickness and a concrete launching area in the angle of the two wings of the building.

The site was well defined by mid-January. Increases in anti-aircraft defences around Sottevast also tended to draw attention to the area more than protect it. According to an "Approximate Bomb Plot" graphic, the site was bombed on 15 February 1944. Since imagery of 7 November 1943 was used as the photo base, there apparently was much good coverage through the fall. As D-Day neared, Allied intelligence and bombing attention on Normandy, and the requirement for ports and dispersal areas in southern England, meant this "probable secret weapons-related" construction would get a lot of

```
                    S.A. 1000
                    SOTTEVAST
                    15.2.44
            APPROXIMATE BOMB PLOT

    •      Well defined bursts
    ///    Smoke obscured area
    A      Long structure
    B      Camouflaged area      36081
```

attention. Eighth Air Force heavies struck on 28 April 1944, and on 5, 6 and 8 May (*Combat Chronology*). Sottevast got enough bombing to discourage further work.

It was never completed and was in the hands of US ground troops on 22 June 1944.

MARTINVAST: Four miles south of Cherbourg on the main rail line and appearing similar to nearby Sottevast, this site was first discovered on 28 July 1943 (*Brit Intel*, vol. 3, p. 593). It was bombed on 11 November and 2 December 1943 as one of a number of "military installations" around Cherbourg. At first thought to be an Army bunker, it was finally associated with the V-weapons deployments and thought to be aligned on Bristol when its long axis was recognized as perpendicular to the prospective target (*Mare's Nest*, p. 219). This V-2 installation was apparently abandoned by April 1944 (*Brit Intel*, vol. 3, p. 439).

SIRACOURT: Near St Pol in the Pas de Calais, the site was discovered on 4 September 1943 (*Brit Intel*, vol. 3, p. 594). It was designed as a 630-foot-long artificial cave for the assembly and launch of V-1s (*V-Missiles*, p. 173). Siracourt and three other "Waterworks" bunkers were expected to launch ninety flying bombs a day. The fifty or so V-1s that could have been stored at this site were to be launched off the bunker roof in volleys. The internal layout of the bunker hinted that Siracourt may have also had facilities intended for possible use of "unconventional" warheads.

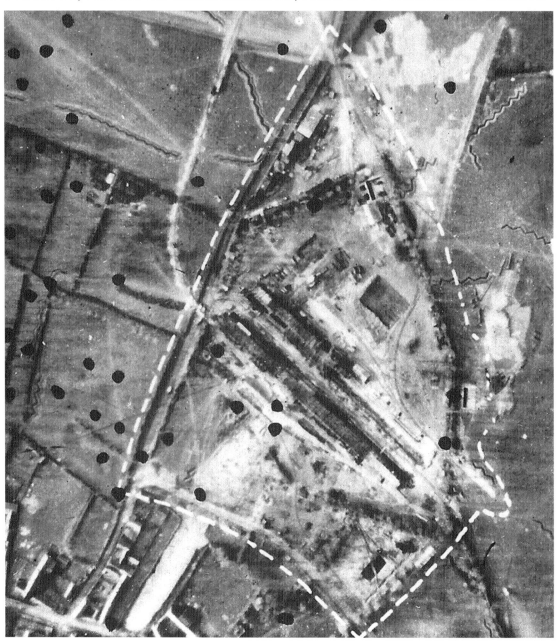

Above–Siracourt,
24 May 1944.

Left–Despite large
bomb hits nearby,
work was still going
on. Siracourt,
15 May 1944.

Bomb plots on imagery from January show that attacks by RAF and USAAF medium bombers were largely ineffective. Plot of attacks in March show strikes on the main construction and April bombing temporarily cut road and rail access by scattered ordnance all over the countryside. A low flyover on 15 May 1944 showed numerous craters close, and some damage to the roof, but the concrete hadn't been penetrated. The rail was back in operation and construction materials were in evidence. By 24 May heavy bombers were turning the area into a moonscape.

Photos from one of the B-17s bombing on 22 June showed ordnance going off in the jumble of craters and gave the impression that the site was obliterated. Post-strike reconnaissance three days later gave the same impression but a mission on 6 July showed work was continuing. In fact, a new support area had been built and the artificial cave was being mounded and banked with dirt, making it harder to see as well as to destroy. This was verified by a US 7GP aircraft overflying the bunker at 100 feet the next day. It looks like the roof had collapsed in several places along each side.

The thick roof protected the lower reaches of the facility from most damage, but repeated

A US 7GP F5 flew Siracourt at 100' to determine status. 7 July 1944.

bombing kept launch equipment on the roof swept away as well as making it virtually impossible to deliver V-1s or construction materials to the site. Additionally, the shock of heavy bombs would probably have damaged the delicate guidance mechanisms of the V-1s, so none were ever sent here. Eighth AF bombed Siracourt eight times between 8 February and 21 June 1944 (*Combat Chronology*). A 12,000lb "Tallboy" bomb eventually collapsed part of the roof, but, surprisingly in the face of the surface cratering, the installation survived the war largely intact. Siracourt was never operational.[3]

LOTTINGHEM: West of St Omer, this was to be another of the V-1 storage/launch bunkers on the Siracourt/Martinvast pattern. It never progressed much beyond clearing the ground for the two long trenches perpendicular to the target, in this case London. First imaged on 24 September 1943, the characteristic footprint caused this site to be deemed threat-related by the Allies. It was bombed by Eighth AF "heavies" on 29 February 1944 (*Combat Chronology*). Henshall and Hölsken call this site Lottinghen.

MIMOYECQUES: Also called Marquise, while not related to either the Luftwaffe V-1 or Wehrmacht V-2 programmes it was a very large excavation and only a few of the "large sites" had any other similarity so it was assumed to be a kindred installation. Allied intelligence had no way of knowing exactly what the site was intended to do but it was clearly aligned on London and that was enough. It was also the closest of the new bunkers to London, more than twenty miles closer than Watten and clearly not in the belt of other "large construction sites" being identified in the Pas de Calais. Construction on two new rail spurs drew attention to the site and it was first identified in August 1943. The tracks led to two parallel tunnels then rejoined the main line on the other side. Light rail had been laid from the standard gauge rail line to the construction sites and large piles of earth spoil gave an idea of the scope of the underground effort.

"Meanwhile on the top of the hill three somewhat bogus-looking haystacks had been constructed. This particular site was watched in considerable detail over the next month or two" (Kendall, p. 90). Mimoyecques attracted serious Allied attention after 18 September 1943. As it developed, activity at Mimoyecques didn't match the size, shape or style of the other large bunkers but it was obviously important to the Germans. Whatever was going on, it was based upon long trenches cut into the hill the light rail lines penetrated. Though at two well-separated locations, the work looked the same at both sites and the Allies considered this one installation.

The trenches were off to the side of the rail axis and an effort had been made to camouflage the work, or perhaps to deny Allied intelligence a look inside the trenches. Almost directly atop the tunnels were unexplained 41' square excavations.

Bombing missions were laid on in hope of stopping whatever mischief the site was designed for and it was struck on 5 and 8 November 1943, stalling work for three weeks. By December 1944 the Allies had designated this site as a high threat along with Watten and Wizernes (*Brit Intel*, vol. 3, p. 413). Apparently the bombing damage was severe enough that when construction began again, one of the two sites was abandoned. Underlining the importance of the location to the Germans, when work began again "Flak defences were considerably increased after the raids and ground reports, which had earlier suggested that rocket projectiles were to be fired from the shafts, indicated that work was continuing" (*Brit Intel*, vol. 3, p. 594). At this time the Allies still didn't know exactly what the site was supposed to accomplish. In fact the Mimoyecques site near Cape Gris Nez was to be the single location for a unique gun called the HochDruckPumpe (HDP) or,

Above – Mimoyecques, site of the V-3
cannon and nearest bunker to England.
Note English Channel at upper left. The
purpose of the site wasn't known until it
was captured, but it was bombed anyway.
4 August 1944.

Left – Mimoyecques was struck on a
regular basis until after D-Day. Here, three
2,000lb bombs are on the way (centre right,
heading left) as others detonate on target.
26 May 1944.

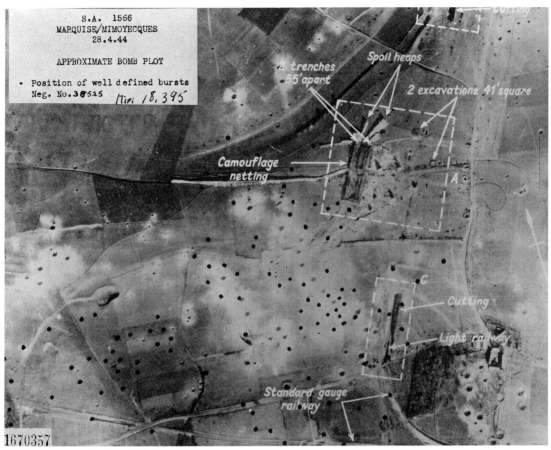

The following text appears within the photograph:

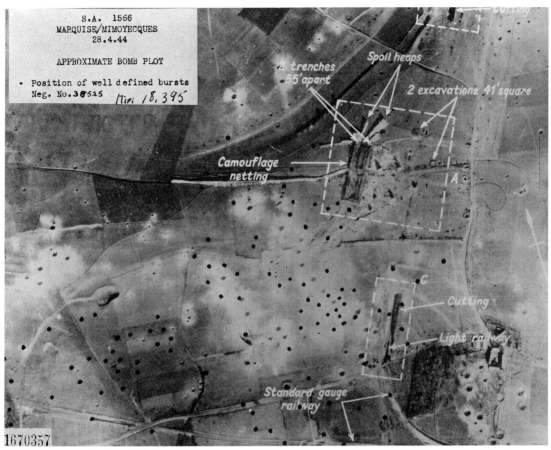

S.A. 1566
MARQUISE/MIMOYECQUES
28.4.44

APPROXIMATE BOMB PLOT

• Position of well defined bursts
Neg. No.38525 /Tipi /8.395

Cutting

Spoil heaps

2 trenches 55' apart

2 excavations 41' square

Camouflage netting

A

C

Cutting

Light railway

Standard gauge railway

1670357

The base photo for this BDA report dates from site discovery in late 1943.

high pressure pump, sometimes referred to as the V-3. We now know it was going to be ten batteries of five 492-foot-long smooth bore barrels. The steeply angling 15cm barrels would launch 300lb finned ballistic projectiles against London at a rate of ten per minute (*Wizard War*, p. 462). Only twenty-five barrels were completed and the first battery was scheduled to fire on London on 1 March 1944 (*V-Missiles*, p. 178). Cannon breeches would be 450 feet below the surface and the whole installation would be under a thick shell of concrete, impervious to Allied bombing.

"Although the 'B 2' Section at Medmenham had heard about a Vergeltung weapon early in 1943 and had been keeping an eye on mysterious field works near Calais, it was not until early summer that serious attention was paid to them. This was because MI6 had learned that the Germans were negotiating with the local French power authority…for power lines and a power supply large enough for a town the size of Hereford or Basingstoke. It was then noticed that spoil from the underground workings was altering the shape of the landscape. Interpreters working on the prints from a tasked air reconnaissance sortie now noted the 50 shafts under construction and the fact that like the (V-1) ramps, they were all aligned on the center of London" (*D-Day*, p. 99).

Photo interpreter Andre Kenny noticed "haystacks" near the tunnels being relocated. They saw one coming apart to reveal a windlass and shaft (*Eye*, p. 210). The shafts lined up with the tunnels and showed how extensive the excavations were becoming. Agents in France reported that this was a long range gun, one called it "a rocket launching cannon", but agents had often said the same thing about other rocket launching sites (*Brit Intel*, vol. 3, p. 435). As late as January 1944 the site was still thought to be part of the rocket programme. Allied intelligence gradually understood that the site had nothing to do with V-1 or V-2 deployments, but that did not cause a lifting of bombing attention. The thing was just too close to England for comfort, and, if the Nazis would put that much effort into it....

Heavy and regular bombing made construction difficult but didn't destroy the site. A strike photo of 26 March showed bombs going off on target and a trio of 2,000 pounders on the way. Good bombing showed again on 24 April with post-strike photos making it look like the area of the trenches had been pretty well obliterated, but the Allies kept at it anyway. A US 7GP recon photo of 4 August not only shows the results of many airstrikes but also how close this site was to the English Channel.

The real purpose of the Mimoyecques tunnels wasn't known until the site was overrun in August 1944 (*Brit Intel*, vol. 3, p. 405 f/n). The range to London was to be achieved by setting off booster charges in side compartments all the way up each barrel just after the round passed, thus accelerating the projectile to 5,000 feet-per-second. With legendary German precision, each round was serially numbered and machined slightly larger than the last to account for wear in the bore. Anticipating operation of the guns, some 20,000 rounds were produced before tests in Germany revealed that the projectiles would tumble at speeds well below the designed muzzle velocity, thus failing to achieve anything near the ranges desired. It was another example of Hitler's decisions sucking up huge amounts of people, material and effort for a dead-end.

Bombproof doors, shell handling equipment, elevators and frames to support the barrels were in place in May and the first barrels were to be installed in July, but it was apparent that the guns would never be completed, and, if they were, would not have the range to reach London. Of course the Allies had no way of knowing that.

Heavy bombing by the RAF on 6 July so damaged the site that it was estimated several months would be necessary to clear the debris and restore driveways so work could continue.

The gun was scheduled for operation in July, but further test firings failed and this programme was apparently going nowhere by late May 1944. Hitler ordered construction to continue because of the bombing effort it was diverting from other, more real, targets. However, this bombing convinced German leadership that the V-weapon bunkers could never be made operational (*V-Missiles*, p. 204-205).

The V-3 never fired at Mimoyecques and the site was in the hands of Canadian troops in late August 1944.

Between 30 December 1944 and 22 February 1945, a two-barrel, shorter version of the HDP fired on Luxemburg in support of ground operations during the Battle of the Bulge. Firing was from an undiscovered location south of Trier, doing little damage.[4]

Much like the V-2, the V-3 was an idea ahead of its time technologically, though experience has proven that "hard installations" can never be built faster than "bunker buster" bombs can be created to breach them. After the war many contemporary British intelligence sources thought that, had it been able to fire on London in 1944, the V-3 would have been the greatest threat to Britain of all the V-Weapons.[5]

MINI-MONSTERS

There were a number of rear-echelon depots built to support the needs of forward sited launch positions. These were generally heftier construction than normal military storage facilities but they were generally built along conventional lines typical of explosive/ammunition/fuel storage. The most typical pattern for storing critical or dangerous items is a lattice or tree of roads leading to a dozen or more small, widely dispersed, buildings. The buildings themselves were usually built low, frequently just simple bunkers of concrete covered with earth.

Other than the timing of their appearance and their robust construction, there was nothing on imagery to allow Allied intelligence to associate these sites with the rocket or flying bomb programmes. Also, they were smaller and less obvious on imagery. Fortunately, agents in France often provided the missing linkage. It is also clear that these storage sites were not as threatening as the launch sites that were occupying so much of the available recce and bombing resource. Even so, seven of the known storage sites were attacked by the summer of 1944. It must be remembered that the time when these depot sites were important to support the V-weapons threat was between 13 June 1944, when the first V-1 was launched at London, and September 1944 when the zone of V-1 launching against England was completely overrun by Allied ground forces. "There were no Allied attacks on the supply sites until after the start of the V-1 offensive on 13 June, because there was no further evidence associating

Even the minor *Crossbow* sites got major attention. Sautricourt, 22 June 1944.

them with either the ski sites or the modified sites. By the time the attack on them began the Germans had already ceased to use them and were instead using underground caves and tunnels for storage" (*Brit Intel*, vol. 3, p. 427 note). Considering bombing priorities on targets in Germany, interdicting the flow of war-making resources to the front, direct support bombing in France, AND destroying the "V" launching threat, it is surprising that any attention was paid to the mini-monsters when they could be identified.

Some examples of these secondary V-1 related sites were:

Beauvais in Normandy, a dispersed storage facility completed in late 1943 and apparently used.

Biennais, a storage site that was abandoned before finished.

Domleger, near Abbeville, dispersed storage site that was bombed.

Equeurdreville, near Cherbourg, originally intended to be a launch site, was probably finished as a storage facility.

Neuville-au-Bois, a storage site abandoned before completion.

Renescure, near St Omer, dispersed storage, apparently not bombed.

Sautricourt, near St Pol, dispersed storage, was probably bombed because of its close proximity to a number of V-1 launch sites. Strike photos of 22 June 1944 show the crater blanketing of a target area that was typical of all of the V-weapons related sites.

St. Martin l'Hortier, another storage site abandoned before it was finished.

Valognes, in the Cherbourg Peninsula, a dispersed storage site for the V-1.

STORAGE, DISPERSAL AND FABRICATION

Since it trailed the V-1 programme in operation, by the time V-2 storage facilities were built in France the Germans were more aware of what concentrated Allied bombing could do, so these depots tended to be in caves, or artificially created caves. One such site was Nucourt, north-west of Paris. That site was bombed in late June, burying or damaging 298 V-1s (*Wizard War*, p. 426).

Bombs detonating at Dannes, France, 20 March 1944.

The largest ad hoc storage was in a mushroom-cave at St Leu d'Esserent, near Paris. Reported by an agent just before D-Day, the cave was heavily bombed in late June without much success. It was bombed again the nights of 4/5 and 7/8 July 1944 using the 12,000lb "Tallboy" bombs, effectively burying or damaging what Allied intelligence estimated might be as many as 2000 flying bombs (*Wizard War*, p. 426-427), denying the Luftwaffe roughly a fourth of the missiles available to them in France at that time. The impact of that strike was apparent over the next ten days. Firings on London fell from 100 a day to "fewer than 70" per day (*Wizard War*, p. 427).

Another such adhoc storage facility was Villiers-Adam, near Paris. This turned out to be a major storage facility to distribute V-2s to forward launch sites. Allied intelligence knew, or thought they knew, about a number of these facilities, but found them unnecessary to strike by the summer. Indeed, General Dornberger had already decided to by-pass the storage and dispersal sites in favor of direct factory-to-launch site movement. This gave a finished V-2 a shelf life of about three days and cut operational failures dramatically. It also significantly reduced the risk of destruction of the weapons by Allied air attack. With a few exceptions, minor fabrication and storage facilities didn't require the extensive construction that made the "concrete monsters" stand out on imagery. Most were based upon pre-existing sites and it is remarkable that many could be identified at all. Most likely, for places this deep in the V-weapons programme, the intelligence source would have been HUMINT, with photo verification.

Too hard to find, too small, overtaken by events, or too hard to strike, most of these sub-contractors, storage and distribution facilities were skipped over in favour of bombing strikes laid on the major surface factories making the V-weapons—those that could be identified from imagery, intercepts or agents.

Factories that did get attention from heavy bombers were:

Friedrichshafen – Zeppelin & Maybach Plants (*V-2*), attacked by the Eighth AF on 18 March 1944 and the RAF on 27/28 April.

Fallersleben – Volkswagenwerke (V-1) attacked by the Eighth AF on 8 April, 20 and 29 June, and 5 August 1944.

Russelsheim – Adam Opel, attacked by the Eighth AF on 27 July 1944 and the RAF on 12 August.

Wiener-Neustadt – (Raxe-Werke) (*V-2*), first attacked by Fifteenth AF on 2 November 1943, and included in eighteen subsequent raids.

Weimar/Buchenwald (gyroscopes), attacked by Eighth AF on 24 August 1944.

Höllriegelakreuth (Hydrogen Peroxide), struck by Eighth AF on 19 July 1944.

Ober Raderach, near Friedrichshafen (Hydrogen Peroxide), attacked by Fifteenth AF on 3 and 16 August 1944 (*USSBS*, p. 20-21).

Most of these strategic targets were out of range for medium bombers and the short summer nights made it more hazardous for less well gunned RAF night-bombers to get in and out on a deep penetration. Even so, RAF Bomber Command allocated 40 per cent of its available sorties to "*Crossbow*"-related targets in the two months following the start of the V-1 attacks on England, including forays into daylight bombing (*USSBS*, p. 33-34).

"Although there is no evidence that bombing caused a decrease in output, failure to meet planned production schedules for V-1 is attributable partly to the direct effects of attacks on

Volkswagen factory at
Fallersleben, Germany (arrow),
made the V-1. 7PG photo,
31 May 1944. Bombed by Eighth
AF on 20 June (Below), adding
insult to injury, the name was
spelled wrong.

(SAV-3858/515 ⁴)(20-6-44)(37966-12-25000)[FALBERSLEBEN)

g plants, partly to the bombing of plants whose connection was

o the gradual disintegration of German industry and transport

and delays in deliveries" (*USSBS*, p. 3).

ETS

ons, rail and road, inhibited movement of V-weapons into the

gland (or other targets), but Allied intelligence was constantly

e the German initiatives.

d out an intensive search for any plants which could be

it unlikely that the enemy had built any special additional

rather they would be using any existing chemical plants

ies. In Germany and Belgium we found 13 plants which

acturing liquid oxygen and we placed all on our target lists

em. In the end, for one reason and another, notably priority

lly bombed any of these sites. There is no doubt that we

nemy considerably by knocking out these 13 plants, if the

t where he was using a great deal of liquid oxygen. This

taliation which we still had available to us but never found

n that at about this time we were using the whole of our

ate the enemy's synthetic oil plants and oil refineries. By

the largest capacity we were able to keep knocking down

sing months of the war, the daily output of fuel was

most of the Panzer units to a halt, notably on the eastern

y the German Air Force that their fighter aircraft could not

m the top and unless our bombers were going over in

force. For this reason single aircraft, such as photographic reconnaissance machines, were left more or less alone at this stage of the war. Earlier in the war they were always subject to attack.

The V-2 rockets also used a considerable amount of hydrogen peroxide as part of the fuel for driving the fuel pumps on the rocket. We felt that the fuel sources in this case were probably less readily available than with liquid oxygen, since pre-war demand for hydrogen peroxide would have been limited. A special investigation was carried out to locate all the sources of production. We found 12 such plants in Germany, two in France, one in Belgium, and one in Italy. All these were targeted in case we decided to attack them. Again, we never did so. In the course of this latter investigation we found a special type of railway wagon on which were mounted in two rows 12 small tanks or carboys. As we had seen this type of wagon at Peenemünde, and also at other points associated with the V weapon program, we felt that it was reasonably likely that this type of wagon was used to carry hydrogen peroxide. We kept a close watch for this type of wagon and looked closely at any plant which had any of them near it. Such wagons were not necessarily an indication of hydrogen peroxide production, as they were also used for the carrying of other chemicals, but at least their presence was enough cause to look closely at any place where they were found.

In the short time which we had available to us to identify and tie down the whole V weapon manufacturing program, we were not able to get a complete picture including, for instance, the full range of subcontractors. Very often it is possible to spot one subcontractor whose elimination can create a major bottleneck in the whole production program. We did identify the main manufacturing points, all the likely sources of fuel, and also the communications system used to move the weapons from the manufacturing area to the front. We had therefore in reserve at least three methods of retaliation apart from attacking the operational area. Of these, the communications were probably the hardest to disrupt in the long term, although they could be temporarily put out of action by the bombing of key bridges or marshalling yards. We found that the enemy was remarkably quick at repairing bombed bridges and getting railway lines back into operation; the most that could be expected from such disruption was a respite of a day or two. Destruction of industrial plants was definitely more worthwhile as it could stop all production for several months at a time" (*Kendall*, p. 129-131).

By 1943, Allied intelligence understood that heavy bombardment was driving German industry underground, starting with aircraft production and quickly expanding to other industries including machine tools, ball bearings, synthetic fuel production and, following the *Hydra* bombing of Peenemünde, the V-weapons industry. "A special underground section was organized at the Allied Central Interpretation Unit (ACIU) at RAF Medmenham, England. This section was known as B-6 Section although its reports were entitled U. Reports. B-6 Section had a maximum strength of seven interpreters and two cartographers as well as the part time services of a geologist. Other sections at ACIU were also available for consultation and assistance. All members of B-6 were British personnel except for one American, the author of the present manual. Before B-6 Section was organized a number of ground reports were received indicating that the Germans were embarking on a large scale underground program. Some photo interpretation work was done as a result of these reports by Industry Section, principally on the large V-2 factory in production at Niedersachswerfen…" (*PI Manual*, p. 6).

This infamous underground facility near Nordhausen, Germany was also known as Mittelwerk. Unfortunately the American officer who authored the USAAF study is never named in the document. The Mittelwerk factory was enormous, as shown by the following three adjoining wartime aerial photos. Annotations are based upon PI and post-war "ground truth" information.

Numerous entrances and structures were carefully noted by PIs, but not always understood. The tunnel alignments were noted by ground information after American troops took over the facility but Medmenham PIs knew quite a bit about the interior structure from identifying the various ventilation shafts. Of course they couldn't know true tunnel alignment or what was going on inside.

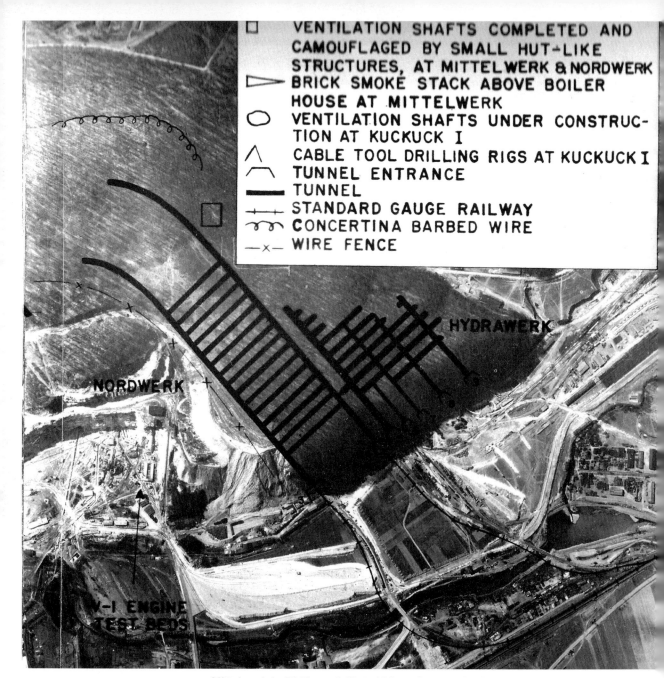

LEGEND (map key):

□ VENTILATION SHAFTS COMPLETED AND CAMOUFLAGED BY SMALL HUT-LIKE STRUCTURES, AT MITTELWERK & NORDWERK

▷ BRICK SMOKE STACK ABOVE BOILER HOUSE AT MITTELWERK

○ VENTILATION SHAFTS UNDER CONSTRUCTION AT KUCKUCK I

∧ CABLE TOOL DRILLING RIGS AT KUCKUCK I

⌒ TUNNEL ENTRANCE

▬ TUNNEL

⊢⊢⊢ STANDARD GAUGE RAILWAY

∿∿∿ CONCERTINA BARBED WIRE

—x— WIRE FENCE

NORDWERK

HYDRAWERK

V-1 ENGINE TEST BEDS

Mittelwerk in PI Manual: Note V-1 engine test-beds.

The Germans were aware of the Allied efforts to locate their U/G facilities and at many sites were unusually careful to move spoil from tunnelling well away from the work and sometimes to cover it with darker surface dirt. Trees above Mittelwerk (right) were provided with wells to prevent them from being killed by the construction. The wells appeared on aerial imagery as small circular pits that actually attracted PI attention to the area. A US Army ground team took the photo of the tree wells shortly after occupation of Mittelwerk in June 1945. The same team took

146

Mittelwerk tunnel entrance (Smithsonian)

Trees in wells to keep them alive as camouflage. June 1945

photos of the main entrance (above) shortly after American troops arrived and the post-war PI manual cited camouflage netting supported by a wooden framework masked the main entrance to the underground V-1 and V-2 factory. The Army caption disagrees with a Smithsonian caption saying the photo shows displaced persons who used the tunnels as an air raid shelter during the chaotic period following the abandonment of the factory by the Germans.

Main rail entrances of Mittelwerk marked "A" and "B".

The post-war PI manual on identification of underground installations (U/G) used this 14 March 1945 106 Group photo of the two main rail entrances to Mittelwerk to demonstrate: "The camouflage here was ineffective because it was too angular in pattern, differed in tone and texture from the adjacent ground and thus did not blend in with its surroundings. The standard gauge railway track leading into the underground factory gave away the presence of the tunnels anyway so that any camouflage of this type, regardless of how good it was, would almost certainly have been a failure."

148

There was no question that something major was going on here.

Similar massive concrete tunnel entrance works can be seen the ground and aerial shots of the main adit at Weisenau, Germany. This U/G factory made launching tubes for the V-1.

The greatest tragedy of Mittelwerk was the way slave labourers were literally an expendable commodity. Some 60,000 prisoners worked here between 1943 and June 1945, and 20,000 died from illness, overwork and starvation.

Two miles from Mittelwerk was Lager Dora, the slave labour concentration camp housing

The graphic below shows a typical massive concrete U/G facility entrance. The ground photo is from 1946. The aerial is 106 Group imagery from 2 March 1945. Weisenau, Germany.

SS operated Lager Dora slave-labour camp, 106 Gp, 14 Mar 45. Note guard towers spaced around camp.

workers needed to make the V-weapons. Guard towers (see arrow) evenly spaced around a perimeter were a long understood PI signature for a prison compound. The SS ran the camp and some 2,000 German technicians supervised roughly 16,000 slave labourers, trying to make 600 V-2s per month in the four miles of Mittelwerk tunnels.

A solid PI signature for a weapons factory was identification of rockets on flat cars. These cars had been seen at Peenemünde and Blizna. Spotting them at Mittelwerk on 14 March 1945 (at right) gave away what was going on inside the mountain.

Rocket shipments were quite distinctive. The V-2 was 46'6" long and the standard German flat cars were 26' to 33' long making it necessary to load each rocket on two cars. Two V-2s were commonly loaded nose to nose on three flats. Tarpaulin covers made the cars appear very long and easily recognizable by PIs.

The same photo coverage caught two train loads of V-2 rockets at Niedersachswerfen,

2 ROCKETS ON FLAT CARS

TUNNEL ENTRANCES

Enlargement of above
photo showing rockets on
train cars at Mittelwerk,
14 March 1945

Germany (Mittelwerk). Even though the rockets cannot actually be seen on these photographs the fact that these trains were carrying rockets was determined by photo interpretation by the spacing and arrangement of flatcars. Note the lack of shadow between units showing the rockets extending beyond the main carrying car. Each train is made up of ten three-car units and is therefore carrying twenty rockets. By the spring of 1945, PIs were getting quite good at identifying rockets in transit.

The photo above shows three trainloads of V-2s after an aerial attack on a rail yard at

Two trains of V-2s, at Mittelwerk. 106 Gp, 14 March 1945.

Trainloads of rockets, Wilhelmshaven, Germany, 10 April 1945.

Wilhelmshaven, Germany. Absence of craters says fighter-bombers did the damage with rockets or guns. Wavy lines of rail cars show equipment destroyed in the attack. The annotations show the seven three-car units on one track that are still covered by tarpaulin (1) and the three adjacent units (2) that are partly unsheeted exposing three rockets. There are ten units on another track that were also attacked (3). These rockets were produced at Niedersachswerfen and were on their way to launch positions in the Netherlands.

Eighth Air Force sent bombers to Nordhausen six times between 7 July 1944 and 22 February 1945. The usual target was the airfield—never the nearly invulnerable nearby Mittelwerk underground factory. The photo below, taken shortly after the American Army took possession of Mittelwerk, shows V-2 rockets on flat cars destroyed on rail sidings near the tunnel entrances. In this case the damage was not done by bombing but probably by slave labourers freed when the Germans abandoned the site.

The task of ACIU's B-6 Section was not only to locate underground installations but to determine what was going on inside them and what sort of geology was involved to estimate the best way to bomb them. Initially, old mines and mushroom caves were expanded, but new construction was quickly spotted. Some of the best tip-offs to U/G installations were unusual

Rockets destoryed at Mittelwerk possibly by released prisoners, June 1945.

activity at otherwise seemingly innocuous sites. Typical indicators were: spoil from the excavations, new electric power or water lines, unusual road and/or rail service and traffic, near-by slave labour camps and the proximity to an existing factory (this was particularly common for the aviation industry).

The two previous graphics demonstrate how much Third Phase PI could accomplish in a

Min-Briefing Chart of Ebensee, Austria. 12 October 1944.

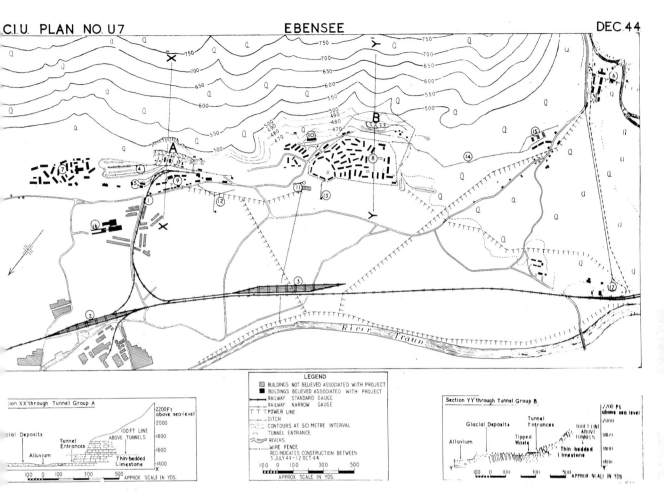

LEGEND
- ▨ BUILDINGS NOT BELIEVED ASSOCIATED WITH PROJECT
- ■ BUILDINGS BELIEVED ASSOCIATED WITH PROJECT
- RAILWAY STANDARD GAUGE
- RAILWAY NARROW GAUGE
- POWER LINE
- DITCH
- CONTOURS AT 50 METRE INTERVAL
- TUNNEL ENTRANCE
- RIVERS
- WIRE FENCE
- RED INDICATES CONSTRUCTION BETWEEN 3 JULY 44 – 12 OCT 44

100 0 100   300   500
APPROX. SCALE IN YDS.

ACIU detailed PI Report on Ebensee showing what PIs could squeeze out of imagery. December 1944.

month. The aerial photo was quickly made into a target graphic but a great deal of detail was dragged out of the imagery to make the ACIU graphic of December 1944. Annotations note entrances, rail lines, waste dumps, maintenance shops, a hydroelectric power station, several camps, warehouses, a sewage disposal plant, wells and water pipes, and foundations for new buildings.

Just a week after collection of the coverage used to make the Minimum Briefing Chart (next page), PIs had determined that the Zipf, Austria underground (U/G) facility was a liquid oxygen plant built in extended beer storage tunnels. After the war it was learned that the factory produced 80 tons of LOX per day. Interpreters were able to determine that research and testing of V-2 engines was also done here. Annotations on the photo below show: entrances 1 (the brewery), 2 (main), 3 (rail), 4 (new, as shown by spoil). A small slave labour camp is at 5. PIs were able to identify 6 as a rocket engine test facility on top of the hill. Both of the Zipf coverages were flown from Italy.

"The degree of faith which the Germans placed in the V-weapon programme is best illustrated

by the decision to put the entire production underground. At a time when Allied bombers were demonstrating their powers of wholesale destruction and frantic efforts were being made to house the most vital industrial processes and machinery in places safe from bombing, a large section of the most ambitious underground project, the Mittelwerk at Niedersachswerfen, was assigned, not to the production of ball bearings, crankshafts, electric motors, fighter aircraft, synthetic oil, rubber or nitrogen, but to the assembly of V-1s and V-2s" (*USSBS*, p. 35).

156

Production underground might be relatively safe from bombing but it had fundamental disadvantages. Limited space, poor lighting and ventilation, and humidity slowed output. Corrosion in electrical systems proved to be a particular problem coming out of the damp caves. In addition, some of the slave labourers did everything they dared to sabotage both production systems and individual weapons moving down the line.

Powys-Lybbe wrote that discovery of the secret factory (Mittelwerk) was "an incredible stroke of luck, railway flats conveniently left in the open were seen loaded with 'cylindrical objects.' Subsequently it was learnt that the factory was the sole source of supply of the V-weapons" (*Eye*, p. 207). It is unlikely that bombing would have hurt the production line deep inside the mountain, but destroying servicing rail yards and lines certainly made it more difficult to move the rockets to the front. Allied bombers simply did not have the information, bombs or accuracy necessary to attack Mittelwerk itself.

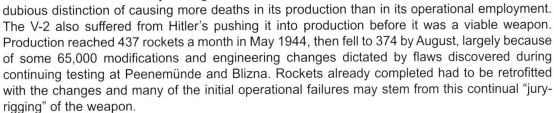

Abysmal working conditions contributed to many failures of the rocket. They also gave the V-2 the dubious distinction of causing more deaths in its production than in its operational employment. The V-2 also suffered from Hitler's pushing it into production before it was a viable weapon. Production reached 437 rockets a month in May 1944, then fell to 374 by August, largely because of some 65,000 modifications and engineering changes dictated by flaws discovered during continuing testing at Peenemünde and Blizna. Rockets already completed had to be retrofitted with the changes and many of the initial operational failures may stem from this continual "jury-rigging" of the weapon.

Douglas Kendall pointed out that PI could not do everything intelligence wished for in the weapons-hunt. "(A) shortcoming of the P.I. source, which I consider more significant, was the utter impossibility of determining what sub-contractors were being used on the V weapon program, particularly for such items as control mechanisms. Destroying these might well have produced a bottleneck in production. The P.I. source had little difficulty in identifying major industrial plants and interpreting, with surprising accuracy, the activity taking place in them. When small machine shops take on significance, the (PI) source has only a small part to play" (Kendall, p. 161-162).

Many of the 227 U/G installations discovered after the war were small machine shops in old mines, extremely difficult to pick-up. ACIU was successful in locating and identifying some sixty U/G installations, including all of the major ones making V-1s and V-2s (*PI Manual*, p. 6-7).

However, targets went very quickly from identification to attack, as the hurriedly made graphic below demonstrates.

Bombing of lines of communications, rail and road, inhibited movement of V-weapons into the threat area and within range of England (or other targets), but Allied intelligence was constantly searching for other ways to damage the German initiatives.

All things considered, the intelligence and air offensive strategy to combat V-weapons manufacture, support, distribution and launch was based upon destroying the most obvious and interdicting or disrupting the rest to make firing impossible or so difficult they were minimized as a threat. Intelligence permitted what was deemed optimum use of airpower. With control of the air, photo reconnaissance and bombing could be executed at will but the underground targets were just not worth the trouble when other targets were easier to hit and produced more results.

Once again, Douglas Kendall has insights on how and why aerial photography was used to examine the infrastructure behind the V-weapons threat:

"From the air, the obvious approach to tracking down where manufacture occurred lay in studying the communications which fed from the firing areas back into Germany itself. This technique proved successful with the V-2 rocket but we never applied it to the flying bomb, first because we were able to keep the firings reasonably under control by attacking the forward storage, as for instance at Creil and, second, because we had discovered that the flying bomb was relatively simple to manufacture, and consequently would be produced by hundreds of small dispersed factories. The only complex equipment in the flying bomb, we felt, was the control unit or automatic pilot which we considered might be manufactured at one or two plants only. We hoped in time to find out what plants were involved in this phase of the operation and to attack them heavily.

Our appreciation on the manufacturing side was confirmed after a number of the flying bombs had landed in England and we were able to study the construction and manufacturing methods. One or two flying bombs actually landed without having detonated.

It was clear from our study of the various components that indeed, as we feared, the flying bomb was built in many places by industrial plants large and small. We were not in a good position to attack the manufacturing units and we never determined soon enough who was making the automatic pilot. With the V-2 we had considerably more success. We assumed that the rocket would have to be brought up to the forward area by railway due to its size, and consequently we studied in great detail all the railway lines feeding back from the area in Holland where firing was taking place. It should be explained that on the air photographs there was no particular problem in identifying all the different kinds of rolling stock, and, in the case of open wagons, noting what was being carried on them. Our railway section at the interpretation unit had evolved very thorough techniques for studying all the various marshalling yards, loading points, sidings and so on in order to determine what traffic was moving, military and non-military, and, by studying such factors as congestion, what effect our bombing attacks were having.

We soon found that the enemy had developed a special kind of railway vehicle for carrying the liquid oxygen needed for the V-2. We first identified this tank wagon at Peenemünde and later found it at various other points in Germany and elsewhere. It was a flat car about 60 feet long loaded with a tank which was 27 feet long. Presumably the tank was heavily pressurized. Between the first of August, 1944, and the 2nd of April, 1945, these special liquid oxygen tanks were seen on 17 different occasions at various points in Holland and Germany but in all cases leading back from Holland to a place called Niedersachswerfen. At the same time we found that a special unit, which we came to know as a triple flat, had been developed for carrying the rocket itself. This was also seen at 29 different points between Holland and Niedersachswerfen. It seemed therefore that Niedersachswerfen played an important part in the whole manufacturing process, although

MiPi 41.916

NINTH AF 2ND IMAGE INTERPRETATION REPORT US10/TV 2003

SORTIE No: US 31/5210 - Photo Nos. 3017, DATE: 12 Oct. 44   T.O.T. 1130A

TYPE OF SITE: STORAGE   1017

REMARKS: Information suggest that the target area is a suspected underground CROSSBOW Supply Depot, and photographic evidence supports this. There are three underground entrances at (A). Two are rail served and of these one is camouflaged with netting. At (B) there is an excavation, also covered with camouflage netting, and containing a circular chimney-like object. A liquid oxygen wagon is observed at (C).

An overhead power line feeds the site from the NORTH, and two Gantry pylons are observed at the head of buried cable trenches which lead towards the excavations.

20th P.I.D. at Hq. 10th P.G.   DISTRIBUTION 'V'

1687413

obviously the fuel supplies would require a separate investigation.

Altogether we examined and reported in detail on 16 industrial plants in Germany which for one reason or another, including reports from agents and prisoners, we believed had something to do with the manufacture of either complete rockets or flying bombs or at least components for them. None of these was of particularly great importance except the one at Niedersachswerfen in the Hartz Mountains. This was a tremendous plant. Built under a hill, the sole indications of its presence were roads and railways which led to tunnel entrances.

In spite of the fact that we could not see the plant itself, there was a surprising amount of detail which we could report about it. First of all, we could definitely say that it was engaged in the manufacture of both V1 and V-2 weapons. This was because on the railway sidings adjacent to the factory we could see railway cars loaded up with these weapons, obviously on their way to France, and later, Holland. We could also make an excellent guess at the floor area likely to be used by considering the shape of the hill in relation to entrances and by studying the geology. Normally tunnelling takes place on a single geological level which will probably be a soft rock like limestone. Again it is necessary that the beds be level as otherwise the tunnelling operation is more difficult. A further factor, which gave a good indication of the size of the plant, was the amount of electric power being fed into it. This could again be measured by studying the power lines which led to the plant. As I indicated earlier, the amount of power being carried can be measured with reasonable accuracy from the size of the transformers which are installed.

We never found any other plant which appeared to be engaged in rocket production on a scale comparable to Niedersachswerfen. As a matter of fact we have since learned that this was virtually the sole source of supply. It was a huge plant and was studied with great interest after the war as we had no comparable underground factories" (Kendall, p. 127-129).

---

1   Writing this chapter I found Philip Henshall's book *Hitler's Rocket Sites*, helpful for dimensions and configurations of the bunkers. Some of his conclusions are rejected by other authors, but I recommend the book to anyone wanting more information on these sites. Mr Henshall walked most of the ruins in the 1980s. While wonderful for the "ground truth" detail presented, his comments on bombing, bombing results and what Allied intelligence knew should be largely disregarded. Time has erased most damage to surrounding areas and some damage to the sites themselves was done post-war. Let the photos presented here show how hard the Allies bombed, how accurate they were, and where these sites stood on target priority lists.

2   *Closing the Ring*, p. 231. Named after Home Secretary Herbert Morrison. Used as tables in homes, these were 6.5' x 4' steel frames that could shelter two crouching adults and several children during an air raid.

3   Notes from the 325th Photo Wing target study. "The purpose to which Siracourt was to be put was never known although long suspected as being designed to launch pilotless planes. The great site, the heavy bomb-proof construction and the regular design made it a very conspicuous object on an air photograph. Cover, exp. 3005, msn 1880 of 106 PG, 4 Aug 44.

4   *V-Missiles*, p. 233 and 298. The HDP barrels firing on Luxemburg were dismantled on 27 February 1945 and sent back to the factory that made them in Wetzlar, Germany, p. 242.

5   See author's comments in *Eye of Intelligence*, p. 208-212 and *Flying Bomb*, p. 164. Before he was mysteriously murdered in Brussels in March 1990, the legendary long-range artillery expert, Gerald Bull, was reportedly trying to develop a gun on this same pattern for Iraq's Saddam Hussein.

Chapter VI

SKIS WITHOUT SNOW

JUST WITHIN RANGE

It eventually turned out that the German rocket programme didn't require an elaborate launching location, and the plan to launch from the "concrete monsters" was a false start, though using the bunkers for storage might have been viable if not for Allied air intervention. Such was not the case for the first of the new weapons to go operational. The flying bomb would also have made good use of the bunkers if the Allies had allowed them to reach completion and their alternative "field launching" sites had several vulnerabilities. While well dispersed over the countryside, they required construction of several structures for checking out and getting the flying bomb into the air that were neither small nor mobile. Few things catch the eye of a PI faster than new construction. German PIs knew that as well as Allied PIs, but apparently the word didn't get to those responsible for making the launch sites. They contracted construction out to French companies that, even if they'd known how, couldn't have cared less about disguising the work.

From its inception, the V-1 programme never envisioned that the bunkers alone would be enough to sustain the kind of rate-of-fire desired. A number of dispersed, camouflaged sites were to be simultaneously constructed on the Cherbourg Peninsula within 140 miles of Bristol and in a band between Dieppe and Calais at ranges from 120 to 170 miles from the centre of London. Other sites would be built closer to England in the Pas de Calais area to take advantage of proximity to several of the centralized launch sites/storage and distribution bunkers being constructed. Fed a regular supply of V-1s from the bunkers, the dispersed sites were expected to keep up a high rate of fire on their targets.

Allied understanding the threat of the dispersed V-1 sites depended upon an understanding of the V-1 itself, and its launch system, and they didn't have that knowledge in the early fall of 1943 when the first dispersed launch sites were being discovered. Agent reports said an aerial torpedo or flying bomb was under development at Peenemünde, and communications intercepts from that area had examples of what seemed to be in-flight tracking of something flying horizontally and relatively low. This was not at all what was expected of the rocket, the weapon Allied scientists were obsessing on, but rockets had been seen and, as yet, Intelligence hadn't seen a single example of the flying bomb weapon. Pieces of the puzzle at Peenemünde and in France didn't match. Enigma intercepts had tied the rocket to Army units and the flying bomb to the Luftwaffe. When intercepted German message traffic identified military units and people related to Peenemünde active in the Pas de Calais, it was presumed they were there for deployment of a V-weapon (*Brit Intel*, vol. 3, p. 393 & 408). Those indicators heightened apprehension that the "new weapons" threat was looming nearer, but the rocket was still the weapon expected. Launching from the bunkers could be envisioned, but Allied intelligence couldn't visualize how the rocket could be launched from the unexplained constructions being found just behind the coast opposite south-eastern England.

Up through the fall of 1943, actually spotting the V-weapons had been like finding a needle in a haystack, but at least Allied intelligence knew the haystacks were Peenemünde and Blizna. Finding the new threat in France presented the problem of searching a haystack that was a 500 mile-long arc from Brest to Antwerp and 60 miles deep from the English Channel. Considering the limited coverage of each photoreconnaissance mission, a limited number of photo interpreters, the high-priority demands for intelligence from the strategic bombing campaign and preparing for the Invasion of Normandy, looking at every foot of this 30,000 square mile "Threat Zone" for new weapons was a monumental task for both PR units and Medmenham. Fortunately, USAAF photo recon assets were just coming into their own. The F4 and F5 photo birds of Eighth and Ninth Air Force Photo Squadrons didn't have the speed, altitude and range to go some of the places Spitfires and Mosquitoes ranged, but the American planes mounted wide-format (9.5") film in Tri-Metragon camera fans covering horizon-to-horizon that were ideally suited to "troll" for targets over a large area—and there was a rapidly increasing number of those planes as new Squadrons became operational.

American photo interpreters didn't yet have all the skills the British had learned in nearly four years of war, but there were a lot of the American PIs becoming available and they were eager to contribute. There were sixty American officers at Medmenham by the end of 1943 (*Brit Intel*, vol. 3, p. 465). By 1944 half of the officers at Medmenham were American. There were also Canadians serving as PIs (Kendall, p. 81). By this time the US had a PI school at Harrisburg, PA, modelled on Medmenham techniques. Medmenham was freely sharing experience on how to get the work done, merging the newcomers into existing teams (*Eye*, p. 189 & 197) so the volume of work that could be accomplished was steadily expanding at a time when speed and volume were about to become more critical than ever.

"Some time before the end of October London had learned from one of its French networks that since August six sites in northern France had been found, each having a strip of concrete and some a line of posts that were aligned on London" (*Brit Intel*, vol. 3, p. 403).

Duncan Sandys decided the rocket danger was so serious that the entire threat area must be rephotographed (*Air Spy*, p. 154). Starting shortly after the 21 October decision, 100 separate photoreconnaissance sorties were flown, each returning from several hundreds to a thousand exposures—every one of which had to be minutely scanned. Douglas Kendall says the actual rephotographing of the threat area began on 28 October 1943. He notes this was the third time that whole area had been studied (Kendall, p. 91). This resulted in a tide of images for Medmenham to print, process, plot, sort, distribute and interpret.

In late October and early November a source in France reported that his construction firm had been hired by the Germans to build eight mysterious sites near Abbeville. "The nature of these sites was not clear to him" (Kendall, p. 91). New photo recon missions were specifically laid on to cover the suspect locations (*Eye*, p. 195). The function of the new sites was a mystery. The Cripps Committee issued a report on 17 November (see below) noting that agents in France were reporting the construction of "as many as 70 or 80 sites, but provided no evidence which enabled them to be associated with the A-4 or any other known weapon." Another appendix in the same

This RAF 541Sq coverage of Bois Carre, 3 November 1943, changed the hunt in France from a general to a specific search. The new, unusual construction was obvious in open country. Note two "skis" outside the wood. Since it was the first identified, all other "ski-sites" were grouped under this name.

Enlargement of first
Bois Carre cover.
3 November 1943.

FIRST V1 LAUNCHING SITE
in France to be analysed by photographic interpretation.

Low-altitude pass by RCAF 400Sq on 9 November 1943 showing Bois Carre "skis" under construction.

report addressed the 'pilotless aircraft' saying "there is no direct evidence of any preparation for the use of this weapon." Nor could they be linked to the Watten-type sites (*Brit Intel*, vol. 3, p. 405 & 407-409).

All eight sites had been photographed by 3 November 1943 (Kendall, p. 91). Though not precisely identical in layout, all eight had the same structures arranged in a crude attempt to fit into the local landscape. "By going back through older photographs, which had been obtained over France by one means or another, we actually found that as early as September 24th, initial ground clearing and the dumping of building materials had been taking place at one of the sites" (Kendall, p. 95). Fortunately the early sites weren't being built with a real eye to concealment. It is relatively easy for a careful, methodical PI search of comprehensive aerial photo coverage to spot something that intrudes on or breaks the natural lines of the countryside. Freshly turned earth halates, showing light and obvious. New paths, roads or cable lines stand out. While the wires are too small to show at most scales, even a new power or phone line can be seen by the light colored "doughnuts" representing earth turned around the base of each pole and the line of dots would lead to the new work. All this facilitated identification of suspicious activity, but that doesn't tell much about the function of a new installation.

Douglas Kendall noted, "It should be remembered that, up to this point in the investigation, it had always been assumed that the object to be fired, presumably a rocket, was so heavy that rail access to the firing sites was essential. This was the brief which had been given to the P.I. unit and consequently not too much time had been seriously devoted by the *Bodyline* section to searching in the areas which were away from the main railway system. This fact should be borne in mind when considering the report written on November 5th, two days following the

photography" (Kendall, p. 91). The speed of completing the Third Phase Report underlines the urgency. The referenced PI Report enumerated the various structures and the orientation towards London. It also noted that, "if these are rocket projector sites, they at present bear little or no resemblance to any installations which have hitherto come under observation in connection with the investigation" (Kendall, p. 91-92). The Medmenham Report went on to note that all eight sites were similar; there were no railway lines anywhere near any of the sites, and each site was being constructed in a small wood, presumably for camouflage purposes, though the camouflage was not very effective. It was pointed out that the sites were reasonably obvious from the air and that there should be no difficulty in detecting any further similar sites should any be under construction. They were significantly smaller than the "large sites" and had a certain commonality that also suggested that there was no relationship to the massive bunkers being built in the same threat zone.

The first of what turned out to be dispersed V-1 launch sites was identified on aerial photography at Bois Carre, near Yvrench in the Pas de Calais, thus giving the new sites that name. The buildings were of a new type that didn't fit anything known about the rocket at a time when the rocket was thought to require "special apparatus both for launching, servicing and handling especially in view of the sort of fuel they would have to employ" (*Brit Intel*, vol. 3, p. 409; citing the Cripps Report). Rudimentary attempts at camouflage and concealment at some sites consisted

The "skie-site" at Maisoncelle provided a good look at all the flying bomb site elements.

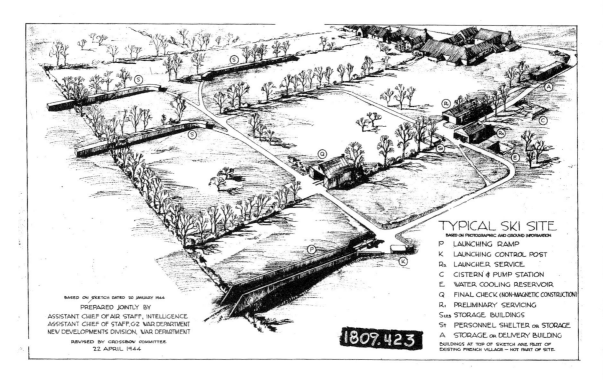

TYPICAL SKI SITE
BASED ON PHOTOGRAPHIC AND GROUND INFORMATION

P   LAUNCHING RAMP
K   LAUNCHING CONTROL POST
R₂ LAUNCHER SERVICE
C   CISTERN & PUMP STATION
E   WATER COOLING RESERVOIR
Q   FINAL CHECK (NON-MAGNETIC CONSTRUCTION)
R₁ PRELIMINARY SERVICING
S₁₂₃ STORAGE BUILDINGS
St PERSONNEL SHELTER or STORAGE
A   STORAGE or DELIVERY BUILDING
BUILDINGS AT TOP OF SKETCH ARE PART OF
EXISTING FRENCH VILLAGE - NOT PART OF SITE.

BASED ON SKETCH DATED 20 JANUARY 1944
PREPARED JOINTLY BY
ASSISTANT CHIEF OF AIR STAFF, INTELLIGENCE
ASSISTANT CHIEF OF STAFF, G2 WAR DEPARTMENT
NEW DEVELOPMENTS DIVISION, WAR DEPARTMENT
REVISED BY CROSSBOW COMMITTEE
22 APRIL 1944

1809.423

The *Crossbow* Committee used Masioncelle's layout as the prototype V-1 site for showing PIs and aircrew what to look for. The graphic seems to have been based upon the imagery on the previous page.

mainly of aligning structures with tree lines and roads, but some of the structures were large and clearly didn't merge well into the normal countryside.

Even more fortunate, at Bois Carre, two of the "skis" and the pad for the launch ramp were built in open fields, guaranteeing discovery. It was quickly apparent that each site consisted of nine uniquely-shaped buildings, some of which initially defied explanation, but early on Kendall and Falcon judged that the oblong concrete platforms were footings for ramps.

It was also quickly learned that the probable ramp at each site was oriented precisely the same as a nearby square building. Plotting the axis of the 150-foot-long ramps (or concrete pads for ramps) and related building, the intersection between sites was noted. They were all clearly aligned, on the centre of London. Even when the launch rail was not installed, the ramp could be identified by the parallel blast walls on either side. The concrete walls were sloped, matching the angle the steel ramp rail would be when installed. Once the ski-sites were related to V-1 launch it didn't take PIs long to guess that the alignment of the square building was to allow for setting the magnetic heading to the target (*Eye*, p. 199). Despite not yet understanding the sites, based upon their orientation alone, they were designated as weapons-related and no one had any doubts as to their objective.

Almost immediately, photo interpreters associated the new sites with the easily seen "signature" of a trio of narrow buildings, just above ten feet wide and 260 feet long, featuring a shallow curve on one end, resembling skis turned on their sides. Look at the 23 June 1943

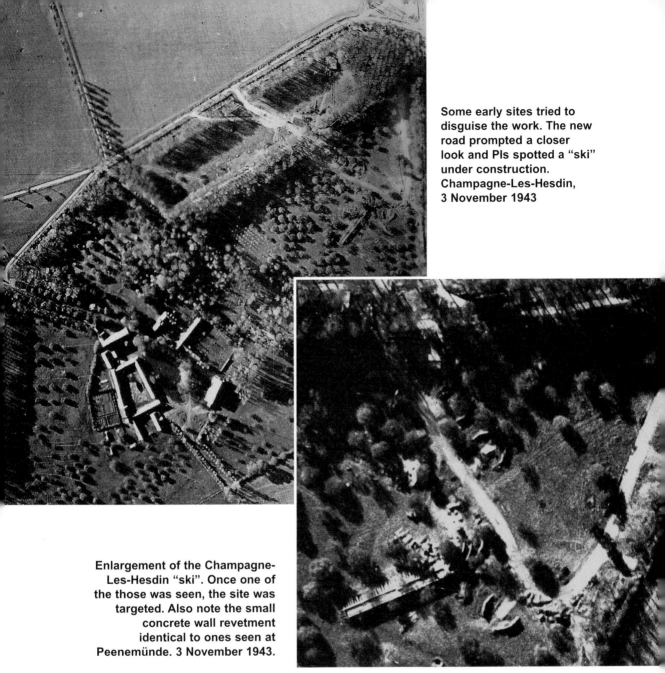

Some early sites tried to disguise the work. The new road prompted a closer look and PIs spotted a "ski" under construction. Champagne-Les-Hesdin, 3 November 1943

Enlargement of the Champagne-Les-Hesdin "ski". Once one of the those was seen, the site was targeted. Also note the small concrete wall revetment identical to ones seen at Peenemünde. 3 November 1943.

imagery of the "ramps" at Peenemünde and note the curious extension of the airfield road just to the south. The curve of that "sidetrack" and its length almost exactly match the length and curved end of the longer "ski" at the field launch sites. I have always wondered if that was intentional or a coincidence.

It seemed that the unusual buildings were windowless and had three-foot thick walls made of pre-cast concrete. Even more curious, one of the ski-shaped buildings at each site was about 30 feet shorter than the other two. All the "skis" had a personnel door at the blunt end and a full-

As in this case, sometimes "skis" were artfully placed in hedgerows but the launching ramp and check-out building stood out and gave the site away. Zudaysques, 4 February 1944.

Pls quickly noted the matching orientation of the launch ramp and check-out building – most were aligned on London. Note blast walls framing the ramp. 5 February 1944

width door at the curved end. Medmenham PIs guessed that the curve in the building was an anti-blast measure because the object(s) to be housed couldn't negotiate a turn behind a normal perpendicular blast wall set a few feet out from the door (*Eye*, p. 197-199). So, the stored objects were long, but could not be as long as the rockets seen at Peenemünde or they wouldn't be able to make the turn of the building.

"Everything seemed to point towards the 'skis' being for storage purposes. We felt that the two longest 'skis' would be used for storing the main bodies of the rockets – or whatever the weapon was – and the shorter one for the tail units. We even did some mathematics and found that the ratio of the amount of rocket body to tail unit worked out approximately right. Anything can be proved statistically!" (Kendal, p. 97).

Some "skis" turned to the left, some to the right, but all had paths that led from the curved end to the larger square building and thence to the London-aligned ramp. Allied "boffins" deduced that no rocket capable of reaching England from these sites could have a body short enough to negotiate the curve in those "ski" buildings. Nor was it likely that a long shallow ramp could be used to launch a rocket. A shallow ramp (or footings for a ramp) suggested a catapult angled to build up lift, and that meant wings. They guessed that the sites must be related to the as yet to be seen flying bomb first suggested in the Oslo Report.

On 4 November, the PM asked Sir Stafford Cripps, Minister of Aircraft Production to chair an ad hoc committee charged by the PM to "examine the facts and decide whether the German secret weapons really existed at all, and if so what was the nature and extent of the threat" (*Air Spy*, p. 156-157).

"By midnight on the 7th of November 1943, no less than 19 Bois Carre type sites had been located but it had not yet been possible to make this information available to the War Office and Air Ministry" (Kendall, p. 93). The search continued with the highest priority for collection and PI.

"About this time, the whole V weapon program was getting much attention from the War Cabinet. The German propaganda machine was making almost hysterical boasts about their new secret weapons, promising that they would shortly prove the complete undoing of the British Isles. Naturally the threats were taken seriously up to a point, but there seemed to be no way of accurately evaluating the significance of the information before us. Mr. Churchill decided to evaluate the evidence himself and it became necessary to send members of the P.I. unit to attend Cabinet meetings to give first-hand evidence. He also called in a number of eminent scientists, who immediately arranged themselves in two teams, those for and those against. Those in favour seemed to be highly pessimistic and concluded that a warhead of at least 10 tons would be possible. Those against were of the firm opinion that the whole thing was a hoax aimed at drawing our bombing efforts from Germany onto useless targets. After some all night sittings, which at times were heated, Mr. Churchill instructed Sir Stafford Cripps to carry out a detailed investigation of all the existing evidence with a view to forming a conclusion. This meeting was called for November 8th, 1943" (Kendall, p. 92). Wing Commander Kendall represented Medmenham at the meeting on November 8th, presided over by Sir Stafford Cripps.

"The meeting started by considering the evidence from non-photographic sources which on the whole was vague and not at all detailed. The evidence from propaganda sources was then considered. It was pointed out by the department responsible for analysing German propaganda that Herr Goebbels never made a major persistent claim of this nature without there in fact being some truth in it. If the German leaders built up a high expectation in the German people that a secret weapon would shortly be available with which to punish the

British, and then they subsequently failed to produce the weapon, the repercussions from a propaganda point of view would be very serious and a great drop in morale would result. Promises of a new weapon with dire threats to the enemy were a useful propaganda tool for about six months, but if they were extended beyond this time without the weapon actually appearing, they in fact produced a negative effect. The conclusions of the propaganda analysers were that secret weapons did exist and that the German plans called for their use during the winter of 1943/44, probably about January of 1944. We now know that the original target day was to be October 20th, 1943, but all sorts of problems caused postponement.

Following this evidence, the bulk of the meeting was given over to a detailed discussion of the photographic evidence with the assumption still at this time that the weapon was a rocket. Having given all the evidence which we had available on the rocket at Peenemünde and elsewhere, Sir Stafford Cripps then asked whether there was any further indication of possible secret weapon activity in northern France. I had the unpleasant task of telling him that during the previous four days we had located 19 sites in the early stages of construction. Sir Stafford Cripps asked what evidence there was for supposing that these sites had any connection with *Bodyline*. I and a couple of photographic interpreters explained that there was no photographic evidence of a positive nature, but a considerable amount of negative evidence. For instance the sites did not correspond with any known military installation, they were all started simultaneously and they did not appear to be in any way connected with the Atlantic Wall defences. We pointed out that the sites had certain common features, such as three ski-shaped buildings and a platform which appeared to be facing always in the direction of London. This evidence naturally produced considerable surprise and the meeting was adjourned for two days so that we could extend our examination to see whether any further installations of this type were under construction.

Immediately following the meeting, a much enlarged investigation group was established (at Medmenham) to carry out the special studies needed. This group was made up of British Army, R.A.F. and U.S.A.A.F. officers. They set to work at once to re-examine northern France from a new point of view. Captain Robert Rowell was put in charge and gave unstinting effort to the investigation" (Kendall, p. 93-94). "Another feature was a concrete platform consisting of heavily reinforced slabs of concrete. Each platform contained 12 studs leading out of it. These pointed directly at London. Later on certain sites were built with platforms pointing in the direction of Southampton, Bristol and Portsmouth" (Kendall, p. 99).

At the 8 November meeting, Douglas Kendall briefed the committee on the nineteen photo-verified new sites scattered throughout the "threat area" and the news came as a shock. He told the Committee that the sites could not be definitively connected with *Bodyline*, but there was evidence that they were unlikely to be anything else (*Eye*, p. 196-197). The meeting was adjourned to let PIs complete their review of the new imagery that was flooding in. Realization that rail was not necessary for the new sites (still presumed to be mandatory for rockets of some sort), resulted in a priority re-examination of recent aerial photos to search for more of the sites.

The ramps and preparation buildings were extremely difficult to spot on small scale area coverage, but the "ski" buildings were almost impossible for the Germans to hide from photo interpreters. Those signature "skis" readily gave away the launch site locations, even early in construction. Once a "ski" was spotted; under construction, aligned with roads, blended into tree lines or hedges, or otherwise camouflaged, the other characteristic buildings, even when better hidden, were quickly located and reported.

"Arrangements were immediately made to obtain low oblique photographs of the Bois Carre site so that the structure could be examined in detail. This task was allotted to a Canadian squadron (400 Squadron, City of Toronto) and the excellent set of photographs which they obtained on November 9th, proved to be highly valuable" (Kendall, p. 92).

When the Cripps Committee reconvened on 10 November, Kendall reported that twenty-six ski-sites had now been found. He also stated that, "In our opinion the ski-shaped buildings were intended for storage, and that there did not seem to be any indication that the sites were intended for the firing of a rocket, which was supposed to weigh 45 tons and would therefore require heavy handling gear" (Kendall, p. 94). Medmenham was convinced that the new sites were for the much rumoured, but still unseen, flying bombs (Eye, p. 197). Powys-Lybbe wrote that Kendall's belief that the ski-sites were not related to the much heavier rocket, which would need heavy handling gear, refuted Professor Jones' "claim that he had to convince the interpreters before they would disallow the rocket hypothesis".

The Cripps Report, however, had "the mistaken assumption, which was due to the lack of intelligence about the nature and design of the V-1, that the pilotless aircraft required no special launch apparatus. It was on this assumption that his report, setting aside not only the earlier correct assumption that Watten was associated with rockets but also the Sigint and SIS evidence that the GAF (German Air Force) was experimenting with pilotless aircraft and was associated with the ski sites, failed to connect these sites with the pilotless aircraft" (Brit Intel, vol. 3, p. 409). Apparently this resulted from assuming the ski-sites were for a smaller, lighter, as yet unidentified, version of the Peenemünde rocket. Cripps felt able to report to the War Cabinet that, "in his opinion V weapons definitely existed, since the amount of activity being devoted to the projects by the Germans was too great to be a mere diversionary hoax. At the same time it was clearly necessary to carry out a detailed study of the 26 Bois Carre type sites located in northern France in order to determine their nature" (Kendall, p. 94).

Of course the Cripps Report was circulating "well above the pay grade" of Medmenham PIs and they continued to assume the new dispersed sites in France were related to the flying bomb. The "skis" were determined to be for storage of the reported weapons as they arrived on site, much like an artillery magazine. There was agreement that, in the face of this fast-expanding threat Cripps reported to the War Cabinet, that whatever the ski-sites were intended to do was apparently a more immediate danger than the long-range rocket and advised increasing coverage frequency of both Peenemünde and the threat area in France. The Cripps meeting ended Bodyline and Sandys' responsibilities for intelligence and countermeasures related to the rocket went to the Air Staff (Air Spy, p. 158).

It was immediately following his return to Medmenham from this meeting that Douglas Kendall asked PI Babington Smith to search Peenemünde for a little plane (related in Chapter III). Kendall set up a sub-section at Medmenham to specialize on the flying bomb aspect of Bodyline, now known as Crossbow. The officer placed in charge was Captain Robert Rowell. Most of his team were RAF and WAAF officers, with a handful of Army officers and enlisted troops from the Army, RAF and USAAF (Eye, p. 197). From the onset they were swamped by the missions covering the new sites (Air Spy, p. 155).

Use of pre-fabricated components for the new structures in France suggested a programme of broad scope. The "ski-sites" were obviously quickly assembled and they were proliferating across the countryside. "Remarkably skillful interpretation of these photographs (the new coverage of the threat zone) revealed that at least 31 'ski-sites' were being rapidly built" (*USSBS*, p. 5). German records indicate that firing was scheduled to begin on 1 December 1943, but technical problems with the V-1 delayed operations. The next scheduled date for V-1 firing was 1 June 1944 for eighty of the simplified sites (*V-Missiles*, p. 178 & 183).

Practically every new photo sortie turned up one or more of the things in one stage of construction or another. The pace and level of effort implied an enemy urgency that was ominous.

"By 24 November, 38 (of the sites) had been confirmed by the PRU and as many as 60 reported by the SIS; all were set back up to 20 km from the coast in a corridor 200 miles long by 30 miles wide in the Sein-Inferieure and the Pas de Calais" (*Brit Intel*, vol. 3, p. 403).

Douglas Kendall put the numbers higher and the date of discovery five days earlier. "By November 19th, following successful photography of the whole area, we were able to identify 96 sites under construction. Subsequently all sorts of rumours came through from different sources giving numbers of sites up to 400. Sometimes these reports caused considerable dismay and resulted in further complete searches of the area, 'just in case.' The P.I unit felt confident that we had not overlooked any sites but naturally this was a matter of opinion. In actual fact, 96 was the exact number of Bois Carre sites built and none was overlooked.

"The figure of 96 seemed to be so arbitrary that British Intelligence felt that there must be more sites in order to reach a sensible number. In fact, the Bois Carre development was a German Airforce unit and therefore was set up along the lines of a conventional squadron. They created for operational purposes 6 squadrons of 16 firing sites each which makes a total of 96 units" (*Kendall*, p. 95). Wing Commander Kendall further noted:

> "Once we had photographs of a considerable number of sites, it was possible to examine these for common features. At some sites, one particular building would be more advanced than the same building at another site, but it was quickly evident that each of the sites consisted of a standard group of buildings to a standard design although, for reasons of topography and tree cover, the layout of the buildings varied slightly from site to site. It looked very much as if a blueprint had been prepared in Berlin and the work had then been handed over to civil contractors for follow through. This was precisely what happened. Each contractor made his own plans for the programming of the construction, some preferring to concentrate on a few buildings at once, while others tackled them all simultaneously but at a slower speed.
>
> This latter fact proved useful since it was quickly possible, by taking one completed building from one site and another from elsewhere to construct, as it were, a drawing of what a completed site would look like. As a matter of fact we made a model. We could, moreover, study the walls before the roof was added to prepare drawings showing the internal division of the buildings.
>
> The problem now was to deduce the type of weapon which would be used from these sites. It did not take many days to reach a solution, but the process of deduction was not as simple as it appears today with hindsight, and we had to go through many hours of argument and counter argument, theory and counter theory. The solution was achieved by considering each separate building, what it could be used for and how it fitted into the whole.
>
> Each site consisted of three ski-shaped buildings, one square building, a concrete platform with 12 concrete studs leading out from it in pairs, a small reinforced concrete building alongside the concrete platform, two rectangular buildings, a sunken building

usually protected with an earthen blast wall and a pyramid-shaped hole in the ground, not unlike a small swimming pool. The whole system was linked by concrete pathways, the layout of which we considered to be significant, since naturally they would tend to show in which direction objects were planned to move. There were buried pipes linking certain of the buildings which presumably could carry either water, fuels or compressed air. Furthermore, electric power was fed into each site and the various buildings were connected by wires hung from overhead poles. Each site also had, a small distance away, one or two reinforced buildings, usually sunk into the ground, which we assumed were the future crew living quarters. These were not completely standard and did not appear to be directly connected with the sites except by road. I might add that the amount of electric power being fed to the sites was small. This we could determine because the power had to feed through a pole-type transformer at the edge of each site, and we could see that this was of a standard 15 KV type. This meant that there was about enough power feeding into the site to light the various buildings and to drive a maximum of seven horsepower of machinery" (Kendall, p. 95-97).

The twelve concrete studs were used to mount the flying bomb launch rail.

Within a few weeks, the number of ski-sites being built seemed to stabilize at ninety-six. According to post-war prisoner interrogations, sixty-four sites were planned (with eight of them in

ACIU plotting V-1 launch ramp alignments as of 30 August 1944 revealed their targets.

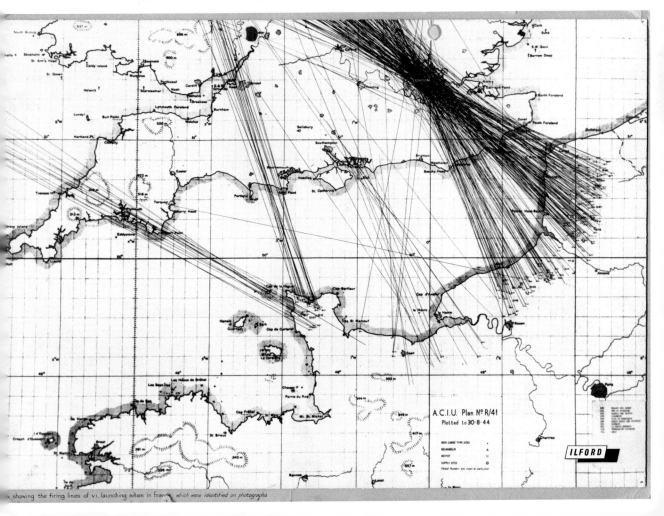

showing the firing lines of v.1 launching sites in France which were identified on photographs

the Cherbourg area), and another thirty-two sites "originally planned as dummies" (*USSBS*, p. 9). Most of those were later "built as real sites". But built to what end? The point wasn't yet proven as far as the Allies were concerned. The huge effort expended to build the "ski sites" clearly identified them as part of a larger threat, but the flying bomb wasn't spotted on the Peenemünde launch ramp until 1 December, and up to that time, the new sites were the subject of considerable doubt, assumption and debate.[1] In addition, no one could predict how many of the ski-sites would eventually be built. So whatever these sites were intended to launch now seemed more worrisome than the possibility of rockets fired from the heavily bombed concrete monsters.

Powys-Lybbe wrote that in the absence of actually seeing a flying bomb (an event that was still a few days away in late November) "The thought of tubes out of which a rocket could be squirted, or rails, or scaffolding or perhaps a ramp, must have acted like some maddening, ceaseless merry-go-round of useless information. Nothing fitted and so much was at stake—possibly fearful destruction in the south of England, and possibly the adverse effect of the mystery weapons on the careful planning of Operation *Overlord* (the Allied invasion of north-west Europe)" (*Eye*, p. 197). Medmenham created detailed architectural plans for each ski-site and practically everything was known about each building as frequent photo coverage of some sites even allowed looks inside before the roofs went on. It was assumed that buildings with the same size and shape served the same function at each site.

Douglas Kendall explained that in early November, Medmenham still believed the new sites were intended for the only weapon they knew about: the rocket. "As we studied each building, we considered it first of all from the point of view of its suitability for rocket firing, and it was only as the evidence pointed increasingly in other directions that we discarded the theory that the Bois Carre sites were destined for rockets" (Kendall, p. 97). He points out that they still expected a 45-ton weapon launched from a steep ramp. "The evidence was there for us to see on the photographs of Peenemünde but we had at this point still overlooked it." (Kendal, p. 97).

"By mid-November, we issued a report suggesting the following:
1. The fuselage on its undercarriage is brought from the larger skis to the square building.
2. The wings are brought from the shorter ski to the square building.
3. The bomb is assembled and mounted on some base while the automatic pilot is set in operation.
4. The bomb is then taken to the firing ramp and mounted on it.
5. Two trolleys then proceed from the small rectangular building, each probably carrying a rocket for takeoff, which is placed under each wing.
6. Instructions to fire are received by telephone at the firing point and radar then presumably plots the course. A central plotting room will no doubt signal the correction to be applied in the square building for the next firing.
7. Immediately before and after firing water will be sprayed at the bottom of the firing ramp to avoid fire to trees from the takeoff rockets.

"After the war we learned that the above general plan was substantially correct, with the one major exception that the trolley which carried the fuselage also carried the wings folded along its side. The reason for one ski being shorter than the other two was something too simple for us to guess. Orders were that 20 flying bombs be stored at the site, fired every night and replaced the following day. 20 is not divisible by 3. Of the three storage buildings at each site, two were built to hold seven flying bombs each and one was built to hold six. Thus by the time that we had finished our studies of the Bois Carre sites, we knew in fair detail the weapon that we were up against, all without ever having seen the weapon itself" (Kendall, p. 99).

Any uncertainty remaining about the ski-sites was shrinking when the flying bomb was identified at Peenemünde in late-November and absolutely settled a few days later in the famous discovery of one at the bottom of a ramp facing out into the Baltic (*Air Spy*, p. 160-165, see Chapter III above). Photo interpreters were struck by the newest of the five Peenemünde ramps, and a similar one at the Zinnowitz Luftwaffe installation down the coast, being very reminiscent of ramps at the ski-sites in France. The Zinnowitz site didn't have the "ski" buildings, but Allied intelligence immediately put two and two together. Powys-Lybbe astutely observed that "it was reasonable for the team to assume that the prototype (V-1) had not been completed until August when construction of the Bois Carre sites had begun. This development was calculated on the evidence obtained from photographic intelligence uniquely, and as Douglas Kendall pointed out: 'It was not difficult to visualize what sort of position we would have been in without it as a source'" (*Eye*, p. 203).

"By the beginning of December 1943 the intelligence authorities had established that Germany was developing both a pilotless aircraft and a long-range rocket, had correctly associated the pilotless aircraft with the ski sites in France, and were concluding, equally correctly, that while the rocket might be the more formidable of the two weapons, the pilotless aircraft constituted the more imminent threat" (*Brit Intel*, vol. 3, p. 415). What's more, PI had established the size, shape and method of launch of the flying bomb and communications intercepts had established its range, speed and flying altitude (*Brit Intel*, vol. 3, p. 417). It was understood that the small size of the weapon meant that small errors in measurements from imagery would result in significant changes in capability (range and payload). This critical information allowed planners to begin thinking about countermeasures, but

Luftwaffe troops moving an assembled V-1. (Bundesarchiv)

bombing of the sites was thought to be the most effective defence (*Brit Intel*, vol. 3, p. 413 & 415), particularly since nothing was known about the intended volume of production or firing anticipated. The only clue to the size of the impending flying bomb attack was the number of launch sites being constructed and an estimate of twenty missiles held at each. Meanwhile, Allied intelligence was gleaning more about the sites each day. The small square concrete building almost completely sunk into the ground near the ramp was probably the firing point. The larger 44-foot square concrete building was also always near the ramp and aligned with it. Appearing like a small hangar, with a 22-foot door, this building was deemed where the flying bomb was taken from a "ski" to have its wings installed. Agents in France reported that this building was made without any ferrous metal so PIs concluded it was where the auto-pilot and compass were aligned, i.e., the V-1 was precisely aimed prior to launch. Fuel storage and vehicle fuelling points were also identified.

In a related PI effort, standard geodetic towers had been recognized along the French coast facing Dover, indicating German engineers were updating the Napoleonic era French maps with a new geodetic survey (*Eye*, p. 199-200). It was now understood that the survey effort was to make their "aiming" of the V-1 more accurate.

Douglas Kendall discussed "ski-site" construction progress with PIs who had been architects before the war and they predicted that the sites might be completed, and the anticipated attack they represented begun, "about six weeks ahead" (*Air Spy*, p. 165). Analysis of construction progress indicated that twenty of the "ski-sites" would be structurally completed in early January 1944 (*Brit Intel*, vol. 3, p. 410). By September Allied intelligence believed the flying bomb would be in operation before the rocket, and that the ski-sites were intended for the V-1.

ADI (Sc) also estimated the V-1 assault would begin soon—mid-January to March 1944. The Allies had no way of knowing that bombing of German production facilities had resulted in supplies of flying bombs to Peenemünde being halted from October 1943 to February 1944 (*Wizard War*, p. 413). This delayed testing and "tweaking" the weapon into an operationally ready status for several months.

Initially the task of bombing the high-threat sites was assigned to RAF and USAAF Tactical Air Forces, "diverting against them (the *Crossbow* sites) the entire medium and fighter-bombers that were being assembled for *Overlord*. When it emerged that they were achieving poor results, in part because of adverse weather conditions, the heavy bombers and Mosquitoes of Bomber Command were called in from the middle of the month and Eighth Air Force was asked to give overriding priority to the ski sites as targets for its daylight bombers" (Army Air Forces in World War II, vol. 3, p. 93-95).

Kendall explained how Medmenham facilitated the attacks. "We set about preparing material on the 96 Bois Carre sites. Target material consisted of a map pinpointing the target, a photograph of each target and surrounding area so the aircrew could plan their bombing photograph of each target and surrounding area so the aircrew could plan their bombing runs, and a detailed photograph of each site taken vertically downward for the selection of aiming points. There were also descriptive reports detailing the amount of flak defending each site and its location. Our group worked hard and fast to collect the large quantities of photographic and printed material needed for the thousands of targets which existed over enemy territory" (Kendall, p. 114).

A programme was developed to systematically destroy the Bois Carre sites and authority to bomb fifty-four of the sites was given on 19 December. The attacks began two days later with an average of ten aircraft for every attack. Sometimes large numbers of aircraft were used. At other times one or two Mosquitoes flying at ground level carried out the raid. Douglas Kendall noted, "I must say they had considerable success with this type of attack" (Kendall, p. 115).

There were seventy-two bombing attacks in December 1943 and 313 in January 1944. That dropped to 196 in February, 127 in March, and rose to 181 in April. As the sites were being significantly damaged the numbers fell to 123 attacks in May, forty in June and only one in July 1944 as bombing shifted to the new Belhamelin sites (which were the ones actually firing). RAF

Naturally Bois Carre was one of the first "ski sites" attacked. This strike of 14 January 1944 was obviously not the first and it seems most of these bombs are wide of the target.

Bomber Command "heavies" made twenty-six attacks; the heavy bombers of the US Eighth Air Force attacked 203 times; medium bombers and fighter bombers of the US Ninth Air Force ran 201 attacks; and the RAF Tactical Air Force struck 623 times from December to June. In June, 105 bombing attacks were made on the new launch sites.

That rose to 129 in July and 142 in August. "Further attacks became unnecessary since our advancing armies captured the launch sites" (Kendall, p. 117).

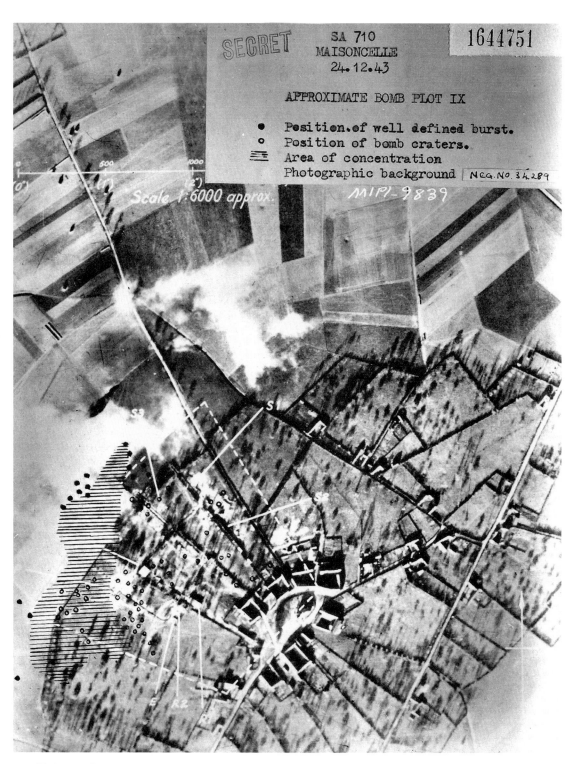

Maisoncelle was attacked on 24 December 1943, the first day of a major missile-site strike campaign by both English and Ninth Air Forces. Half of the bombs were inside the target area – no small feat considering the small size of the installation.

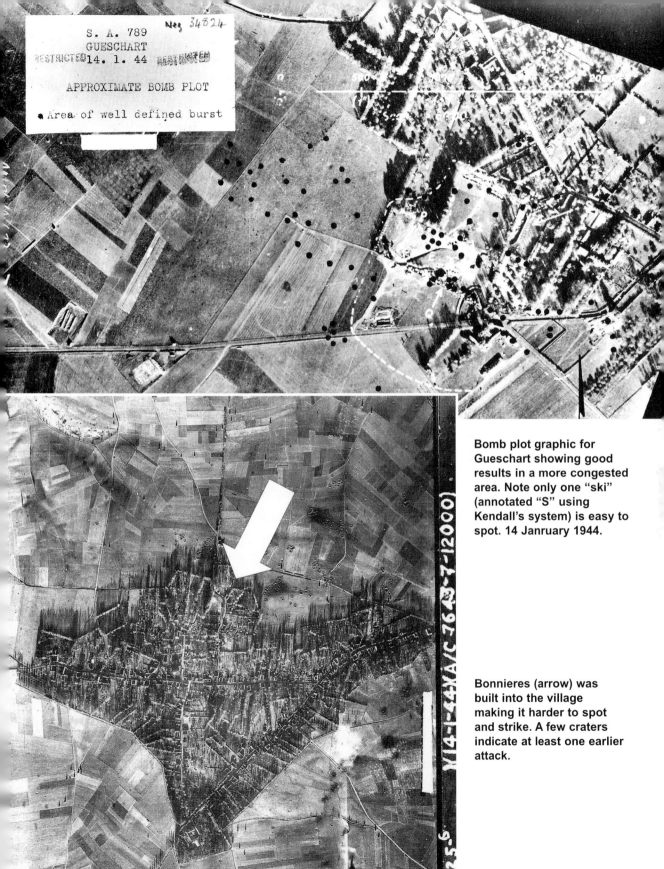

S. A. 789
GUESCHART
RESTRICTED 14. 1. 44 RESTRICTED

APPROXIMATE BOMB PLOT

• Area of well defined burst

Neg 34824

Bomb plot graphic for Gueschart showing good results in a more congested area. Note only one "ski" (annotated "S" using Kendall's system) is easy to spot. 14 Janruary 1944.

Bonnieres (arrow) was built into the village making it harder to spot and strike. A few craters indicate at least one earlier attack.

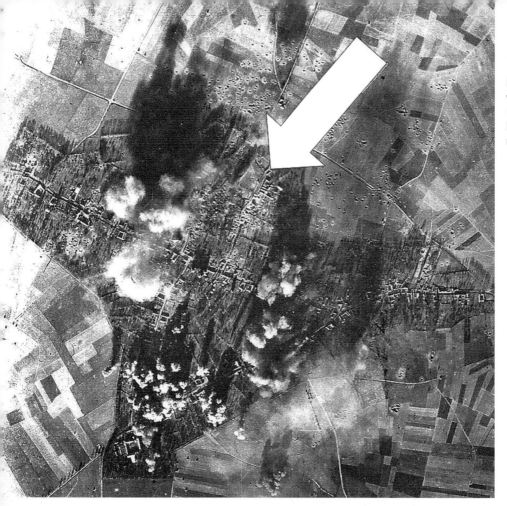

Bonnieres V-1 site (arrow) was first attacked on 14 January 1944. It looks like the village suffered more than the target.

Aside from finding the launch sites, creating target materials to help the strike aircrews, and follow-up with Damage Assessment, photo interpretation was useful in determining the best access of attack for each site by identifying enemy anti-aircraft gun positions. "Our P.I. unit was asked to examine all sites for anti-aircraft defenses. We were fortunately able to send a signal that same night to all units advising them that no flak defenses had been moved into any of the sites. The Air Ministry advised us to maintain a continual watch for flak defenses and to report

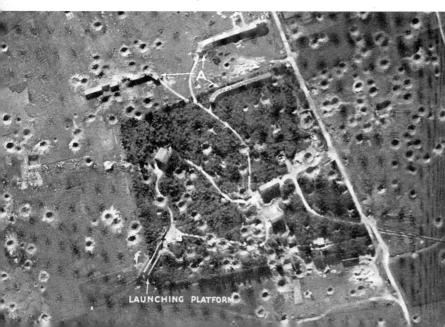

LAUNCHING PLATFORM

Results were better at Bois Carre. However the ramp and check-out building were intact so the site was still a threat.

any immediately to command headquarters" (Kendall, p. 116-117).

Kendall added, "The American Flying Fortresses were particularly effective in these attacks since they operated by day and were better equipped for attacking small targets. The R.A.F. night flying tactics were better suited for attacks on large targets."

As soon as the bombing began the

Left: "Skis" might be disguised but the launch ramp was almost impossible to hide. 5 February 1944.

Below: The same site on 7 March 1944 showing false-work and camouflage netting.

Germans were forced to recognize that the launch sites were too easy to find. They began to build the "skis" and launch ramps more carefully into the pattern of the land, making them harder to identify. Camouflage was used, but if the shapes and new roads disrupt the surrounding patterns, no amount of netting and leafy branches will fool a PI.

The best techniques for hiding a site were building the final assembly building inside an

The Germans tried to complete Bois Carre after it was attacked. Note buildings built beside and over a "ski" to mask its characteristic shape (arrow), and camouflage paint on another. False-work (arrow) also attempts to hide the check-out building and its orientation. Bomb craters made the site easy to find

182

existing barn or house, or to erect a square structure over the characteristic turn of the "ski". It is doubtful if any of that worked to mask a site under construction very long. It was too little, too late. If there was any question about a possible camouflaged installation, a PI could always look at previous cover for signs of construction. Allied PIs were carefully scanning the extensive coverage of the threat area, and all of the first generation flying bomb launch sites were annotated on Allied target maps.

In December, General Eisenhower was advised that "the threat was so serious that he should consider the need for *Overlord* bases outside the range of the flying bomb, as alternatives to Portsmouth, Southampton and Plymouth" (*Brit Intel*, vol. 3, p. 417).

A handful of the original ninety-six sites were near Cherbourg and aligned on England's South Coast ports. Since those were the ports destined to support the Normandy Invasion, those sites were slated for destruction early in the Allied V-weapons offensive.

Once the "ski-sites" were determined to be flying bomb launch sites the aerial recon search in France was widened and intensified under the code-name *Crossbow*. By that time it was decided to try to bomb these sites just as they reached superficial completion, letting the Germans expend time, effort and material uselessly. Medmenham began producing drawings, photo-mosaics and other materials needed by aircrews to strike the sites.

"Still there was a certain amount of opposition to our raids. Some people found it difficult to justify diverting aircraft and bombs from targets in Germany to bomb some insignificant concrete buildings in Northern France. However, the Joint Chiefs of Staff felt that serious devastation to

Right: Flak towers made low altitude recon and bombing more hazardous as defences were upgraded. 5 July 1944.

Below: Low altitude recon gave a look at a launch ramp under construction and inside a "ski". 8 February 1944.

**Bombing from lower than usual altitudes, B-17s put more bombs on a target.
Heudiere, 5 July 1944.**

London would hinder the war effort. Moreover, many of our raids took place on days when weather conditions did not favour deep penetration into Germany. The flying bomb sites were an excellent alternative, especially for new flight crews just starting their bombing operations" (Kendall, p. 115).

Kendall's Medmenham *Crossbow* team established a system of points given for construction of various aspects of a flying bomb site with 100 indicating site completed and ready for operations.

"The threat was considerable. Remember, each site stored about 20 bombs and 96 sites existed in all. In theory, the enemy was capable of firing nearly 2,000 flying bombs at London every single night. However, we did not have the resources to waste on attacking the Bois Carre sites prematurely. We studied the time it took to complete the construction of a site. Of course, this included a bit of guess work and some luck, but we concluded that construction would take from 120 to 140 days. Since different contractors using different construction methods worked at the various Bois Carre sites, the only way to assess the state of completion of any one site was to invent a point system. We took the various components which made up the site and allotted to each component a certain number of points" (Kendall, p. 114).

"As new sorties covering the area were examined, each item was re-assessed and points added according to progress. When the total reached 70 (or 70%), the moment had come to pass on the information that the site should be included in the next bomber hit-list" (*Eye*, p. 203-204). The seventy per cent estimate for attack was deemed prudent since bad weather could deny imagery of any number of the sites for days or even weeks.

"It sounded simple. In practice, it was more complicated. We had to consider periods of bad weather when photography was impossible. During these gaps, the construction continued. We gave an extra three-quarters of a point for each day, so a site which had 65 points on the day we photographed automatically came on our bombing list one week later even if we had been unable to continue photographing it. Following an attack, the site was photographed and assessed once more. Once a site fell below 60 points- that is, 60 percent of completion- it was automatically taken off the bombing list" (Kendall, p. 114).

Photo interpreters were still having considerable success in locating the launch sites and as fast as they were identified, they were bombed and bombed repeatedly under the code-name "No-Ball". Film from bombing sorties also frequently carried the mission number prefix "SAV".

The post-war analysis of USAAF bombing says that:

"a. An analysis of the rate of construction showed that at least 20 "ski-sites" would be structurally complete by 1 January 1944. It was then decided that direct countermeasures were necessary and a series of bombing attacks was launched. These attacks resulted in the eventual abandonment of the 'ski-sites' of which 96 had been identified by 22 January 1944. Not more than two of these original sites were ever used operationally.

b. It appeared that the Germans had seriously underestimated the competence of our photo-intelligence and the potential accuracy and weight of our bombing attacks, for the 'ski-sites' had not been designed to be bomb-proof, but were of elaborate blast-resistant construction, reliance having been placed on skillful siteing and camouflage to avoid detection" (*USSBS*, p. 6).

Detailed full-sized replicas of sites and various buildings were constructed at Eglin Air Base in Florida, then attacked with a variety of aircraft, weapons and tactics. "American experiments had indicated that low-level fighter-bomber strikes were the most effective weapon against the "ski-sites," but in their desperate anxiety to save the British people from another Blitz, the Government insisted that the 'heavies' be thrown into the counterattack as well" (*Bomber Command*, p. 331).

Extensive bombing of the initial sites was followed by a period of inactivity on the Continent while German authorities assessed the damage and probability for success of the ski-sites. This was followed by work to complete the sites not struck and to repair some of the least damaged of those hit. An estimated "ten sites could be regarded as operational but that, as the enemy might operate from sites that were not complete, he might have twenty sites operational by the end of the month (March) if that figure was not reduced by further bombing" (*Brit Intel*, vol. 3, p. 422). The number of sites capable of operations had risen to forty-one by the end of the month but was revised to twenty-five operational sites in mid-April.

The Allies used a policy of major strikes on a "ski-site" just prior to its completion so the renewed German effort was rewarded by more bombing. A favourite time for attack was just after the Germans had poured concrete footings and slabs. This had worked so well at Watten that it was adopted as policy. The bomb-scattered wet concrete was virtually impossible to clean up or work around. Sites so struck were almost always abandoned.

The farthest along of the ninety-six "ski sites" identified by mid-January 1944 were struck before the month was out, most of them thought completely destroyed. In fact, of the fifty sites struck by 27 December, BDA imagery showed direct hits on essential elements at thirteen of them (*Brit Intel*, vol. 3, p. 419). The strikes continued. By mid-March, fifty-four of the ninety-six sites had received major damage. Nine of them were under repair but at thirty-one of the sites there were no signs of repair work. There were no signs of new sites and the number of sites that could

First of a new breed. It was a nasty surprise when Allied PIs found a launch site with just a ramp and check-out building. The frst "modified site" was Belhamelin, near Cherbourg. April 1943.

be completed was diminishing, therefore so was the threat—or so it seemed. The other side of that coin was that during the last several months, signals intelligence indicated steady improvement of flying bomb accuracy at Peenemünde (*Brit Intel*, vol. 3, p. 421).

The German response was to intensify camouflage and defenses.

"Once the enemy no longer considered it worthwhile to repair certain buildings, we had to change our point system. We changed to an A/B/C/D system of categories. The "A" sites were those seriously damaged with at least one essential building destroyed and low points. "B" sites were less seriously damaged. "C" sites had only slight damage while "D" sites had no damage at all. The policy then became to bomb only the "D" sites and once they had been eliminated to start on the "C" sites. In early March 1944, the enemy virtually gave up trying to repair the sites and by the end of May, the battle was won. Every single site had been reduced to a safe category and the Germans abandoned the 96 sites for good. Unfortunately, the war was not yet over" (Kendall, p. 116-117).

German attempts at repairs of the Bois Carre sites in the face of continued bombing focused on the firing point (the ramp) and the small square building nearby and oriented in the same direction. This told PIs that those two elements were most essential to launching the flying bomb (*Air Spy*, p. 166).

When the Germans understood that the "skis" were too easy to identify on aerial photography and they were "giving away" the launch sites, they first countered by making the sites harder to find, taking more care to blend the "ski" buildings into the surrounding land-patterns, use of camouflage, and changing the shape of characteristic buildings with lightly constructed shells. However, the "skis" were simply too long to blend well into the countryside, even with artful camouflage, and photo interpreters had seen enough Bois Carre sites that they were quite good at spotting new ones.

Based upon the Allied bombings of December and January, the German commander of V-1 and V-2 units in France had apparently already decided that "the ski sites were both too conspicuous and too vulnerable" (*Intelligence in War*, p. 283). General Erich Heinemann also abandoned the "large structures" in favour of caves to house weapons and fuel. Dropping the "skis" didn't mean giving up on V-1 launch sites. It just gave Allied intelligence a new set of problems, and a new launch configuration to identify.

SANS SKIS

At least some of the continuing construction or activity at the original "ski-sites" may have been a ruse to draw Allied attention away from the real threat for on 28 April 1944 a new launch site pattern was identified on aerial photos (Kendall, p. 105). Other sources say this occurred on 27 April (*Piercing the Fog*, p. 221 and *Brit Intel*, vol. 3, p. 423).

As usual, the hardest part of the PI task was spotting the first of the new configuration. Once interpreters knew what to look for, the task was still methodical, tedious and stressful, but finding the new sites was mostly a matter of aerial coverage and PI time.

Having thought they had at least delayed the V-1 launch threat for several months, this new discovery was quite a shock to the Allies because of the credible threat the flying bombs posed to London and the "*Overlord*" ports, depots and troop concentrations on the south coast of England. It was feared that a new German bombardment campaign might upset the all-important timetable for the invasion of France. Critical timing included troop movement to debarkation areas, ship arrivals across the Atlantic, the moon and tides. This giant clockwork might be upset by even minor destruction at any one of dozens of places

The Allies intensified reconnaissance in the "threat zone" with a "max-effort" to search the entire area yet again (*Brit Intel*, vol. 3, p. 425). This PR effort involved RAF Sq. No. 106, the 2nd Tactical AF Recon Sq., the U.S. 7th Photo Group and Tactical Recon Squadrons of the U.S. Ninth Air Force. "SIS reports and PR indicated that work on them (the ski-sites) was indeed being abandoned when damage was very heavy, and that the enemy was increasingly giving camouflage priority over repair, but they also left little doubt that the sites were being abandoned only when repairs were impossible, and there had been some reports to the effect that craters were being left unfilled to give the impression that sites had been abandoned when in fact their launching areas were being repaired" (*Brit Intel*, vol. 3, p. 425).

"Considering offensive countermeasures as a whole, the attacks on 'ski-sites' were the most effective measures against V-1s. They forced the re-planning of the entire launching procedure and the design and construction of an entirely new system of sites. The exact delay entailed is not yet known but available evidence indicates a maximum delay of three or four months" (*USSBS*, p. 22. This conclusion was written in 1945).

Suddenly, just before the *Overlord* Invasion, "modified sites" were cropping from Normandy to Calais, and being bombed as fast as they were found. This bomb-plot graphic of Belmesnil shows a few nearby hits. We have to admire the skill of PIs who identified a launch site this well hidden, January 1944.

As hundreds of ships, tens of thousands Allied troops and millions of tons of material began concentrating in the all-important ports along the south coast of England, "All but one of the 93 Mark I launching sites, designed to hold a large number of flying bomb components to be assembled on the spot, had been completely destroyed, and there was now intense activity in woods and forests where hundreds of makeshift ramps were being built under cover of foliage hiding them from photographic interpreters in Britain. These too, soon attracted attention. Being built on the edge of woods, so that the flying bombs would have a clear flight beyond the end of the ramp, the misfires—and there were many—made craters in the open ground in a direct line with the hidden ramp" (*D-Day*, p. 161. This is the only author using "Mark I" for Bois Carre sites, and the correct number was 96). Of course those craters didn't help locating the new sites until after they had fired, and that was still some weeks in the future. Another post-firing tip-off was the pits and skids left by the launch pistons hitting the ground following separation from the flying bomb, but again that only helped after a site had fired.

As early as February, SIS agents were reporting construction of a new type launch site at as many as 120 locations, and that many would be operational by May (*Brit Intel*, vol. 3, p. 424). Since the new V-1 sites were much harder to find, several were well underway when identified.

Another surprise, call it an Intelligence confusion factor, the first new sites were not found in the Pas de Calais high-threat zone aiming at London. First identified at Belhamelin, near Cherbourg, the new launch locations threatened the very coast where *Overlord* was assembling. They had only the concrete pads for the assembly building and ramp.[2] Once those critical elements were in place, activity at the site was held to a minimum.

"At first glance the sites looked as if they had been abandoned..." (*Eye*, p. 206). The new sites were simplified, smaller and heavily camouflaged, carefully sited to blend into the patterns on the ground. Even so, alert Medmenham PIs began finding them. Five of the new sites were located in the next five days, most near Cherbourg. Once again, it was a matter of finding the first one; from then on PIs knew what to look for. Kendall explained: "The Belhamelin sites were simplified

After a site fired, launch ramp pistons fell to earth leaving a skid-trail of small impacts (B, D, E). Three larger craters between "B" and "C" were where V-1s failed to "fly" on launch and crashed. The ramp is annotation "A". Random craters are from Allied bombing. (Imperial War Museum)

versions of the original Bois Carre sites. They were aimed not at London, but at Bristol and Portsmouth. Only the foundations were laid at Belhamelin. The firing ramp was there along with a slab of concrete which we assumed was (the) foundation for the familiar square building. In addition, each site contained the foundation for a rectangular building. Both buildings were situated well away from the firing ramp and in some cases were built inside existing farm buildings.

"Once again, the search began. But we had a new set of problems. The invasion of Normandy was close at hand and aircraft were needed for other intelligence work. We simply could not afford to re-photograph all of Northern France. Making do with incidental photography, we found twelve sites by the 3rd of May and reduced our program to four main objectives:

1. How long do the simplified sites take to build?
2. How many are there and where?
3. What is the method of construction?
4. What is the exact orientation of each firing ramp?

The new sites had virtually no servicing or storage facilities. This indicated that supplies had to come from main depots further back. Since the Belhamelin sites represented such poor targets, we redoubled our efforts at studying the whole storage and supply pattern" (Kendall, p. 105).

Babington Smith characterized the new sites as "horribly difficult to spot, but within a few days twelve had been identified" (*Air Spy*, p. 166). She went on to explain, "These finds sounded off a new *Crossbow* alarm, and for the fourth time a special flying program was laid on. The whole area within 130 miles of London, Southampton, and Plymouth was to be photographed yet again. At Medmenham, Kendall put fifteen more interpreters onto *Crossbow* work" (*Air Spy*, p. 166-167). By the time troops were ashore in Normandy, sixty-one of the new sites had been identified, thirty-eight of them north of the Somme (*Brit Intel*, vol. 3, p. 426). SIS reported 110 launch locations prior to the first firings on 13 June—thirty-one of those were subsequently photo-confirmed.

One can only imagine the pressure felt by the PIs at Medmenham with the enormous high-priority workload from the bombing campaign, looking for new defensive threats to the great invasion just weeks away, the continuing assault on the flying bomb sites…and now, a new, possibly imminent, threat to south-east England. The new sites had to be destroyed, but first they had to be found, and meant eyeballs on prints for long shifts.

It is hard for imagery interpretation to be fast, comprehensive and meticulous all at the same time, but that was the challenge of finding such small, elusive targets in such a large area. Here I must disagree with the "official history" which states: "It must be repeated that the new sites were well hidden and possessed no distinctive characteristic, as the ski sites had done" (*Brit Intel*, vol. 3, p. 424). Actually, the Belhamelins did have a signature: concrete pads for a standard size assembly building and launch ramp (or provision for erecting a launch ramp). Albeit much harder to spot than the "skis," the PIs did have characteristics to look for. The authors of that history then opined: "There must be more than a suspicion that there was some delay in finding the first of the new sites because the interpretation of the PRU photographs had been influenced by understandable concentration of AI and CIU on the search for additional ski sites and on the study of the damage and the repair work done at sites already known" (*Brit Intel*, vol. 3, p. 424-425).

That is another example of historians writing about something they'd never experienced and didn't understand. Since the new sites were in close proximity to known launch locations near Cherbourg and in the Pas de Calais, and since those areas were being meticulously scanned for

Another PI tour de force identified the "modified site" at Ruisseauville. It was photographed in January and bombed on 13 February 1944.

anything new, in addition to the "ski sites", that might bother the invasion; I find it unlikely that there was a PI version of "target fixation" hindering interpretation. The work was hard and long hours, but had to be thorough and the act of looking for new ski-sites would alone have turned up anything else that was new and different. I submit that a more likely cause of the two month "delay" between agent reports of construction and PI identification of the first of the new sites was a combination of bad weather and the fact that there was nothing to identify in the early stages of site preparation. Only when the ramp signatures were on the ground did the site reveal itself. Prior to that, without "skis", the construction had nothing to tip-off its presence or purpose. A square concrete pad might be for a barn. Only when it was matched with a long rectangular pad or a series of concrete studs was added, and both aligned on a target in England, was the site obvious.

Because of the lighter, pre-fabricated construction of the assembly building and ramp, many of the new pattern sites were well along toward completion when first identified. "The phenomenal success of CIU in discovering all the Bois Carre sites was not to be repeated in the case of the Belhamelins. In May 1944 the Normandy landings were only about a month distant, therefore it was necessary virtually to switch the whole of the reconnaissance effort to essential targets in preparation for Operation *Overlord*, therefore bombing attacks on the V-1 sites had to be decreased in order to fulfill these new commitments. As a result, the interpreters had to face the added burden of examining hundreds of previous sorties (new cover not being available) and only twelve of the Belhamelins had been discovered by 3rd May 1944 (*Eye*, p. 206). In May and June, aerial photo coverage concentrated on coastal defences and lines-of-communication deeper in France. Unfortunately, the flying bomb sites tended to be hiding between those two zones. By mid-May, none of the sites was as yet completed and their final form remained uncertain (*Brit Intel*, vol. 3, p. 426).

Prefabricated buildings, and fewer of them, were quickly erected and thus harder for PIs to find in time as well as space. If photoreconnaissance was weathered out of an area for several days, a site might not be spotted before becoming ready for operation. Launch ramps were also of a new type, consisting of a simple rail without the easily seen blast walls on either side. Use of small concrete footings suggested that the launch ramps too were quickly set up when needed, then possibly disassembled to help hide them. These new launch locations were called "modified sites" and "more than 60 had been identified before 12 June 1944" (*USSBS*, p. 6). Since the first one was found near Belhamelin, many people, particularly those in PI, knew them by that name (*Eye*, p. 204). By the time the first flying bomb was launched at London on 12 June, 156 of the new-type sites had been discovered (*Eye*, p. 206)

The other importance of the Belhamelins was that, absent "skis" for on-site storage, this meant PR had to look elsewhere for forward storage of the flying bombs in locations where they could quickly resupply firing sites. Those storage locations would presumably be rail served to receive large shipments of weapons from production plants, and near clusters of the new launch positions. As early as January the Germans had decided, based upon the utter failure of the "bunker effort", to use existing tunnels and caves for weapons storage (*Brit Intel*, vol. 3, p. 423).

In the spring of 1944 a PI circled suspicious activity on the print at lower right with his grease pencil, probably based on the alignment of the two structures. I don't know if this ever became a V-1 launch site, but it shows how thorough and careful the search had become.

"The whole question of supply to the Belhamelin sites became vital. The size and permanence of the Bois Carre sites had made them ideal targets for our bombers. With the destruction of these sites, it became unnecessary to launch a major bombing offensive against their supply system. When the Belhamelin sites became active, it was obvious that some sort of supply organization had to exist. Conditions had changed. The less permanent nature of Belhamelin sites made them easier to camouflage. The Germans realized that their installations were being spotted. But for some odd reason, they thought it was the work of secret agents. They never realized the remarkable and surprising details that we learned via air photographs" (Kendall, p. 111).

Intelligence was proving that the flying bomb threat was creeping steadily closer, spurring authorities in England to prepare. "During the early months of 1944, we developed our plans for

NOBALL XI/A/187
FRESNOY
LOW OBLIQUE
G.S.G.S. 4040/??
PINPOINT 02H16

R1

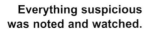

CAMOUFLAGED
RAMP

Camouflage at Fresnoy shows
how hard it was to locate the
new V-1 launch sites. The
recon plane was at 100'
altitude. 7 July 1944.

Everything suspicious
was noted and watched.

B

This photo is labeled Falby, but I think it's another low pass over Frresnoy, perhaps even from the same mission included above. The launch ramp (B) is set back into the wood and heavily camouflaged. (Medmenham Club)

meeting the flying-bomb attack. It was decided that the defenses should be laid out in three zones—a balloon barrage on the outskirts of London, beyond that a gun belt, and beyond that again, an area in which the fighter aircraft would operate. Steps were also taken to hasten the supply from America of the electronic predictors and radio proximity fuses, which, when the bombardment eventually started, made it possible for the gunners to take a heavy toll of the flying bombs" (*Closing the Ring*, p. 239-240).

Below: with all the photo coverage of the threat area it was inevitable that one would be caught launching. Mount Louis Ferme. Note the utter simplicity of the site. (Medmenham Club)

FLYING BOMB ON
LAUNCHING PLATFORM

"On 10 June a Belgian source reported the passage of a hundred 'rockets' by rail through Ghent towards the Franco-Belgian frontier; on the 11th new photographic intelligence revealed 'much activity' at six of the modified sites, with rails being laid on ramps and buildings completed" (*Intelligence in War*, p. 284). Clearly what was seen was a shipment of V-1s on the way to France.

"Meanwhile, the British and American Air Forces continued to bomb the hundred or so 'ski-sites' in Northern France. This was so effective that at the end of April aerial reconnaissance indicated that the enemy was giving up work on them. But our satisfaction was short-lived, for it was discovered that he was building instead modified sites which were much less elaborate and more carefully camouflaged and therefore harder to find and to hit. Whenever found these new sites were bombed. Many were destroyed, but about forty escaped damage or detection. It was from these that the attack was ultimately launched in June" (*Closing the Ring*, p. 240).

Hard as they were to spot, the new sites were being steadily found thanks to intense aerial recon and PI work concentrating on the "threat area". F/O Babington Smith observed that sixty-eight "modified sites" had been found by early June. She observed that once concrete bases for ramp and assembly building were laid the sites were left uncompleted. One reason was undoubtedly to try to avoid detection, but the answer was found in cover of the Luftwaffe flying bomb training site at Zinnowitz (Zempin) on the Baltic coast south-east of Peenemünde. "New cover showed that an additional launching site, of the modified type, was being completed there. So Kendall and Rowell were able to observe the manner in which one of these sites was made ready for use. Sections of rail six meters long were brought to the site, and there they were fitted together and erected: while prefabricated parts for the square building were also assembled on the spot" (*Air Spy*, p. 167). Rail sections and prefab building components could make a seemingly abandoned or dormant site operational in two days after the critical pieces arrived.

Just four days before the scheduled Normandy Invasion (five days before it actually occurred), the military chiefs were told that eighty-four of the original ski-sites had been heavily damaged, but fifty-two new sites had been found. The Air Ministry was informed on 5 June that it was estimated that the "modified sites" could be finished/erected in forty-eight hours (*Brit Intel*, vol. 3, p. 427). Allied military units were already moving to concentrations in the invasion ports, and the power and volume of the anticipated German assault was still unknown. At this point neither side knew how effective the new weapon would be—the crunch point was almost at hand.

Because they could be established so fast, and the invasion of France was already considered so precarious, the only viable response for the Allies was to attack. This again took much-needed bombing sorties from targets that had to be destroyed in support of the Invasion and the smaller new flying bomb sites were more difficult targets. The "modified-sites" were bombed as fast as they were identified. Once again Douglas Kendall set up a system for warning. When the necessary components were spotted at a "modified site" and firing was imminent, he would signal the code word "Diver" (*Air Spy*, p. 167). Unfortunately, "PR sorties over the sites had been suspended since 4 June, partly as a result of bad weather and partly on account of the opening of Operation *Overlord* on 6 June" (*Brit Intel*, vol. 3, p. 430).

D-Day had priority for all tactical photo recon during the first two weeks of June and *Crossbow* photo sorties, deeper inland, didn't begin again until 11 June. Six days after the Normandy Landing, and the day before the first V-1 was launched at London, sixty-four of the new sites had been discovered—presumably using re-looks at earlier imagery. German sources say there were eighty sites that would be completed by 1 June (out of 144 under construction) (*V-Missiles*, p. 183). If that total is correct, clearly Allied PIs hadn't found many of them. This could be because some construction was in such early stages that it didn't show up, and/or because the Germans were working hard to keep the new construction unobtrusive and concentrating heavily on camouflage. Characteristic buildings were held to a minimum and kept in proximity to pre-existing structures— sometimes the key buildings on a site were even built inside existing farm buildings. The ramps were usually surrounded by trees (Kendall, p. 107). Necessary paved roads to the assembly building and the ramp followed existing paths where possible and were often covered with sod to avoid detection. Recent German writing now claims that some of the launch sites that had never been activated were hidden so well that Allied troops later rolled over them without realizing they were there (*V-Missiles*, p. 183). I am a confirmed skeptic about the effectiveness of camouflage under repeated scrutiny from aerial reconnaissance and PIs using stereo, so I question that claim (See my book, *To Fool A Glass Eye*).

I have never seen aerial photography of one of those supposedly well hidden V-1 launch sites so I don't know if there was coverage, how good the camouflage actually was,[3] and why or how Allied PIs might have missed them. Without a specific location of an "undiscovered" launch site it is impossible to tell if recent German assertions of Allied failure to discover them are true or revisionism. Nor have I ever seen a ground photo of a perfectly camouflaged and not activated "modified site", so I find this claim impossible to resolve. What I do know as a PI, after researching for this book and looking at thousands of frames of pre-invasion coverage of France, suggests the claim is false.

Douglas Kendall agreed. "Our reconnaissance efforts were elevated to other targets in preparation for D-Day. For the same reason, bombing transferred to other targets such as bridges and supply routes. Had we been able to devote the same effort to the Belhamelin sites as we applied to Bois Carre, we would have been just as successful in their destruction. The sad fact was that we had to face the firing from flying bombs in order to be successful at Normandy" (Kendall, p. 108).

On 12 June, with the weather partially cleared and immediate invasion requirements relaxed, photo interpreters finally got new "area coverage" of the threat zone. Kendall took one look at nine of the "modified sites" and, even though some of the basic elements of the launch sites had changed, the Medmenham *Crossbow* team was quite sure about the threat. They saw "much activity" at six of the "modified" launching sites, the only ones that could be photographed because of bad weather elsewhere. Three of them appeared to have their launch-rails in place (*Mare's Nest*, p. 231).

Douglas Kendall was instrumental in pulling all the available photo-intel together. "During the night of June 11/12th, 1944, the first suggestions of the imminence of firing were received. Photographs had been taken on the 11th which showed that the installation of the firing ramp was taking place at three sites. If our predictions were correct, then installation would take place only a day or two prior to firing. The bombs could be expected with 24 to 48 hours. An immediate signal was issued to the Air Ministry. And the next morning, I had the unpleasant task of advising senior officers in the Air Ministry in person that the bombing was imminent" (Kendall, p. 107).

The PI "point" system suggesting certain sites were almost operational when the ramp rail was installed (*Eye*, p. 206), led to Douglas Kendall's "Diver" signal (*Air Spy*, p. 167), accurately predicting that firing from the "modified sites" would begin early on 13 June 1944 (*Eye*, p. 206). All of the new sites identified as operational were "first subjected to bombing and later to harassing attacks" (*USSBS*, p. 19).

FLYING BOMBS ARRIVE

For weeks the Allies anticipated that V-weapons would be used to interfere with the invasion of France. When that didn't happen it was next assumed that the flying bombs would come in retaliation for the Normandy Invasion. The number of launch sites suggested that London could expect a high volume of fire, starting with a volley from every operational site. Indeed, the Germans wanted to do just that, firing in salvos, knowing that multiple targets would be much harder for the Allies to track and interdict. "This promising method, however, could never be put into practice, as synchronization of the launching sites failed to function" (*V-Missiles*, p. 198). It is also true that Allied bombing of German road and rail lines in France and Germany, to isolate the Normandy Bridgehead area from German reinforcement, serendipitously delayed or denied delivery of flying bombs to the surviving V-1 launch sites (*Brit Intel*, vol. 3, p. 430).

"After the initial attacks, the Germans made frantic efforts to repair (launch sites) and continue. But it became impossible to keep up. A directive from Berlin instructed commanders to forget repairs to non-essential buildings and concentrate on the launching platform, the square building and the two rectangular buildings. These were the only buildings essential to the launch of the bombs--all the others were for storage. Of course, this meant that the Germans had to bring in their bombs by truck each night. Instead of firing 20 bombs per night per site, the actual launches were greatly reduced" (Kendall, p. 115). "A maximum of 300 V-1s launched in 24 hours was achieved from the Belhamelins, whereas the planned objective for the Bois Carre sites was 2,00 flying bombs for the same period" (*Eye*, p206).

Ten flying bombs were launched the night of 12/13 June. Five crashed immediately and only four made it to England.

Lord Cherwell, who had been a consistent skeptic of the V-weapons, uttered his famous disdain, "The mountain hath groaned and given forth a mouse!" (*Wizard War*, p. 417). Others readily agreed and after a collective sigh of relief among the upper echelons in London, the Chief of the Air Staff decided to reduce the 3000 heavy bomber sorties allocated against V-1 sites to 1000,

The large dome is Methodist Central Hall in Westminster. With Nelson watching from his column at left, this buzz-bomb is pretty well on azimuth but a little long if Tower Bridge was the aiming point.

shifting the balance back to direct invasion support (*Bodyguard of Lies*, p. 719-720). That same day Hitler assured his generals that the V-1s, launched the day before, "would be decisive against Great Britain" (and his jet fighters would drive Allied planes from the skies)—but Hitler didn't have enough fighters or flying bombs partly because so much of his resources were being poured into V-2 production (*Rise and Fall of the Third Reich*, p. 1040).

Initial euphoria in London lasted until the night of 15/16 June. After a few days to assess the initial results and mistakes, the Germans began the V-1 assault in earnest at 11:45 on 15 June, firing from fifty-five sites (*V-Missiles*, p. 202). Within twenty-four hours, seventy-three of the flying bombs hit London. The V-1s flew at altitudes between 2,625 and 4,921 feet (*V-Missiles*, p. 199) so they were just above the effective range of small-calibre, fast-firing guns. Large calibre anti-aircraft guns, most of them 3.7-inch, had a difficult time training on the fast, low-flying attackers. They still brought down eleven. At first the new weapon seemed almost unstoppable and was made more frightening because of the "buzzing" sound of its pulse-jet motor and the random nature of the attack. When the Fi 103 reached its programmed distance, the motor stopped and the silence was deafening because everyone knew the bomb would dive and the next sound would be a large explosion. There was no one within the range of the bomb who could feel safe, day or night. As the attack progressed, barrage balloons were reset to intercept the flying bombs close-in to London and anti-aircraft guns were positioned right on the coast. Radar stations at Swingate, Rye, Pevensey, Poling and Ventnor were augmented to track the new weapons (*Triumph and Tragedy*, p. 229).

It was quickly discovered that some Allied fighter planes had the speed to shoot the bombs down if they could intercept without much of a chase. That resulted in aircraft with good low-altitude speed, such as late model Spitfires and Tempests, patrolling in zones over the channel and inland between the guns and the balloons. Crossing the English coastline, the speed of the Fi 103 was below 370 mph. Shortly before reaching London, maximum speed of 400 to 408 mph was achieved (*V-Missiles*, p. 199).

It was soon learned that shooting down a flying bomb as though it were an enemy fighter was a dangerous proposition. Blowing up a V-1 put the intercepting aircraft in serious danger from the blast and debris. "The defenses against the flying bombs themselves, fighter patrols, anti-aircraft guns and balloons, organized before launchings commenced, reached a high degree of efficiency and destroyed a progressively greater proportion of V-1s before they reached the London area." (*USSBS*, p. 6-7).

Londoners felt they were reliving the Blitz, only with more terror and more destructive power. The V-1 had an 850kg warhead. Heinkel He 111 bombers that bombed London in 1940-42 could carry six 250kg bombs. The V-1 warhead had an explosive (Trialen 105 or 106) that was seventy to eighty per cent more powerful than the same weight of earlier warheads, (see *V-Missiles*, p. 188). Therefore each V-1 had more destructive power than a Luftwaffe bomber, and accuracy was only a little worse. The same source (p. 199) states "Due to the light construction of many English buildings, there were cases where a single flying bomb devastated an entire street of houses."

With the arrival on British soil of the highly destructive flying bomb, British response was rapid but initially not particularly effective. All available anti-aircraft artillery was rushed to London and south-eastern England. Few of the V-1s were shot down by the London guns but the sound of their firing was valuable for morale purposes.

Several RAF units with aircraft fast enough to overtake the V-1, became rather good at "tipping" the flying bombs out of the sky. Eventually, the closely held first RAF jet unit, No. 616

Squadron at Manston, flying Gloster Meteors, was committed to the battle against the V-1s on 10 July, achieving the first of thirteen victories on 4 August 1944. To maintain secrecy, the jets were

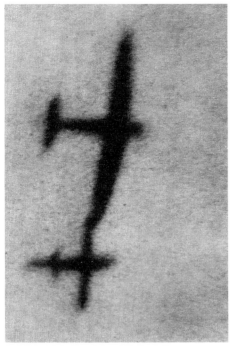

forbidden to fly closer than fifteen miles from the enemy-occupied coast (*Flying Bomb*, p. 105-106). Ironically, the first RAF jet fighter unit went operational the same month as the first Luftwaffe Me 262 unit.

On the other side of the Channel, Hitler was elated by the assumed results. On 17 June 1944 he directed that production priority be placed on the V-1, at the expense of the rocket programme (*Rocket and the Reich*, p. 230, and *Brit Intel*, vol. 3, p. 431). He did not rescind that directive until August when many of the flying bomb launch sites were about to be overrun on the ground and firing rates were falling off dramatically. Also on the 17th, Hitler had his own "close encounter" with a V-1. "Shortly after the field marshals had departed from Margival (where they were meeting with Hitler) on the afternoon of June 17 an errant V-1 on its way to London turned around and landed on the top of the Fuehrer's bunker. No one was killed or even hurt, but Hitler was so upset that he set off immediately for safer parts, not stopping until he got to the mountains of Berchtesgaden" (*Rise and Fall of the Third Reich*, p. 1040-1041).[4]

By the time of the first V-1 firings, Medmenham had identified 156 of the modified sites in France (*Eye*, p. 206). Of course not all of them were yet active. Kendall noted that many of the first indications of a site were from agents on the Continent. While invaluable for a tip-off early in the construction process, multiple and sometimes conflicting agent reports also made for a level of confusion that could only be resolved by aerial photography.

"When attempting to obtain precise information from enemy occupied territory, the problems are multiplied tenfold and it is only too easy for the same information to be reported differently from different sources. Ground sources tend to be very unreliable in giving exact positions and numbers."

"It can be appreciated how utterly impossible it would be to attack a target of the Bois Carre type without the P.R./P.I. source. Admittedly since 1945, tactics, particularly in air warfare, have changed fantastically and the targets of today are presumably mass targets such as major cities. If, as in 1944 and 1945, the weapon being fired against us came from hundreds of small installations scattered over a vast area, it would be inconceivable to use atomic weapons on their supply dumps or the manufacturing facilities behind them. Certainly in the last war (WW II) we found it impossible to attack any target at all without first obtaining air photographs in order to pinpoint it and plan the attack. No other source could replace the P.I. function" (Kendall, p. 158).

The flying bomb, or as the Londoners called it, the "doodlebug" or "buzz bomb", was having an impact. "This new form of attack imposed upon the people of London a burden perhaps even heavier than the air-raids of 1940 and 1941." The Prime Minister went on to note that the suspense and strain were more prolonged than in aerial bombing. "Dawn brought no relief, and cloud no comfort. The man going home in the evening never knew what he would find; his wife, alone all day or with the children, could not be certain of his safe return" (Both quotes from *Triumph and Tragedy*, p. 39).

On 18 June, a V-1 hit the Guards Chapel at Wellington Barracks during a service, killing eighty people and injuring 120. Churchill ordered the RAF to make maximum effort strike against Berlin in retaliation. The night of 21/22 June 1944, 2500 RAF bombers hit Berlin, followed by 1000 Eighth Air Force bombers escorted by 1200 fighters the next day. The bombing raids completely dwarfed the destruction wrought by the flying bombs but no one thought the tit-for-tat attacks were at an end.

Expecting more destruction in London, the government began evacuation of women, children, elderly and patients in hospital. That put a terrific strain on rail and roads needed to move loads to ports in support of the Normandy landings. By June 27, V-1s had blown out millions of windows. If the glass industry couldn't replace that window glass before winter, more lives would be lost to the cold (*Bodyguard of Lies*, p. 722). Of course all of this also put a tremendous strain on the morale of the people. No one who lived through it has failed to note the rising fear and feeling of helplessness.

Remembering those tense days, General Eisenhower wrote shortly after the war: "The effect of the new German weapons was very noticeable upon morale. Troops worried too" (*Crusade in Europe*, p. 259). He also remembered, "Defensive measures against the V-1 soon attained a very high degree of efficiency, but even so, the threat of their arrival was always present at all hours of the day and night and in all kinds of weather" (*Crusade in Europe*, p. 260). Ike wanted the flying bomb threat neutralized quickly. On June 18, Eisenhower ordered that *Crossbow* (V-1) targets would now rank higher than anything for the Allied bomber force right after direct support of the Invasion (*Bodyguard of Lies*, p. 720).

Naturally preoccupied with the success of *Overlord*, which was still far from decided in the final weeks of June and early July, Eisenhower wouldn't hear of objections to his directing more aerial attacks against the V-sites. He feared that the new weapon would "dislocate the war effort" (*Masters of the Air*, p. 297). Along with Ike, Commanding General of the US Army Air Forces, H H Arnold understood that the flying bomb was not a precision weapon, but he worried that they might be directed in large numbers against the concentration of troops and supplies in the target-rich invasion support ports or even the beachheads themselves (*Masters of the Air*, p. 297). Of course we know that V-1 azimuth of fire was tied directly to the orientation of the immobile launch ramp. Firing at the Normandy Beaches could only have happened through new construction after June 6th and photo recon would have found those sites immediately.

Allied attacks on V-1 logistics and launch sites became the top priority for both intelligence and strike aircraft of all types; heavy and light bombers, fighters and recce. The "No-Ball" sorties were short hops from bases in England and it was not unusual for aircraft to fly several strike missions per day. "One of the most obvious results of the V-weapon campaign was that it caused the Allied air forces to turn aside from their primary offensive mission and commit part of their forces to essentially defensive operations. This commitment was very substantial" (*USSBS*, p. 27-29).

The reconnaissance emphasis, in turn, led to an almost paranoid level of photo interpretation in which every suspicious excavation or building orientation in the "threat area" was carefully noted and probably a few innocent sites were bombed. The only bright spot was that once they fired, even the best camouflaged V-1 launch sites in France were easy to locate because of craters from failures. PIs quickly learned to identify the scars directly in line with the launching ramp. "Once the Germans had fired their flying bomb, the piston flew out off the end of the ramp and fell to the ground a few hundred feet away. The grooves left in the landscape were very evident on our photographs. Also German engineering did not always work as expected. Often their rockets[5] would stall as they left the ramp. In one case I examined, the bomb must have just got to the top of the ramp and then toppled off. The resulting explosion must have been a shock to everyone at the site.

"As it was the flying bombs did considerable damage to London and were particularly effective as an anti-morale weapon. They had such a peculiar throbbing noise, so menacing and so very personal" (Kendall, p. 107-108).

In spite of Allied bombing, flying bomb rate-of-fire increased rapidly as more of the "modified-sites" became operational. Firing rates were undoubtedly lower from the modified sites than they would have been from the ski-sites which had storage, assembly, fueling and launching all in one place. Within a few days 244 V-1s had been fired, 144 of them reaching England. Aside from ducking Allied air patrols over France, the two greatest difficulties for the V-1 sites were supply and consequences. Allied aircraft damaging road and rail lines and vehicles in and behind the Threat Zone, severely impeded delivery of Fi 103s and fuel to the launch sites (V-Missiles, p. 201). A lack of current, frequent intelligence made it almost impossible to assess results of the firings.

The Germans had no fast, reliable, "on demand" method of knowing how many bombs were getting through, much less where they were going. Reports from German spies or "neutral sources" in England provided some information on impact locations but there was a significant delay in getting that intelligence, which hindered correlation with firings. To gain an idea of the success of the V-1 attack, radio transmitters were fitted on 440 of the 6,046 flying bombs delivered before August. The signals could be triangulated from three tracking stations in France, giving a good idea of where the transmitting bomb went (V-Missiles, p. 200). Of course it was only a rough indication of what the overall assault was accomplishing because some of those Fi 103s failed on launch and others were interdicted short of London. Each of the recovered plots was annotated on a map of London. The new data, "at no time provided information that would have justified a change in firing with regard to range or direction" (V-Missiles, p. 200). In any case, change of direction would have been almost impossible even if the flying bomb's compass was offset to make the weapon deviate slightly from the angle of the launch ramp. However, distance could be adjusted (more on that below).

The devastation was steadily increasing on both sides. The Allies were bombing day and night and steadily pouring ground forces into the Overlord beachhead. The Germans were just as determinedly launching the V-1s while trying to hold the line and win a war of attrition in France. Launch crews and anti-aircraft units protecting the V-1 sites in the Pas de Calais might have been more productive had those men and weapons been available to stem the fast-growing Allied tide in Normandy—but they weren't, and the damage done by their flying bombs wasn't accomplishing much. Both sides gritted their teeth and held on, hoping the other would blink first.

June 26th saw the south coast of England under attack with fifty-five V-1s fired at Southampton. Though much smaller targets, Portsmouth, Southampton and other coastal locations were more vulnerable than London because, being on the coast, they had no potential for defence in depth. Now the threat was to the Allies' capability to maintain the force so tenuously planted in Normandy. Fifty-three flying bombs were launched against Southampton the following day, then German command in the west ordered all launches be against London (an order confirmed by Hitler) (V-Missiles, p. 204). This was the same mistake Hitler made in 1940, going after

London rather than staying on RAF fighter bases. Attacking the invasion assembly areas, hoping to randomly hit targets that were an actual threat to German forces in France, would probably have been more useful.

For seven weeks in June and July 1944 the V-1 rate-of-fire approached 3000 a month. "The enemy achieved an average of just under 100 launchings in every 24 hour period, or about one every 15 minutes – day and night. In practice, all the launches took place at night. The story of death and destruction would have been very different without these (Allied) excellent counter measures. And—heaven forbid—if the enemy had ever achieved their target of 2,000 firings per day instead of 100, London would have been annihilated" (Kendall, p. 117-118).

Reconnaissance searches for new launch sites, and regular bombing, did not abate.[6] No launch crew wanted to make themselves conspicuous, so Allied command of the air over the launch zone probably held down V-1 firings to some extent, but firings in bad weather or darkness were unaffected. Meanwhile, considerable damage was being done in England by the random landing of these weapons.

The following day was the first meeting of a special War Cabinet Sub-Committee with the brief to coordinate all counter-measures against the V-1 threat. Duncan Sandys presided. This was essentially shifting the *Bodyline* priority against the rocket to deterring the flying bomb, which was now recognized as the most immediate threat. The search effort, analysis, and all associated ops were called *Crossbow*. A week later, General Eisenhower rejected Allied air commander's pleas to get heavy bomber sorties back on German industrial targets, ordering attacks on the flying bomb launch sites that were threatening his base of operations.[7]

While the V-1 was not a precision weapon, for all its flaws, remaining parts and examples of flying bombs that weren't totally destroyed impressed the Allies. The V-1 was simple, cheap to produce, and effective. Imitation being the most sincere form of flattery, the US was sufficiently impressed, or awed, to rush to create its own version of the flying bomb, the V-1 look-alike Ford/Willys-Overland JB-2 (which was rushed into production but never used operationally).

In 1948, with the memories of V-weapons attacks still fresh and strong, General Eisenhower wrote, "It seemed likely that, if the German had succeeded in perfecting and using these new weapons six months earlier than he did, our invasion of Europe would have proved exceedingly difficult, perhaps impossible. I feel sure that if he had succeeded in using these weapons over a six-month period, and particularly if he had made the Portsmouth-Southampton area one of his principal targets, *Overlord* might have been written off" (*Crusade in Europe*, p. 260).[8]

A recent German author says of Ike's quote, "This claim, which decisively has contributed to the rise of a V-weapon legend, is simply a misjudgment which Eisenhower could have avoided if he had taken a closer look at the matter" (*V-Missiles*, p. 307). Is this true or really just an excuse for a German failure? Part of the impact of a weapon is its effectiveness and part is its perception. All the post-war criticisms of the V-weapons are valid—both the flying bomb and the rocket were inaccurate, produced in insufficient numbers, and ate up too many scarce resources all out of proportion to their results. But the Allies certainly didn't know any of that in June-July 1944, and people act/react based upon what they believe at a point in time, not what they (or some scholar) learn long afterward.

What I would call revisionists have made much of Ike changing, or not mentioning, the statement quoted above in later editions of *Crusade* or his other books. Hindsight is wonderful for understanding events, but it can be poor history when used to judge actions in retrospect— or when the author is faced with other, more pressing, challenges and threats. I am inclined to pay more heed to the General's memories and reactions closest to the events for his state of mind and concerns as the flying bombs were landing in England.

In *Closing the Ring*, Churchill called Eisenhower's quote (above) an overstatement. "The average error of both these weapons was over ten miles. Even if the Germans had been able to maintain a rate of fire of a hundred and twenty a day and if none whatever had been shot down, the effect would have been the equivalent of only two or three one-ton bombs to a square mile per week. However, it shows that the military commanders considered it necessary to eliminate the menace of the "V" weapons, not only to protect civilian life and property, but equally to prevent interference with our offensive operations" (*Closing the Ring*, p. 234-235). But Churchill was writing from the safety of three years after Ike's book and seven years after the bombs were causing him to take extreme, sometimes draconian, measures, including evacuation of London. Clearly some of the impact of the V-weapons was mellowing with time.

By the end of the June 200,000 houses had been damaged, water, sewer and gas lines ruptured and 1,769 killed (*Mare's Nest*, p. 242). Evacuation of a million women and children, elderly and hospitals was straining a bureaucratic and line-of-communications infrastructure already stretched to the limit by invasion requirements (*Bodyguard of Lies*, p. 721). Taylor says 1.5 million people were evacuated before the end of July (*England 1914 – 1945*, p. 505).

The Allies kept striking back at the only targets they could. "Our bombing forces carried out a systematic destruction of the railway network in northern France as a preliminary to the D-day invasion. This meant the Germans had to rely on the roads to bring up the bombs. It seemed likely they would move their supplies by rail to the Paris area, which they still controlled, and from there go forward by road or railway, whichever was working. Therefore, we started looking for storage depots in the forward areas.

"The first indication of what we were looking for came on July 1st, 1944. This consisted of two piles of rubble near Beaumont, clear indication that excavations were being made into the side of a hill. A lot of care had been taken to hide any signs of activity. Large areas were covered with camouflage netting. However, we could see a new electric power line built to supply the site. If Beaumont was a possible storage site in our *Crossbow* investigation, it was obvious there would be more. So as the bombs continued to fall on London, we began a major effort to identify other sources of supply" (Kendall, p. 111. This quote encompasses pre-invasion to four weeks later).

Despite bombing of launch sites, storage locations and lines of communication, the flying bombs still kept coming but the new weapon was proving to be far from unstoppable. A complex, but effective, system of conditions was established to allow fighter planes to intercept the flying bombs without running into the AAA-belts (See *Flying Bomb*, p. 106-107 for a discussion of this capability). Defences were having some success, but more had to be done. The night of 16/17 July, some 1,596 anti-aircraft artillery guns were moved from other positions in England to the south coast (*Mare's Nest*, p. 254-255). Thousands of miles of communications and control cables, 23,000 people and 60,000 tons of equipment, ammunition and supplies were shifted overnight to set up a defense line (Also see *Wizard War*, p. 427-428 and *Flying Bomb*, p.116-118). This new belt of AAA was made more effective by the new SCR.584 gun-laying radar and one of the first operational uses of the proximity-fuse. "The success of the anti-aircraft guns was based on the combination of radar predictors with proximity fuses. Our radar would have been useless if the enemy had succeeded in jamming it. But through our photographs, we were able to identify every radar station on the French coast. Our fighters attacked these installations systematically from about D-Day minus 20. Out of 100 radar stations which might have picked up our ships or aircraft or been used for jamming, only five were left operational. Our work was a big factor in achieving surprise on D-Day and some weeks later, it enabled us to use our anti-aircraft radar predictors undisturbed" (Kendall, p. 118-119).

Not long afterward, US Army 90mm guns were added to the gun-belt along the coast. When linked to radar and a "predictor", the gun could be automatically trained and fired, all the crew had to do was load.

A few days later, the Luftwaffe began launching V-1s at London from He 111 bombers based in the Netherlands; about 50 during 18-21 July 1944 (*V-Missiles*, p. 206). Eventually some 300 V-1s were air-launched against London, ninety against Southampton, and twenty against Gloucester.

Anti-aircraft artillery fire was steadily improving. On 28 August 1944, they shot down ninety-three of ninety-seven V-1s that crossed the coast.

By late July the Allies had the most effective solution to the flying bomb. Troops in France cut off all V-1 sites in the Cotentin Peninsula. Heavy and nearly continuous bombing by RAF and US long-range and tactical aircraft, and ground advances, cause the Germans to abandon all the V-1 launching sites west of the Seine. This took away the threat to the invasion support ports along the South Coast. New sites were built and many of the original sites, plus some decoys, were left to draw off air attacks. Hölsken cites the effectiveness of the decoys: "The Allies, in fact, repeatedly fell for these deceptive maneuvers again. Some of the mock sites were attacked up to 35 or 40 times. The real danger, therefore, did not come from the raids against the launching sites, which could be replaced at any time. Far more effective were the attacks against the lines of communication" (*V-Missiles*, p. 209). Once again I must question the assertion.

Throughout the war, Allied photo interpreters routinely identified "decoy" oil refineries, factories, airfields, storage areas and the like—and Medmenham was quite good at finding them. It is also true that, though being briefed, aircrews often fell for the decoys anyway, particularly at night. Without knowing where any of those "decoy" V-1 launch sites were, I have no way to look at imagery to see if Allied PIs did, or could have, identified them. I suspect, even if they had identified the sites as decoys, tactical air would have attacked them, since fast, low-flyers didn't bomb coordinates; they bombed based upon recognition of a target, so even reasonably good decoys would likely have gotten plenty of attention. In addition, Hölsken may not have appreciated that the Allies quickly had squadrons of tactical aircraft, such as P-47s, operating from fields in France. The huge number of Allied fighter-bombers available to harry the area adjacent to the expanding Normandy lodgment (and the inability of Luftwaffe resources to stop short range fighter-bomber runs in the "threat area"), made it possible to "waste" sorties on mock or dormant sites "just in case". Many of these Allied tactical units flew missions roaming over an area, and simply shot up or bombed anything that moved or looked suspicious.[9]

August 2/3 saw the high point for V-1 launches with 316 within twenty-four hours from some sixty sites, but Allied defences were getting steadily more efficient. Professor Jones cites 28 August as an example. "...of the 97 bombs which approached England, 13 were destroyed by fighters out to sea, the guns then shot down 65, with another 10 brought down by fighters over land, leaving 9 to continue towards London. Two collided with balloons, three fell outside London, leaving only four to reach it" (*Wizard War*, p. 428). Kendall (p. 117) wrote it was ninety-four flying bombs with sixty-five shot down by anti-aircraft guns, twenty-three by fighters, two by balloons and only four succeeded in getting to London. Meanwhile, Allied ground forces were about to surge out of the Normandy beachhead. Remaining V-1 launch sites were in increasingly precarious locations.

In addition to active methods to combat the V-1, British intelligence used passive methods. ADI

(Sc) had already superimposed Peenemünde tracking plots on London and noted that the impacts were routinely short. The opening bombardment had a good correlation with the intercepted Baltic tracking. In a brilliant analysis, early in the "buzz-bomb" onslaught, British plots of impacts indicated that half of the bombs would have landed in built-up areas with a shift of four miles to the north-west. It was assumed that the nominal aiming point was Charing Cross, the "official" centre of London (it turned out to be Tower Bridge), and therefore the Germans were firing short—the identical tendency of the V-1 observed in signals intercepts from Peenemünde. If the Germans could be convinced they were actually firing "long" they might shorten flight duration, causing bombs that made it through the defensive belts to dive to the ground in open country southeast of London (*Wizard War*, p. 420-421). The story of the deception, and the reasoning behind it, are well told by Professor Jones.

It was quickly apparent that the Germans badly wanted information on where the flying bombs were going. "On the night of the opening of the assault both a Junkers 88 and a Messerschmitt had been shot down...and daylight launched bombs continued to come across under observation from the crews of the new Messerschmitt 410 twin-engine fighter. The purpose of these was obviously to monitor the accuracy of the V-1 which had to have its course predetermined and set 'blind' and it has only been recently revealed that agents in this country deliberately fed back to the Nazis information which could mislead them into believing that the course setting which had in fact caused a cluster of the weapons to fall on central London were bombarding an area to the north of the intended vicinity so that the resultant 'correction' would actually cause future missiles to fall short of the intended target" (*Flying Bomb*, p. 107).

Details of bomb detonations beyond London were "leaked" back to the Germans using agents who had been "turned" or were Allied double-agents from the start. Other "long firings", real or bogus, were planted in British newspapers with detonation times and locations carefully matched to time and azimuth that actual V-1s could have achieved. Since the Germans had no way of knowing how many, or which, flying bombs were being shot down, much less where the successful ones were landing, this information led the V-1 launch crews to conclude they were being more successful than they actually were, but firing long. They began to shorten range. This drew bombs away from London proper but caused more damage in working-class areas south of the Thames (*Bodyguard of Lies*, p. 725). The deception was successful in large part because the RAF so thoroughly denied the Luftwaffe photo coverage of London. Professor Jones wrote, "In this helpful conclusion, Wachtel was supported by the evidence of photographic reconnaissance, which incidentally revealed one of the biggest surprises of the whole war. It turned out that there seemed to have been no German photographic reconnaissance of London from 10th January 1941 to 10th September 1944" (*Wizard War*, p. 422). Colonel Wachtel was commander of Flak Regiment 155(W) which Allied signals intelligence had associated with the flying bomb at Peenemünde and responsibility for launches in France.

When a Luftwaffe reconnaissance jet finally got photo cover of London on 10 September, it was limited by clouds and, without recent comparative coverage, German photo interpreters assumed damage from bombing north of the Thames in 1941 was caused by the V-1 offensive (*Wizard War*, p. 423). *Intelligence in War* says the first Luftwaffe photo recon flight since January 1941 occurred on 6 September 1944 (p. 292).

The elaborate deception methods were devised by ADI (Sc), Professor Jones, who wrote: "When we overran Wachtel's headquarters two and a half months or so later, we were able to see the results of our work, for he had recorded the points of impact of the flying bombs, both as reported by the agents and as plotted by his own organization on sample bombs which had been fitted with radio transmitters" (*Wizard War*, p. 422).

Of course the Allies knew about the V-1 tracking radios, but I have found no reference to jamming them or using the frequencies to send bogus data back to France. In any case, the radio-equipped V-1s represented a statistically insignificant number of weapons (3%). Allied deception methods not only confused the Germans at the time but make it difficult (if not impossible) to assess the true operational accuracy of the V-1 today. Even in an "after action" context, since the actual London aiming point may have been changing over time, the firing accuracy can't really be measured to a solid CEP (Circular Error Probable).[10] If the Allied deceptions were indeed as successful as reported, the actual accuracy of the V-1 may have been better than some recent authors want to believe. Hölsken cites interviews with members of Flak Regiment 155(W) who deny that the Germans fell for the deception (*V-Missiles*, p. 295-296). Again, I am inclined to rely on memories recorded closest to events. Professor Jones had Wachtel's records and the quotes in Hölsken are clearly answering Jones' claims but without documents to support them. Jones had the Allied view and Hölsken the German. Jones wrote thirty-four years after these events, but he lived them. I respect Dr Hölsken's scholarship but he was born eight years after the war and wrote forty years after it ended (the English version of his book came out ten years after that). He had no experience of anything remotely similar to what was going on in 1940-45. The "we fooled them but they didn't fool us" statements negating the effect of Allied deception seems a bit revisionist—like the "stab in the back" arguments after the First World War, but that's just my gut feeling. Actual results suggest Jones' version of the story is correct.

Other unusual but thorough measures taken to deny the Germans information on the accuracy of the bomb or means to disrupt anti-bomb defences were:

--Limiting obituary notices, which the Germans had used initially, assuming large numbers of deaths in a given location meant a bomb hit (*V-Missiles*, p. 200).

--Big Ben tolling on the BBC was changed to recordings "lest any sound of an approaching V-1 should be caught by the microphone and prove of use to the enemy" (*Flying Bomb*, p. 74).

--Papers and radio correspondents were not permitted to give information about the new gun-laying radar or proximity fuse, and could only discuss results of defences in general terms (*Flying Bomb*, p. 119-120). Actually the prohibition came too late; the innovations had already been reported.

--Tactical aircraft bombed German electronic jammers that might have interfered with British AAA radar and/or air intercepts (*Wizard War*, p. 428).

Going into summer, the flying bomb launch sites were further simplified with less concrete, a smaller signature for the catapult and several of the buildings replaced by tents (*V-Missiles*, p. 209). One of the best recent books on the V-weapons attributes faltering success to supply problems, faulty equipment and failures of the steam generators that launched the missiles. Little mention is made of roving Allied aerial patrols hunting activity of any sort and bombing to damage launch capability, though the author admits that fifty-one launching sites had been destroyed by air attack and eight more from V-1s exploding during launch (*V-Missiles*, p. 210).

The maximum firing rate of 316 V-1s in one day was achieved on 2/3 August. By late August Flak Regiment 155(W) was in retreat for Germany.

When Allied ground forces began to overrun the original launch area, V-1 attacks were maintained by air-launching the flying bombs from He 111 bombers, and at least six launch ramps were built in the Netherlands. Air-launching against the south and east coasts of England went on into October in spite of extremely poor accuracy. Some of the degradation of accuracy was a natural result of the longer range from the ground sites and less precise launch location from the aerial platforms.

Manchester was attacked on Christmas Eve and air-launches against London continued until mid-January 1945, but weapon accuracy was so poor and random that little damage was done.

For all practical purposes any possibility of the V-1 program altering events in England, or combat operations in Europe, was over in mid-August. According to USSBS data, 7,500 V-1s were launched at England from June to September 1944. From September until the end of the war another 7380 were launched, mostly against continental targets, with Antwerp getting most of them. After mid-September 1944, both German and Allied emphasis shifted to the more dangerous, and even more elusive, V-2. Late October saw hundreds of flying bombs fired against Brussels and Antwerp. New models of the Fi 103 had longer range and the V-1s were used against targets they could reach, including London, until 30 March 1945 (*V-Missiles*, p. 247). As many as 275 of the longer ranging Fi 103 F-1s had been launched at London from sites near Delft. But those attacks were too few in number and too random to be anything but harassment. By late January 1945, the launch sites had retreated so far that some short rounds and failed launches were landing on German soil (*V-Missiles*, p. 239).

In ten months of assault, 7,500 V-1s "reached or approached" England, and another 6500 or more were reported against continental targets (chiefly Antwerp) (*USSBS*, p. 1).

Seven hurriedly established, minimum configuration, heavily camouflaged sites in the Netherlands fired at the start of the Battle of the Bulge (*V-Missiles*, p. 235), but contributed little or nothing to the combat.

As the Allied ground surge into Germany began again after the Bulge, swarms of fighter-bombers working with and ahead of the advancing troops were stumbling on V-1 launch sites and disrupting their supply lines. Allied intelligence seemed to play less of a role in this phase than the large numbers of Allied aircraft roaming freely over the battle area.[11] Talking to Second World War fighter pilots over the years, they all said that toward the end of the war in Europe, anything moving in Germany would be strafed. Allied mastery of the air also denied German photo reconnaissance any chance to see where their weapons were falling. Luftwaffe aerial photoreconnaissance was extremely limited but what they could see indicated few V-2s hitting the city, with most in the outskirts of Antwerp (*V-Missiles*, p. 246).

The last V-1 battery closed up shop on 25 March 1945.

Once again, Douglas Kendall provides an overview from a key position in the battle against the flying bomb.

"On the whole, one attack in ten on the Bois Carre sites was successful in doing serious damage. The P.R./P.I. source was absolutely critical in damage assessment following attacks. No other source could have effectively performed this function and it is difficult to see how air warfare could be conducted without effective follow-up by P.R. It is worth examining the size of the P.R./P.I. needed on the *Crossbow* investigation alone. First of all it involved close to 4,000 special photographic sorties. Since losses on P.R. operations throughout the war ran about two percent of sorties flown, it would appear that the cost in P.R. aircraft was about 80. Actually I doubt if it was this high and I would guess at a figure closer to 30, since most of the *Crossbow* sorties were over North France, involving shorter flights with less hazard than deep penetration into Germany. Of course, these losses were still significant enough.

These flights produced approximately 1,600,000 photographs which had to be examined in detail. Ultimately 363 sites were targeted for potential attack, each target involving a considerable volume of printed and photographic material. Sufficient copies had to be produced so that each bombing aircraft in each squadron, British and American, could have a copy of the material for briefing purposes. Consequently hundreds of thousands of photographs had to be reproduced. To keep pace with the investigation and what was being discovered day by day, no less than 2,322 signals (PI Reports) giving urgent information had to be handled and a total of 3,450 separate reports were issued. As each report had on an average, a distribution of about 100 copies in order to cover all the interested parties from the Prime Minister's offices to the Pentagon, 345,000 reports had to be distributed.

The actual size of the P.I. effort varied according to the emphasis of the investigation and the state of the weather. If there had been a spell of clear weather resulting in a large number of photographs coming in, it became necessary to increase the number of interpreters allocated to this project and consequently to reduce investigations in other directions. In general perhaps 20 officers were permanently assigned to this project out of a total of 550 officers but at times this increased to about 80. The officers engaged on the project consisted largely of members of the British Army, the Royal Air Force, the Women's Auxiliary Air Force, and the U.S. Army Air Force. They made a magnificent team.

Looking at the results of the intelligence war against the V weapons I think in retrospect it is fair to claim that it was highly successful. The enemy's intentions were clearly seen well ahead of the time they were put into practice, in spite of every effort on his part to conceal his activity and intention. This definitely constituted an intelligence victory. Whether the intelligence information was put to good use by the operational arms and thus resulted in military victories, is not really of direct concern to whether or not the intelligence war had been won, although the military victory justified the intelligence effort. With the flying bomb, we knew substantially what we were up against by November, 1943. We knew that the enemy intended to use this weapon against us in January or February, 1944, and by providing the necessary information to the operational forces we were able to deny the use of this weapon to the enemy until June 1944" (Kendall, p. 158-160, quote edited for brevity).

The official post-war analysis of Allied bombing noted, "Another activity which should not be overlooked is the part played in the campaign by photo-reconnaissance and interpretation. Approximately 4,000 reconnaissance sorties flown by British and American aircraft contributed directly to 'Crossbow' intelligence. Brilliant interpretation of the photographs obtained confirmed the reports of experimental work on the Baltic, pin-pointed and identified launching and supply sites in France, definitely established the purpose of the 'ski-sites', provided the material for the targeting of more than 300 objectives, analyzed the results of attacks and, in general, provided the framework for the planning and execution of offensive countermeasures. In all, 4,070 interpretation reports were issued on these subjects" (USSBS, p. 17).

Professor R V Jones aptly summed up the V-1 campaign. "But before we leave the flying bomb, we should remark its technical excellence as a weapon. Its simple construction made it cheap to produce, and it was designed to exploit the extraordinarily favorable situation in which the Germans found themselves, able to shoot at such a great target as London from an entire 90 degree arc running from east to south. The bomb was hard to shoot down, and if we had not had so much prior warning our defenses would have fared poorly. (He explains that the cost of

208

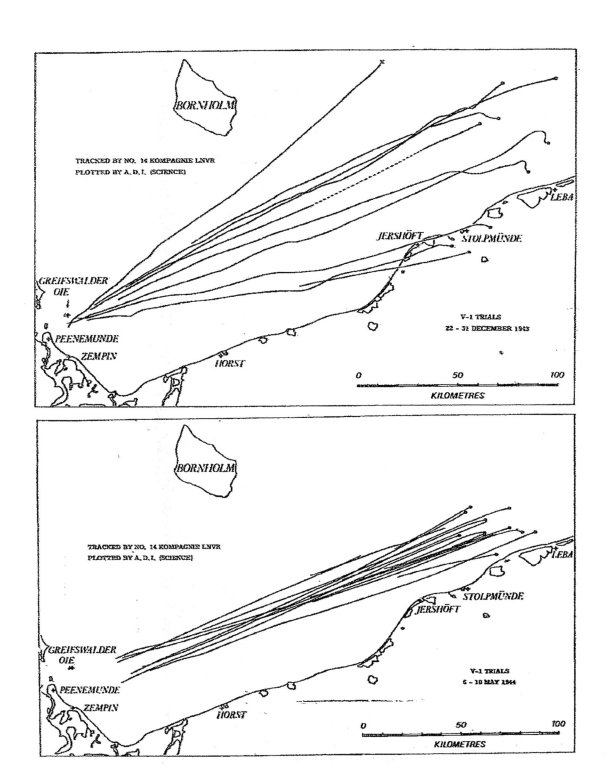

Comparisons of V-1 tracking showed improvement in accuracy between
December 1943 and May 1944.

countermeasures exceeded the estimated cost of the campaign to the Germans)...the balance on which judgment must be passed is not between British and German expenditure but between our expenditure on countermeasures and the damage that would have ensued in lives, material and morale if those countermeasures had not been undertaken" (*Wizard War*, p. 429).

Comparisons of V-1 tracking showed improvement in accuracy between December 1943 and May 1944.

Most V-weapons damage was done by the V-1 between 13 June 1944 and 29 March 1945, a total of 9,251 flying bombs were plotted of which 2,419 reached London. Flying bombs alone killed 6,184 people in London and seriously injured about 18,000. The total number of flying bombs destroyed before reaching their target were 4,261 of which 1,971 were destroyed by anti-aircraft guns, 1,979 by fighter aircraft, 278 by balloons and thirty-three by the Royal Navy. German records showed that by 7 April 1945, 1,190 V-2s were launched against London and of these the Allies detected the fall of 1,115, of which 501 fell in the London Civil Defense Region.[12]

In addition to the loss of life, some 23,000 homes were destroyed (*Flying Bomb*, p. 174).

V-1 ASIDES

At the request of ASDI (Sc), SIGINT captured German radar tracking of flying bomb tests between December 1943 and May 1944. Assuming the same launch ramp and aiming point, this shows considerable improvement in accuracy, particularly in azimuth, just prior to the weapon going operational in June.

Douglas Kendall remembered, "We were still mystified that we had not found a so-called ski site in Germany. It appeared amazing that the Germans would build 96 sites in northern France without a single prototype site in Germany. We felt happier two months later (after Dec 43) when we photographed a military training area on the eastern Baltic coast near Konigsberg and found three firing ramps, two square buildings, a pair of rectangular buildings and one 'ski'" (Kendall, p. 101).

Powys-Lybbe added, "To everyone's delight there had just been a malfunction when the photograph had been taken, resulting in the top end of a ramp being blown to smithereens" (*Eye*, p. 203).

Douglas Kendall wrote about the devastation and cost of the flying bomb, citing results slightly different from the previous statistics. "In total, 8,564 flying bombs took off against England. Just over 1,000 of these crashed on takeoff due to lack of sufficient speed. The flying bombs killed 6,184 people in London and seriously injured about 18,000. The number of houses damaged was about 750,000. For every flying bomb launched, one person died and three others were seriously injured. In addition, 2,000 British, American and Canadian airmen lost their lives in our counter offensive. And a total of 50,000 tons of bombs were dropped against the V-weapon sites" (Kendall, p. 117). Another author says 500 aircraft and 3,000 airmen were lost their lives in these operations (*Bodyguard of Lies*, p. 723). Yet another has attacks on the V-weapons costing 399 heavy bombers, about 100 other aircraft, and nearly 2,000 aircrew (*Flying Bomb*, p. 174).

I realize that the V-1 was intended to cause fear, to punish the British in London for the bombing of German cities, but that can only be viewed as an act of desperation. German leaders knew the English hadn't buckled during the more intense, more destructive bombing of 1940-41, and could see their own populace holding on through the massive Allied bombing raids of 1943-44. I find it curious that Nazi leadership still believed the "buzz-bomb" would have the desired result as a terror weapon. Perhaps they might have been more effective if they had been operational earlier, if there had been enough of them and they had attacked multiple targets— and if Allied air and ground attacks hadn't cut short their operational life.

Though the Luftwaffe was developing a rocket fighter at the same place the pulse-jet flying bomb was being tested, and the Army's nearby long-range rocket programme had a zero-launch system, but no one thought to apply those concepts to the V-1. Apparently it wasn't realized how readily the elaborate launch rail and check-out building, let alone the "skis," would be found by Allied intelligence. A small rocket launch-booster would have permitted a short, perhaps even truck mounted, launch rail that would have been extremely difficult to locate. Such a launching system would also have made it possible to change the target by simply reorienting the ramp.

I also find it curious that the Germans were obviously aware of the range accuracy limitations of the V-1, yet didn't take advantage of the relatively better azimuth accuracy. They might have had more productive results in early June 1944 had they fired almost due west from sites in the Pas de Calais, letting the flying bombs fall at random into the invasion support area along the

Vehicle parks, supply and munitions dumps like this abounded in southern England, in the spring of 1944. They held all the fuel, ammunition, food and other items necessary to support Operation *Overlord* and the bombing campaign. These extremely lucrative and vulnerable targets were never attacked or even located by the Germans.

south coast of England. Long shots would have threatened Portsmouth and Southampton and shorts might have hit camps, dumps and assembly areas dotting the landscape along the way. Ah, but they didn't know where the invasion assembly areas were. Allied deceptions had fooled the Germans into thinking the Cross-Channel attack would come from Patton's shadow army in East Anglia, and RAF fighters had kept Luftwaffe photo reconnaissance at bay, denying German photo interpreters an opportunity to spot the massive build-up from Kent to the Severn. Perhaps the Germans expected all the troop and material build-up would be in safer territory north of the Thames. In any case it is apparent they and didn't understand the "target rich" environment immediately across the Channel.

---

1   *Brit Intel*, vol. 3, p. 412, says the P20 was seen on the Peenemünde ramp on 28 November, the "same night" as the mission. The time line related here is more likely considering aircraft recovery in Scotland, courier to Medmenham, time for film processing and printing, print distribution and subsequent photo interpretation in Third Phase.

2   Notes from the 325th Photo Wing study. "Belhamelin Site at Eckfeld. This was one of the 1st of the Belhamelin sites to be built. Note the characteristic black smudge from the forward end of the ramp. Here an effort had been made to conceal the skid marks by directing the fire over the constructional spoil of an autobahn. Cover, exp. 3017, msn 3744 of 7 PG, 1 Jan 45."

3   This is like not knowing when you didn't find a quarter in the parking lot on the way to work? Camoufleurs on the ground always think they are doing a better job than they really are when their work is viewed from overhead and over time. See my book *To Fool A Glass Eye*.

4   I have not seen this story reported anywhere else. One of two "Hitler Bunkers" (Fuhrerhauptquartier) in Western Europe, Margival, near Soisson (also known as Wolfschlucht 2) was built in 1941-42 for the invasion of England.

5   He means flying bombs.

6   Nearly fourteen per cent of bombing sorties from England, and forty per cent of reconnaissance flights, were directed against *Crossbow* targets.

7   *Mare's Nest*, p. 241: Memo of 29 June. Over forty per cent of Allied bombing was against *Crossbow* targets.

8   Text varies slightly from Hölsken who used the German translation.

9   From conversations I have had over the years with pilots who flew those missions "attacking the big green ball".

10 The radius within which fifty per cent of the weapons will impact.

11 The German wife of a comrade-in-arms once told me she was sure after the war "every man, woman and child in America could have their own P-47" since there were so many of them overhead when she was a girl.

12 There are almost as many different statistics on the V-1s and V-2s as there are sources. These came from the British Military Intelligence Museum, by way of Chris Halshall.

Chapter VII

OUT OF NOWHERE

On 15 July 1943 a telegram from "our man in Stockholm" stated that "German scientists at the research station at Peenemünde were under orders from Hitler to devise ways of mass-producing long-range rockets so that he could carry out his threat to 'plaster London with thousands of missiles a day' till it was razed to the ground'" (*Silk and Cyanide*, p. 351). British agents were told "We urgently need a description of the rockets and their emplacements, and as much information as possible about the scale of rocket and projector production at the research station" (*Silk and Cyanide*, p. 352).

Operational use of the rocket was serendipitously delayed by air attacks on transportation aimed at the V-1, by the Peenemünde bombings, and by technical problems with the weapon and its manufacture. Winston Churchill noted that in the spring of 1944, "A second threat drew near. This was the long-range rocket, or V-2, with which we had been so preoccupied twelve months before. The Germans however had found it difficult to perfect, and in the meantime it had been overtaken by the flying bomb" (*Triumph and Tragedy*, p. 49). He also referred to the rocket as "an impressive technical achievement" (*Triumph and Tragedy*, p. 52).

Rocket testing had begun again at Peenemünde in late 1943. Over the winter of 1943/44, test firings of the V-2 from Blizna and Peenemünde had ironed out most of the launch problems (*Rocket and the Reich*, p. 220). "The attack on Peenemünde, for which such sacrifices were made, therefore played an important and definite part in the general progress of the war. But for this raid and the subsequent attacks on the launching points in France, Hitler's bombardment of London by rockets might well have started early in 1944. In fact it was delayed until September. By that time the prepared launching sites in Northern France had been overrun by General Montgomery's forces. In consequence the projectiles had to be fired from improvised positions in Holland, nearly twice as far from the target of London, and with much less accuracy. By the autumn, German communications became so congested by battle needs that the transport of rockets to the firing-point could no longer secure high priority" (*Closing the Ring*, p. 234).

In spite of thousands of technical "teething problems", with the V-1 assault faltering it was decided to make the rocket operational. "Its complexity and high cost were offset by the simplicity of its launch system, which allowed it to depart from any point where a few square feet of hard surface to sustain the thrust of its exhaust gases could be built or even found. Indeed, in some respects, the Meillerwagen, which both transported the weapon and raised it to the vertical, was as brilliant a conception as the rocket itself" (*Intelligence in War*, p. 288). As the flying bomb assault tapered off, Duncan Sandys announced that the "Battle of London is over" (*England 1914-1945*, p. 506). Unfortunately he was a day premature.

On the evening of 8 September 1944 the first V-2 was fired at England (*V-Missiles*, p. 220-221). It wasn't launched from a fortress, a bunker or a dispersed, well prepared site. It came from an essentially unimproved position in the Netherlands. The V-2 assault on London was supposed to begin the morning of 6 September. The first two attempts failed but other rockets were launched that same day. Meanwhile, two rockets were sent against Paris on 8 September (Paris had been liberated on 25 August). Hölsken quotes an official German record saying: "The A4 was effective with two shots against London on September 9, 1944." Many Allied sources say the first rocket landed in London on the 7th, others say it was at 6:43 pm on the 8th. Himmler ordered cancellation of fire against French targets so concentration would be on London.

The rocket programme had stalled with emphasis on the flying bomb, but regained momentum when it was obvious that the V-1 sites were about to be pushed out of range. The Allies expected to see the rocket eventually, but had no warning when it arrived. It was immediately apparent that barrage balloons, anti-aircraft artillery and fighter planes that worked well against the flying bomb were useless against the new weapon. It was particularly terrifying that the rockets impacted without warning and detonated with a powerful blast made more destructive by the supersonic speed of the falling missile. There was no radar warning. There was no sound warning. There was no way to predict even a rough area of impact. Seemingly out of nowhere there would be a sonic boom followed instantly by a huge explosion. Nor was there a way to bomb the launch sites. Author Hölsken correctly points out that not even one V-2 launching site was identified early enough to be attacked before a rocket was fired (*V-Missiles*, p. 216).

Suddenly the rockets were showering down and it was quickly clear that the only defence was to stop the rockets from being shipped within launch range or find the rockets at launch sites before they could be fired. Even when the same area was used for a launch, the crew would fire and retire, all of which took from an hour-and-a-half to two hours.

"Having found out something of how the rocket was fired, we became aware that even in open country no launching sites could be confirmed from photographic evidence alone, unless the rocket could be actually photographed during the process of fuelling and in the vertical position, immediately before takeoff. In wooded areas, even this chance was small. In any case the launching site had little meaning. Although it might be convenient for the Germans to use the same site regularly unless disturbed, if only to simplify their plotting procedures, they only had to move to some other flat section of ground as soon as they felt that they had been observed" (*Kendall*, p. 122).

Airborne patrols might suppress launches, but there was a large area to patrol and plenty of flak available to make such patrols very risky. The V-2 launch sites were so small and so basic (any stretch of paved road would do) that increasingly frustrated photo interpreters couldn't find them. They didn't know what to look for beyond the characteristic fuel and support vehicles. The Allies couldn't come up with a way to stop the new threat and had no idea how much worse it might become. A major English history study summed up with, "These (rockets) were a greater danger than the flying bombs, though less alarming psychologically—they fell without warning. They caused more destruction, and no defense was found against them. Plans were laid to abandon London, and indeed London survived only because the rockets were few and late. They were expensive to produce, and the advance of the Allied armies overran most of their launching sites soon after the attack began" (*England 1914-1945*, p. 506).

It was obvious that the cycle of an aircraft returning film, processing and PI that had been so effective against the V-1 was too slow to catch the V-2 as it was being set up for launch. It quickly became apparent that the only solution to the rocket was to attack the means to bring it into range. The other response was to push hard on the land, driving the launch sites out of range. Indeed, in one of the few real impacts the rockets had on the conduct of the war, Field Marshall Montgomery set his sights on Operation *Market Garden*, starting the day after the V-2s began landing in England.[1] The 17 September 1944 airborne assault (*Market Garden*) in eastern Netherlands was costly, and contributed to the general Allied offensive (setting up conditions for the more costly *Battle of the Bulge*), but it did force the V-2 launching units to quickly relocate. That resulted in London being out of range until the V-2 batteries came west again after the Allied failure at Arnhem. Meanwhile, Liege, Maastricht, Hasselt and St Quentin were also targeted and rocket potential further diluted by using them as long-range artillery against point targets in France, Belgium and the Netherlands (*V-Missiles*, p. 222). But, by this time, even the most optimistic advocate must have understood that the V-2 was far from being the equivalent of "long-range artillery".

Once again, German leaders were scattering a resource rather than focusing everything they had against a single objective. The closest the Germans came to "remaining on point" was firing on Antwerp starting on 21 October, trying to deny its use as a port to shorten Allied logistic lines for ground operations. After October 12, 1944 the fire had been concentrated on Antwerp and London (*V-Missiles*, p. 229).

Meanwhile, the Allies were frantically trying to come up with ways to deter or interdict the rocket. RAF 11 Group sent armed reconnaissance sorties "over the forward storage depots and their associated road and rail communications…and transport movement was to be immediately attacked" (*Flying Bomb*, p. 57-58). Finally, with the blanket of Allied planes over the continent, reports started coming in of sightings of launches. It didn't take long to determine that there were no fixed launch sites to attack. The biggest surprise for the Allies was that, unlike all predictions, the rocket launch did not have to be rail served. The V-2 launching system was brilliantly simple and efficient. Everything was on road-capable wheels. A little convoy of vehicles would move to a pre-selected flat spot; a road or open field, anything would do.

The Meillerwagen would erect a rocket or rockets over "Lemon Squeezers", they would be quickly fuelled and fired. The entire process literally took only a few minutes, minimizing the chance of Allied air intervention before the launch crew packed up and headed for a protected location to refill fuel tanks and pick up fresh rockets. Re-firing from a given location occurred simply because once the trajectory and azimuth had been worked out it was easier to use them

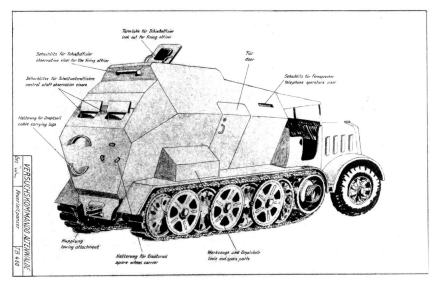

Armored mobile control vehicle.

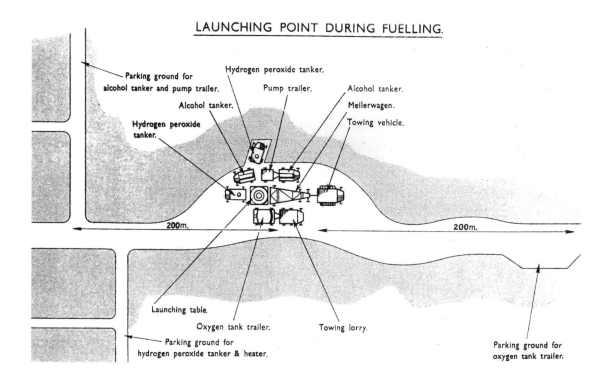

Parking ground for
alcohol tanker and pump trailer.

Hydrogen peroxide tanker.

Pump trailer.

Alcohol tanker.

Meilerwagen.

Towing vehicle.

Alcohol tanker.

Hydrogen peroxide
tanker.

200m.

200m.

Launching table.

Oxygen tank trailer.

Towing lorry.

Parking ground for
hydrogen peroxide tanker & heater.

Parking ground for
oxygen tank trailer.

again. Some tree cover at the launch site was helpful, as were good egress routes for the crew and equipment to escape Allied aircraft that might have seen the firing.

With this understanding of the V-2 launch process, Allied air reconnaissance and combat patrols had something to look for: convoys with characteristic fuel transports, and, of course, the 40-foot-long rocket. Unfortunately the search area was huge and knowing what to look for and finding them were not the same.

**Alcohol, Hydrogen-
Peroxide and Liquid
Oxygen were loaded from
high-pressure trailers.**

Flight Officer Babington Smith remembered that from the start of the "drizzle of rockets" in September, "innumerable sorties were flown to pinpoints that had been reported as launching sites, and the interpreters searched thousands upon thousands of photographs. But in only two cases where clearings in woods were found at the suspected spots—could any suspicious signs be reported. Not one single operational launching site was found. In fact they did not exist" (*Air Spy*, p. 170).

"The only positive results on firing points which we got during the early stages of firing, that is, in October and November 1944 were at Rijs in Holland where two fresh clearings were seen among trees in an area which we knew from radar plotting had been used for rocket launchings, and at Metelen Ribers where a clearing and turning loop were seen in a wood from which one of our pilots had seen a rocket emerge. It should be noted that in both these cases the photographic evidence was of no value, and would certainly not have been found, without some evidence to direct it to the spot from some other source, in this case radar plotting and visual observation. Nevertheless, in a vain attempt to get some clue which would give us a lead to counter measures,

Rare chance of a camera-equipped plane over-flying a V-2 site seconds after launch. The fighter in the photo appears to be a Hawker Typhoon. Photo date isn't given.

V-2 set-up and launching was simplicity itself with everything on wheels. Note erected Meillerwagen used as a ladder for access to guidance and warhead during final missile check-out.

we continued throughout September and October 1944 to examine thousands upon thousands of photographs without any positive results" (Kendall, p. 122-123).

"If Hitler's ideas of sticking to massive concrete 'launching shelters' had prevailed, the tale would have been very different. There would have been something (for PIs) to bite on. But the plain fact of the matter is that General Dornberger's almost ridiculously simple conception of how the V-2s should be launched defeated Allied photographic reconnaissance" (Air Spy, p. 171).

Agents near The Hague reported loud roaring noises and fire trails in the sky. In late December, reconnaissance caught what appeared to be rockets on the ground in The Hague's main park. "It was not until December 29th, 1944 that rockets were seen on photographs in the operational area. By this time the enemy had been driven out of most territories within range of England and with good enough communications, by road and rail, to permit supply. They were compelled to use the Haagsche Bosch, which was a wooded park in the middle of The Hague, the summer capital of the Dutch Government. On this particular day, we saw at least 13 of the V-2 rockets dispersed under the trees on their wagons. Unfortunately for the Germans, it was winter and the leaves had fallen, no longer giving any cover. The Haagsche Bosch became the main firing area for the V-2 rockets and in an attempt to make the area reasonably untenable, we started sending fighter aircraft over the woods at frequent intervals, briefed to fire at anything which they could see moving in among the trees. In many ways, the rocket was more vulnerable to fighter attack than to bombs. Eventually, the enemy abandoned the Haagsche Bosch. The abandoning of this site caused a few days of complete relief from the bombing, but it soon resumed from elsewhere" (Kendall, p. 123).

On the afternoon of 26 February 1945, a V-2 was finally photographed in launch position and being fuelled (below) (Air Spy, p. 170). It was on an unimproved road at Duindigt race course, in a north-east suburb of the Hague, proving how little was required of a rocket launch site. The area was bombed and both photo and "armed" recon continued, with the same general lack of results.

Duindigt Race Course, Belgium, 26 February 1945. Can you find the V-2 being prepared for launch?

Enlargement of above, the only photo coverage of a V-2 setting up for firing. Black arrow drawn by an Allied PI in 1945 points to the erected rocket on the road. Some craters may be from failed launches.

"There had been no time to build either underground or covered storage and in any case underground storage in Holland, with the high water table, would have been virtually impossible. The standard method for storage was for the enemy to disperse the rockets on their now familiar wagons, at various points throughout the woods. Naturally as we found these points, they were attacked by both fighters and a small part of our bomber force. Needless to say, however, since the main responsibility of our bombers at this stage of the war was to support the army, we could not divert large numbers and had to accept a small volume of firing on London. A typical day would be 10 rockets but not all would reach the target areas" (Kendall, p. 123).

A month later the V-2 offensive was, for all intents and purposes, over. Troops on the ground had pushed the weapon out of range of any target large enough for the rocket to hit with reliability. "From time to time we found the odd indication of the areas being used for firing and storage, but everything was on a very small scale and no targets which, if destroyed, would substantially reduce firing were found. Our only real defense at this stage was to overrun the firing areas or to attack the communications and manufacturing systems to the rear" (Kendall, p. 124).

As the rocket offensive progressed through the end of 1944, it was obvious that the weapon was impressive technology for its day. It also had impressive destruction capability, but was less than impressive in accuracy. In his detailed examination of the V-missiles, Dieter Hölsken put the "average deviation from the target" at eleven miles for the V-2s launched at London (V-Missiles, p. 219). A more recent author puts the average error at 8.8mm (Rocket and the Reich, p. 225). Hölsken also mentions that German troops at Remagen were told to pull back nine miles when rockets were to fire in an attempt to destroy the Ludendorf Bridge, that being the impact deviation experienced to date (V-Missiles, p. 243).

It is only fair to note that most Allied "precision" aerial bombing wasn't much better. "In the summer of 1941, an alarming government study of bombing accuracy was released. Its author, a civil servant named D M Butt, claimed that only one-third of British planes reaching their targets that June and July had dropped their bombs within five miles of the Aiming Point. In the heavily defended Ruhr, with its permanent cloud of industrial smoke, the number was only ten (Masters of the Air, p. 54).

Air Force historian Dr Richard Hallion observed that only one of 376 bombs hit Japan's Yawata steel mill during a B-29s raid in 1944 and it took 108 B-17s dropping 648 bombs to guarantee a ninety-six per cent chance of getting just two hits on a Nazi power plant (see Hallion article, p. 57). Bombing accuracy was sometimes much better, but the RAF and Eighth Air Force compensated for inaccuracy by having large numbers of aircraft and bombing frequently.[2]

By November, the V-2 was more harassment than threat. The rockets played no role in the Battle of the Bulge. Continuing to attack London and Antwerp, caused some destruction but made no impact on the conduct of the war. The last attacks against London and Antwerp were on 27 March 1945. In April V-2 launch personnel were ordered to duty as infantry (V-Missiles, p. 244). Author Hölsken quotes a German source claiming the final two rockets were launched at London on 28 March.

Medmenham PIs were in the thick of things chasing down the elusive rocket. Their assessments of the weapon are interesting.

"In all, 1,190 V-2 rockets reached England. Of these about 500 actually hit the London area killing 2,724 people and injuring 6,467, a far higher percentage than the flying bomb. On the other hand the manufacturing effort needed to build one V-2 was equivalent to about six or seven fighter aircraft, whereas a V1 flying bomb only represented a small fraction of this work. As a

Left: A rare German photo taken at 0938 hrs on 24 February 1945, shown at near original scale. "Margate" is a German annotationn. My arrows point to damage noted by Luftwaffe PIs.

Below: Enlargement of the "Margate" photo shows German PI annotations of probable rocket hits (boxes and circles with "X"). The taking unit was 1 (F) 123, a long-range Recon Squadron based at Rheine airfield just east of the Dutch border. To get this close to London in 1945 the taking aircraft was probably a high-flying Arado 234 jet.

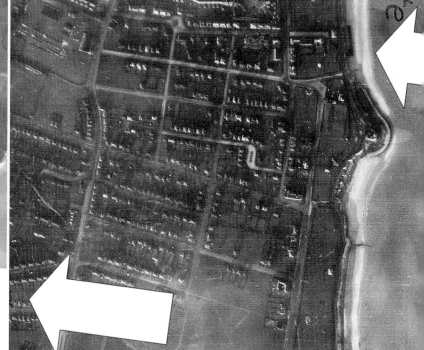

method of delivering one ton of explosive the V-2 was very costly and ineffective. Yet as a forerunner of the future, it was a remarkable engineering feat, years ahead of its time. I should mention that the rate of firing from October 1944 onwards built up to 500 V-2 rockets a month, of which 200 were fired against London and 300 against Antwerp. V1 flying bombs were also sent in quantity against Antwerp and Liege, resulting unhappily in many Belgian deaths. However the disruption to the overall war effort was minor (Kendall, p. 126).

However, indeed. The rocket does not stand up to cost-benefit analysis. The unit cost of a V-2 was as much as twenty times that of a V-1 and the damage done by the rocket was not proportionate to this greater cost (USSBS, p. 24). "Even our Mosquitoes, each of which was probably no dearer than a rocket, dropped on the average 125 tons of bombs per aircraft within one mile of the target during their life, whereas the rocket dropped one ton only, and that with an average error of fifteen miles" (*Triumph and Tragedy*, p. 54). The flaw in this analysis is that in a life-or-death struggle it doesn't matter what a weapon costs if it gets the job done. In sufficient numbers the V-2's value as a terror weapon would likely have overridden the high cost and poor accuracy. The oft heard argument; "you don't use a sledge hammer to kill a fly" is used by people who have never had to "kill the fly", much less faced flies capable of killing them. Those under fire will use anything that works, no matter the cost. Unfortunately for the Nazis, the rocket just didn't get the job done. There were too few of them, they were operational too late, and they were too inaccurate to attack high-value targets.

---

1   Montgomery, p. 251-252. "Military History Magazine", October 2004, p.28, "It is debatable whether it was necessary to go to Arnhem at all. In lieu of that, many men on Montgomery's staff wanted a drive toward Wesel, just north of the Ruhr, which would have entailed fewer river crossings. Dempsey suggested just such a move on September 9. The day before, however, the first German V-2 guided rockets hit London, and Montgomery began thinking that an advance to the Ijsselmeer region would cut off the western Netherlands and isolate the launching bases. That assumption turned out to be another mistake, but only because the drive to Arnhem, Operation Market-Garden, failed."

2   This reminds me of a favourite saying of the General I worked for in Saigon: "Quantity is quality...if you've got enough."

Norsk-Hydroelectric plant, Rjukan, Norway. This 1934 photo shows it would be a difficult target to bomb.

Chapter VIII

WARHEADS

Throughout the war it was almost universally believed that Hitler would use any and all means at his disposal to win—or forestall defeat. What special resources did he have?

From the start of the war the Allies assumed that Nazi Germany had stocks of lethal gas—mustard and phosgene upgrades of gas types used in the First World War. These could be dispersed in artillery shells, pressurized cylinders, grenades, aerial bombs or sprays (*Brit Intel*, vol. 2, p. 674). What the Allies didn't know was German policy for use of chemical weapons (*Brit Intel*, vol. 2, p. 116). Of course the Allied side also had stocks of gas and neither side wanted to be the first to open that 'Pandora's Box'. Hitler had personal experience with gas on the western front during the First World War and knew it to be unreliable, dependent upon particular circumstances of temperature, humidity, wind direction and surprise, so he was unlikely to use it near the forward edge of the battle area. He might have considered using lethal or debilitating gas against targets well removed from his ground forces (such as London), but he also learned early in the war that the Allies could put large numbers of aircraft over almost any location in Germany, so a chemical-weapons stand-off resulted in the west.

The new fear was that the Germans would not be so circumspect in the east. Enigma intercepts indicated they were afraid that the Soviets would use gas and were fully prepared to retaliate. This led the Soviets to similarly prepare (*Brit Intel*, vol. 2, p. 116). In 1942 it was known that the Germans had stocks of gas artillery and mortar rounds but as yet they were just a threat (*Brit Intel*, vol. 2, p. 676). By 1943, the fact that lethal gas had not been used by either side at Stalingrad led the Joint Intelligence Committee to conclude that "the likelihood that Germany would use gas was becoming more remote; except in retaliation…" (*Brit Intel*, vol. 2, p. 118-119). The Allies would not have been so comfortable in that assessment had they known that German scientists were developing three strains of nerve gas more lethal than anything our side had (*Brit Intel*, vol. 2, see footnote, p 119). We didn't know about most of this effort until after the war.

The upshot was that lethal gas was deemed too unstable, too unreliable and too dangerous for those loading and dispersing it to be of value, even as a 'last ditch' weapon. The fact that this truth survived the Cold War, and all the smaller World Power Surrogate Wars since (excepting the "home grown" Iran-Iraq war) proves that even in the intensity of the Second World War, some sanity prevailed.

Use of nuclear weapons was another thing entirely. There was a great likelihood that whichever side got the bomb first would use it to end the war, and the Germans had a good start.

The basic concept was understood in the spring of 1939, but no one on either side of the Atlantic was working on an atomic bomb at a war-driven pace. However, the threat was believed

S.A.661
HYDRO ELECTRIC POWER STATION
RJUKAN, NORWAY
16.11.43. Neg. N° 31918

APPROXIMATE BOMB PLOT

• Position of well defined bursts
/// Area of concentration
Photographic background 5.8.42 N/60?
Photo. 5 10
LEGEND
A. Power Station
B. Water Electrolysis House
C. Possible Water Cooling Units
D. Pentstock

626826

Allied post-strike graphic showing bomb hits. Note damage to penstocks and main building. The base imagery was from an RAF recon mission of 5 August 1942.

serious enough for physicists in America (Leo Szilard, Enrico Fermi and Eugene Wigner) to cajole well-known pacifist Albert Einstein to write to President Franklin Roosevelt about the need for a programme to create a nuclear bomb. Einstein's 2 August 1939 letter to FDR suggested that the Germans had a head start,[1] and America better get into the race (Roosevelt didn't see the letter until October). Despite its esteemed signatory, the letter had little effect for two years.

Bureaucratic skepticism finally buckled on 6 December 1941 and the "Manhattan Project" was born in August 1942. In 1942 no one on the Allied side knew anything about the German rockets and no one knew that the successful Allied atomic bombs would weigh four to five times more than the V-2 could lift—so heavy that only a handful of Luftwaffe bombers could have carried them. The intense pace of Allied effort was assumed necessary to beat the Axis to the bomb. It was expected that the Germans knew an atomic weapon was being vigorously explored in America, but, like the Allies, the Axis could only guess at the progress being made by their enemy. Concern was heightened because atomic research had been mentioned in the Oslo Report, and almost all of the other weapons programmes mentioned in that document had come to pass (*Bodyguard of Lies*, p. 370).

Allied intelligence knew that, thanks to their control of Belgium, German scientists had access to "the largest stock of uranium oxide in Europe" and were increasing production of heavy water (*Brit Intel*, vol. 2, p. 123). Reports trickling out of Europe seemed to indicate rapid German progress on harnessing the atom for war.

The Norsk Hydro electric plant at Vemork (sometimes referred to by the name of the nearby town, Rjukan), Norway, was built early in the century to support production of fertilizer and generate electricity for much of southern Norway. Norsk Hydro was one of the world's largest hydro electrical power plants when it went into operation in 1911. In 1934 the installation was up-graded with a seven story reinforced concrete building that also produced heavy water—a by product of manufacturing ammonia fertilizer using electrolysis. Heavy water was necessary to the operation of a nuclear reactor so the Germans took over Norsk Hydro in 1940. The perceived need to deny that resource to German scientists made Norsk Hydro a target. It was photographed by 1PRU on 20 May 1942, and again on 5 August. From then on it was watched carefully by aerial recon and agents on the ground.

A British-Norwegian commando raid on 19 November 1942, Operation *Freshman*, failed when one glider crashed in the sea and the other, and its Halifax bomber tug, crashed in the mountains behind Vemork. All the raiders were killed in the crashes or following torture by the Gestapo.

In Operation *Gunnerside*, six Norwegian commandos parachuted into the mountains and linked up with the group that landed before the failed glider raid. This small, combined force achieved some demolition in the electrolysis chambers on 27-28 February 1943, but British intelligence learned in August that the damage was repaired by April (*Brit Intel*, vol. 2, p. 127). This repair effort convinced the Allies of German determination to continue nuclear progress.

Norsk Electric was built on concrete piles embedded in solid rock so only direct hits would do real damage. It was determined that the relatively small target didn't lend itself to night bombing so 143 Eighth Air Force B-17s were sent to the plant in a daylight raid on 16 November 1943. They dropped over 700 bombs on the Norsk Hydro plant but the small complex clinging to the side of a steep, narrow valley proved to be a daunting target and only a few of the bombs did real damage.[2] A few hits on the main building probably did less to slow production than hits on the penstocks (large pipes bringing water to the plant from a lake higher in the mountains). However, the air raid convinced the Nazis to move the remaining stocks of heavy water to Germany by rail.

On 20 February 1944, Norwegian agents intervened again, planting explosives that sank the

Photos of bombing damage to Vemork, taken by Norwegian agents on 27 November 1943.

1659359

ferry in deep water as it carried the heavy water railroad tank cars across Lake Tinn. The Norwegian saboteurs used a timed detonation and escaped but fourteen civilians were killed when the boat sank. Collectively, these bombing and sabotage efforts probably further delayed the German attempt to create a nuclear weapon. The sinking of the Lake Tinn Ferry sank German aspirations for an operational nuclear bomb completed in time to influence the war. "As Dr. Kurt Diebner, one of the main figures in the Reich's research and development program, acknowledged after the war, '...it was the elimination of German heavy water production in Norway that was the main factor in our failure to achieve a self-sustaining atomic reactor before the war ended'" (*Bodyguard of Lies*, p. 376-377). Allied Secret Intelligence activities in Norway had not only ended a potential technological threat but the operation convinced Hitler that Norway was vulnerable to Allied attack. The Germans kept reinforcing Norway with arms, construction and troops right up to the end of the war—resources that were not available to strengthen defenses in Normandy or repel the D-Day Invasion.

In a parallel effort, at the request of ADI (Sc), Wing Commander Kendall initiated an exhaustive photo search for the home of Nazi nuclear research. Agents had identified some of the key players as being at Hechingen, a large country house near Stuttgart, so the search centreed in that area. Power plants and grids were mapped to find concentrations of electrical demand. All the large buildings in the Stuttgart area were examined for power and possible size or shape needed to perform nuclear research. The work would have been impossible without complete, repetitive, good quality and scale aerial imagery. The study took three months and the final report said that "there was no indication from aerial photographs available at Medmenham that the Germans were working on the production of an atomic bomb at the time Hechingen became the main centre for atomic research in early 1945" (*Eye*, p. 175-176).

Douglas Kendall remembered:

"The vehemence of German propaganda led some British officials to think that the weapon might be destined to carry an atomic warhead. I was therefore summoned to a highly secret meeting where this fantastic new development of the Allies was explained to me. I was instructed to set in motion an investigation to find if the Germans had any similar programs. I was told that two well known German professors had been carrying out research in this direction at the Kaiser Wilhelm Institute in Berlin but that, as far as we knew it had been moved to the Stuttgart area, where they were supposed to be carrying on their research in a country house. Obviously continued research was not feasible in Berlin, under the bombing to which it was being subjected.

I unfortunately could not, for reasons of security, advise the officers carrying out the photographic interpretation of the main purpose of their studies. I was able to arrange for complete photography of the Stuttgart area with our photo reconnaissance units and assigned to our electrical engineers a study of all the power facilities available in the Stuttgart area. A study was also carried out of all the industrial plants within a 100 mile radius of the city. The only suspicious activity we found was the erection of 14 new factories, all identical in shape, in a valley not far from Stuttgart. Each plant consisted of a grid pattern of pipes lying on the ground, one or two tall chimneys and some tanks, similar to oil tanks, for storage. There also appeared to be open pit mining operations associated with each plant.

A curious feature of the plants, which we observed at once, was that they were all on the same contour level. This factor, together with the open pit mining, immediately pointed to some geological reason for their existence. I therefore sent one of our geologists to go through the German records held in the Geological Museum in London. He quickly found that in this area, before the war a German geologist had reported a thin bed of low grade oil shales. It was apparent that the Germans, faced with their acute oil shortage, were exploiting this low grade and expensive source of fuel in order to supplement their supplies. The plants were in fact very crude refineries using the system of laying out the shale in piles over the pipes and setting fire to it. The gases given off were drawn into the pipes and then brought into the refinery for treatment. Following the investigation we felt quite confident that these plants did not represent an atomic menace to us. Curiously enough we had a day of qualms immediately following this conclusion as someone produced a report that in Sweden uranium in reasonable quantities had been found in the oil shales. But a second look at the plants persuaded us that their sole purpose was oil.

By the time we had finished studying in the Stuttgart area, we felt that we could report with reasonable certainty that there was no sign, in this area at lest, of any developments which looked like the preparations for atomic weapons. As we had reasonably complete photographic coverage of the whole of Germany we also felt that there were no suspicious plants anywhere else. With some relief I was able to give a qualified but reasonably optimistic report on the subject to the officer on the Prime Minister's staff who was investigating this problem" (*Kendall*, p. 124-126).

A recently published "expert" on the German rocket programme read an early manuscript of this book and wrote that he was "appalled" by my discussion of the possibility of German nuclear weapons. He cited the backward state of that programme, but that observation was made from the comfort of decades of hindsight while people in London were making decisions with warheads going off around them. That author, who has no active duty military experience, also ignored, or didn't understand, the tension felt by all senior officers as the Invasion Force remained in tenuous conditions for many weeks. The responsibility for committing resources and lives in war is something you have to experience (or witness close-in) to understand and appreciate. To discount the possibility of a German nuclear weapon discounts the natural Allied fears of what the German scientists could achieve—after all, much of the work done on our own A-Bomb was being done by German scientists. The V-weapons were unquestionably technologically advanced. It was German rocket experts that gave us working ICBMs and sent us into space after the war. The Allies simply couldn't take a chance on being wrong on German progress with either weapon or warhead.

Some researchers, who actually inspected the V-weapons launch complexes after the war, such as Watten in France, say there were rooms with provisions for special isolation, suggesting anticipation of nuclear or chemical warheads—others vigorously disagree with that assessment. But there is no indication that the nay-sayers have ever set foot in one of the destroyed V-2 bunkers.

Short of the sacrifice of incredibly brave and determined Norwegians and RAF crews, the Germans might also have been a lot farther along in producing a nuclear bomb. Of course there is no way of knowing if Nazi science, without interruption, could have produced a weapon, let alone something small enough to be a warhead for the V-2. If they had, and if even one or two nuclear warheads had been detonated in England, it is not hard to visualize a truce—certainly there would have been no Normandy Invasion.

Eminent British military historian, John Keegan, summed up the German nuclear research programme as, "dissipated between too many competing research organisations. There was no Dornberger, no von Braun, no Peenemünde and never enough money. The world, nevertheless, had a very narrow escape" (*Intelligence in War*, p. 294. Quoting David Irving, *The Virus House*, London, 1967). The Allies may have had their suspicions that there was no German nuclear threat, but they weren't sure until intelligence teams found Nazi atomic research papers at the University of Strasbourg in November 1944. Operation *Alsos*, an Allied programme of sending teams right behind frontline troops to recover German nuclear documentation, personnel and materials to determine progress and deny it to the Soviets, verified that Germany did not have, and was not likely to have, an atomic bomb in time to influence the war (*Budiansky article*, p. 27).

The remaining warhead options for the V-weapons were high-explosive (HE) or fragmentation, such as used in conventional artillery shells and aerial bombs. Frag warheads would have diminished the weight of explosive and not increased the damage from weapons designed for terror and area punishment, so HE was the obvious choice. Amatol, a mixture of ammonium nitrate and TNT, was the explosive of choice; 1,870lbs for the V-1 and 2,150lbs for the rocket. Not the most powerful explosive available, amatol "was apparently chosen because it was less likely to detonate from the heating effect as the missile passed into the atmosphere at supersonic speeds (for the V-2)" (*German Secret Weapons of the Second World War*, p. 37). The same author notes that "The fuzing system (for the V-2) was so efficient that only two incidents of unexploded warheads are known between 8 September 1944 and 9 January 1945 in which time 1,150 rockets had landed in England" (*German Secret Weapons of the Second World War*, p. 37). The V-1 fusing was also quite efficient with only four failures in the first 2,700 incidents monitored in Britain. Additionally, the V-1 had a clockwork time delay fuse adjustable up to two hours (*German Secret Weapons of the Second World War*, p. 21-22). A time-delay fuse was impossible on the rocket because of the speed of impact.

---

1   Isaacson's article, p. 63. "Einstein said a few months before his death in a conversation with the American chemist Linus Pauling, 'because we all felt that there was a high probability that the Germans were working on this problem and they might succeed and use the atomic bomb and become the master race.'"

2   Some sources refer to subsequent air raids but Combat Chronology doesn't indicate any more USAAF attacks. Brit Intel, vol. 2, p. 127-128, indicates that the USAAF raid convinced German authorities that "they could not produce a nuclear weapon in time for use in the present war."

Chapter IX

LOOKING BACK

There is an enormous difference between being surrounded by books and papers telling how the war came out and waking up not knowing how the events of the day would play out, let alone the outcome of the conflict. From this distance it is easy (and tempting) to play the game of "what if," "they could have" or "they couldn't", or the "why didn't they", but that is all speculation and opinion, not history (though I'm going to fall into that trap a little bit later on). In hindsight, we can see that a German nuclear bomb/warhead was never a real possibility, but the Allies couldn't know that in 1940, and didn't know it even mid-1944. Nor had the Allies any way of knowing that technical and production limitations would keep the Germans from launching the V-weapons early enough or in numbers large enough to compensate for the lack of accuracy. The other side of that coin is that the Germans couldn't guess that the Allies would be so good at finding and stymieing their original launch schemes, or that Allied air attacks would be so intense.

What we can know is that the V-weapons were conceptually well ahead of anything the Allies were developing. That they were viable concepts is attested by their great-grandchildren—the long-range ballistic and cruise missiles of today.

It is wise to be wary of revisionism, particularly on the rocket. Let's get something straight—the "Vengeance Weapons" were not just a little side-trip on the way to space, nor was their failure simply because of inherent weaknesses in both programmes. A recent book used German archives for a minute and scholarly dissection of the V-2 programme, its problems and progress, hardly mentioning warheads or results (other than poor accuracy), seemingly ignoring the purpose of the V weapons to deliver high explosives into cities to kill civilians.

Other recent authors have more correctly observed that the V-weapons were never intended to be militarily decisive. They were not employed for strategic advantage, just revenge (*Bodyguard of Lies*, p. 728). Authors writing about the V-1 seem to be more honest about the "vengeance" or "retaliation" intent of the weapon than those writing about the V-2. The rocket programme tends to get the same "white wash" Wernher von Braun got after the Second World War (Operation *Paperclip*) when the US Army needed him for the Cold War and ignored all the people killed in England, Belgium, and as forced labour making the V-weapons or their facilities.

No matter how they began, or the various motives of their developers, the flying bomb and rocket were funded and deployed not as long-range artillery against specific military targets but to be unanswerable weapons intended to punish an enemy. They were made and employed with full knowledge that the target would be—could only be—the population of large cities, in particular, the 692 square miles of "Target 42" – London. Of course the RAF and USAAF, were doing the same thing to Germany, applying punishment to non-industrial targets—mainly Berlin, then Hamburg in July 1943. On both sides, area targets were struck partly because of accuracy limitations.

German propaganda filled soldiers and civilians with hope that the punishment of the enemy would be so great it would influence the conduct, even the result, of the war.

Anyone can guess, but no one can know, what might have happened if Allied intelligence hadn't identified the V-weapons threat when they did, and if RAF and USAAF air attacks hadn't slowed the deployment and operations of the weapons until after the Normandy landing and ground advance through Europe. As historian Dennis Showalter aptly summarized, "*Overlord* was an operation that could only be mounted once. Britain, its morale and material resources exhausted by four years of total war, was in no position to repeat any disaster suffered on the beaches of France. The United States for its part had committed an unexpectedly large amount of its national effort to a single action. In an election year, with President Franklin Roosevelt standing for an unprecedented fourth term despite his declining health, failure in Normandy could have incalculable political and strategic consequences" ("World War II" magazine, October 2004, p. 76-77).

Had either of the V-weapons been operational as originally planned by the Germans, they might well have forced a delay or postponement of *Overlord*. I maintain that a major reason for the V-weapons not having more influence on the war, was the outstanding work by intelligence, particularly photo analysts at Medmenham. Their work was instrumental in keeping the V-1 and V-2 from becoming more serious threats than they were, and helped stop the V-3 from happening at all.

Operations steered by Intelligence kept the flying bomb and rocket out of the equation during the critical months prior to the Normandy Invasion, and kept them from doing more than moderate and random damage following D-Day—though there was certainly nothing random or moderate for the people directly impacted. Speculation, "what if," and "couldn't have," are all well and good (usually from authors who've never heard a shot fired in anger), but the terror of those new weapons was very real to the people living through the assault. What Allied Intelligence and air operations accomplished to delay or stop the V-weapons and limit their numbers is a FACT. The Allies did impede, interrupt and destroy German plans for employment of the V-weapons, diminished the number of weapons fired and upset the already tenuous accuracy with subterfuge, then finally pushed the V-weapons back out of range.

If I had to pick one compressed period in which this enormous and significant struggle was decided it would be from the time photo interpreters identified the first "ski-sites" in early November 1943, through the first actual sighting of a V-1, then seeing it on a ramp at Peenemünde at the end of the month, followed by the intense December-January bombings of the original "ski-sites." This three-month period of discovery and destruction set the style and pace for the rest of the V-weapons battle.

Considering that the Allies began this "Second Battle of Britain" without knowing what the enemy weapons looked like, how many there were, how they would be employed or when, their range, or what their launching points looked like, there was a lot of catching up to do. The Germans had a significant head-start in the race and were feverishly pouring concrete for elaborate firing sites when they were first spotted. If the Allies hadn't been able to stymie the initial V-1 and V-2 production and launch plans, and hold the V-1 firing down as far as they did, it is possible that England might not have been able to withstand the increased urban damage at a time when everything south of the Thames was under considerable stress from preparation for, and support of, the Normandy Invasion. It is certainly possible that crucial ports would not have been able to function to capacity, thus jeopardizing overall conduct of war on the Western Front.

Intelligence and air strikes enabled the Allies to push back the true dawning of a decisive "Missile Age", but only just....

General Walter Dornberger, the German officer in charge of the A-4/V-2 program, wrapped up his book admitting that "operational employment of the A-4 in the autumn of 1944 could not of itself win the war. But what would have happened if, during the period since the summer of 1942, by day and night, more and more long-range rockets with ever-increasing range, accuracy, and effect had fallen on England?" (V-2, p. 236). He then avers, "The use of the V-2 may be aptly summed up in the two words 'too late'" (V-2, p. 237) assigning blame to high-level lack of foresight and failure to understand the science involved. Dornberger doesn't appear to acknowledge the impact of Allied countermeasures in his assessment.

Looking at the V-weapons from the safety of decades of hindsight and well-removed from the fear and tension of their assault, it is easy to claim the rocket in particular could never have been decisive because it was inaccurate and could not be produced in sufficient numbers.

Granted, the V-weapons were expensive and of dubious operational value, but they were not much less accurate than aerial bombing. However, planes could be shot down and there was no effective defence against the V-2 in particular.

Douglas Kendall had a different view of why the rockets failed to change the war. "On the V-2 rocket, we were already in the early stages of investigating the enemy's intention by April, 1943, and by June, 1943, had identified the weapon as a rocket 38 feet long. The rocket did not fire against us until September, 1944, the delay in part being due to the counter-measures against Peenemünde by our air forces" (Kendall, p. 160—quote edited). General Dornberger said essentially the same thing without deigning to acknowledge the Allied victory.

I agree that it all comes down to timing. In my judgment, winning the war over the German operational use of the V-weapons ranks as one of the great achievements of the Second World War—and combined triumph for fighting forces and intelligence. It wasn't an event of a few minutes such as USN dive-bombers changing the Pacific War by sinking the heart of Japan's carrier fleet at Midway in June 1942. Rather it was a term of gradual steps unfolding over months, involving skill in analysis, patience, attention to detail and luck; the luck of something being caught in the open on aerial imagery, and the luck of that object being understood. It also had a goodly share of mistakes and misunderstandings, but these were overcome in time.

There are many parallels with the epic air battles over southern England in 1940, only in a sense the roles were reversed. In both cases, rather than initiate a plan of attack and stick to it, the Germans changed emphasis, this time shifting priority from the V-2 to the V-1 and back. Ironically, in both cases, a cross-channel invasion was at stake.

Without question, a lot of chance was involved in this epic struggle. Who could have foreseen that bombing the V-2 "concrete monsters" to a standstill would result in the weight of "V-weapons" operations being quickly shifted to dispersed launching sites for the flying bombs. Who could know that within three weeks of finding the first "ski-sites" Allied aerial reconnaissance would catch a flying bomb on a ramp at Peenemünde, thus fully explaining the new threat? Who could have foreseen that the Allies would be so successful in finding and identifying the initial V-1 launch sites, and destroying them—all of them? This meant that instead of firing at England in March of 1944, the first V-1s weren't launched for another four months, and then not one of them came from one of the original launch sites. How could the Germans have guessed that all their V-1 (and a few V-2) launch sites would be flanked and driven back on the ground by August? The Cherbourg sites that most directly threatened the invasion forces in France were shut down quickly and some of the southernmost launchers were within Allied artillery range by mid August.

In the first week of September 1944, Allied ground forces rolled up through north-west France, reaching the Albert Canal, in Belgium, on the 4th.

The one thing the Germans should have been able to foresee was that, based upon recent history, the English people and government would stand firm even in the face of the terrible damage done by weapons they couldn't effectively counter.

Between July 1943 and July 1944, this "Second Battle of Britain" was effectively won by intensive intelligence work rapidly identifying sites and the RAF and USAAF actively bombing them, delaying both rocket and flying bomb programmes. "Another activity which should not be overlooked is the part played in the campaign by photo-reconnaissance and interpretation. Approximately 4,000 reconnaissance sorties flown by British and American aircraft contributed directly to "*Crossbow*" intelligence. Brilliant interpretation of the photographs obtained confirmed the reports of experimental work on the Baltic, pin-pointed and identified launching and supply sites in France, definitely established the purpose of the "ski-sites", provided the material for the targeting of more than 300 objectives, analyzed the results of attacks and, in general, provided the framework for the planning and execution of offensive countermeasures. In all, 4,070 interpretation reports were issued on these subjects" (*USSBS*, p. 17).

"However, we have abundant evidence that the Germans were bold planners in other fields, and actually achieved a rate of production of 4,200 aircraft per month in July 1944. Speer, Koller and Frydag have stated that production of V-1 did not compete with that of aircraft and that the production cost was only a fraction of the cost of a single-engine fighter. The production of sufficient weapons to assure the weekly rate of fire given the above was, therefore, well within the capacity of industry. Messerschmitt said that he believed a monthly production of 100,000 was possible" (*USSBS*, p. 13-14).[1] Interruption of production, transportation and launching insured that firing rates for the V-1 never reached anything like enough needed to collapse the Normandy Invasion, nor was the weapon accurate enough to do the job. By September the weapon was driven out of range by success on the ground. German emphasis shifted back to the V-2, which was, by that time, almost out of range of the invasion-critical areas of England.

Without a good way to find the small, mobile rocket launch locations, with no fixed launch support sites to attack, had the V-2 remained the German "weapon of choice" in 1943, things might have been quite different. As it worked out, Allied intelligence, command of the air and forward movement on the ground, eventually bested the rocket as well. The Allies learned how to destroy the rockets in transit, and pushed them out of range.[2] Luckily for our side, the war ended before the V-2 could be range-extended or supplied with a more destructive warhead.

Considering the rate and location of Allied ground advances, other than attempting to deny the Allies use of Antwerp as a port and trying to destroy the Remagen Bridge, the 14,758 casualties from V-weapon bombardment of targets on the continent can only be attributed to terrorism and spite.

IMPACT OF THE V-WEAPONS

By 1943 Allied intelligence and decision-makers were persuaded that Hitler was holding back some wonder weapon to repel an invasion of the Continent, something that would have a devastating effect on ships, planes and troops. That weapon or weapons hadn't been identified, but many believed they existed (*Bodyguard of Lies*, p. 362). No one can ever know much the impact of those rumours stiffened the will of German soldiers in increasingly hopeless situations, causing them to stand and fight a month, a day or an hour longer than they would have otherwise. This aspect of morale is often mentioned in memoirs or first person interviews of German soldiers in books and magazines such as "World War II", and it is not possible to know how many Allied soldiers died because of that German propaganda-driven false hope, or how many Allied tactical decisions were changed because of enemy resistance born of wishful thinking.

Allied suppositions about the "new weapon" reached the status of paranoia (*Bodyguard of Lies*, p. 362).

Allied fears of expected but as yet unknown weapons were reinforced when the Luftwaffe sank an Italian battleship, damaged Italian and British battleships, plus damaged USN and Royal Navy Light Cruisers off Sicily and Salerno in September 1943 using rocket-boosted, radio-controlled bombs. About this same time the Allies began to see large concrete installations of totally new designs cropping up close to the English Channel, suggesting some form of long-range artillery that might threaten English cities and Invasion staging areas, even the necessarily concentrated ships during the Invasion itself. No one knew what warheads to expect from the mystery weapons, but the worst case had to be considered (biological, chemical, nuclear). British HUMINT organizations strained every nerve to learn what these weapons and installations were, what they presaged, where were the weapons were made and how best to destroy them (*Bodyguard of Lies*, p. 362).

General Eisenhower observed that the drive to take Antwerp, badly needed as a port, also cleared the area being used to launch V-1s and V-2s. Denying Antwerp to the Allies was also one of the main objectives of the German Ardennes Offensive in December 1944. Unfortunately the obvious importance of Antwerp also called down rockets on the Belgian city as the Germans sought to deny the Allies a supply point closer to the northern front. Ike's assessment of the V-weapons campaign was: "The development and employment of these weapons were undoubtedly greatly delayed by our spring bombing campaign against the places where we suspected they were under manufacture. Peenemünde, in Germany, was known to be one of the largest of the German experimental plants and periodically we sent large formations of bombers to attack that area. There were other places indicated to us as suspicious. One was Trondheim, in Norway, where we thought that the Germans were engaged in atomic development. We also bombed the suspected launching sites along the coast of northwestern Europe, where our reconnaissance photography showed numerous facilities and installations that could not be interpreted in terms of any known weapon. These areas were continuously hammered" (*Crusade in Europe*, p. 259. The Trondheim reference is probably Vemork/Rjukan).

Countermeasures taken against the V-weapons were certainly massive. "The Strategic Air Forces based in England dispatched 36,795 aircraft on offensive counterattacks and dropped 102,491 long tons of bombs…. The Tactical Air Forces were also heavily involved during the autumn and winter of 1943. Nearly all of this effort was applied against launching sites and the supply organization in northern France. The reconnaissance effort was likewise substantial; 4,000 sorties or 40 per cent of those flown from the United Kingdom in a 23 month period (from May 1943 to April 1945) contributed to the '*Crossbow*' campaign" (*USSBS*, p. 3).

Post-war bombing analysis concluded, "Although there is no evidence that bombing caused a decrease in output, failure to meet planned production schedules for V-1 is attributable partly to the direct effects of attacks on known or suspected manufacturing plants, partly to the bombing of plants whose connection was unknown at the time, and partly to the gradual disintegration of German industry and transport which led to shortage of materials and delays in deliveries" (*USSBS*, p. 3).

A recent author characterized the *Crossbow* campaign as a failure, because of the losses and diversion of heavy bombers from strategic targets. Almost 2,000 aircrew and 400 four-engine bombers were lost. He then quotes Adolf Galland's observation that, "The best way to fight the German V-weapons system, would (have been) to paralyze the German war industry" (*Masters of the Air*, p.303). This opinion was written with the hindsight of six decades after the events. From the perspective of those in England in 1944, disrupting the V-1 launchings was an immediate priority because they had no idea how many of them there would be and how much (or little) damage they might do—and they were landing RIGHT NOW.

Criticism of failure to destroy the V-weapons infrastructure is also misplaced. Those attacks were limited because the

Above: Damage done to an English urban area by a single V-weapon, probably a rocket. The devastation is better understood with a wider look at the same area (Below). (Official British photos).

For comparison to the scope of damage, this was what was being done to German cities by heavy bombardment. You are looking inside the walls of burned-out buildings.

Allies didn't know many of the places where the weapons were being made until late in the war. It ignores the difficulty in identifying all the various small, dispersed locations where the V-weapons, or their components, might be made (cottage industry). Nor does it recognize the "hardness" of some of the most significant potential targets (e.g. Mittelwerk). General Galland was undoubtedly correct, and Allied bombing of the German petroleum and transportation industries was the best that could be done to interdict the V-weapons.

"There is good evidence that countermeasures delayed the beginning of V-1 attacks by three months or more, but after attacks had begun, bombing had little effect. Delay in the beginning of V-2 attacks amounted to approximately six months. Factors contributing to this delay were (in order of occurrence):

    a. Bombing of the experimental establishment at Peenemünde on the Baltic.

    b. Technical difficulties with the weapon.

    c. Bombing of factories at Wiener-Neustadt and Friedrichshafen.

    d. Bombing of launching sites at Watten and Wizernes on the French coast" (*USSBS*, p. 2).

Professor R V Jones remembered summarizing the probability of a rocket assault in a late-summer report. "Our threat to their launching area and to their lines of supplies may, however, cause the Germans to make an earlier, but smaller effort—if they can. And, indeed, this was clearly going to be a 'near run thing', as our armies were now racing north-eastwards" (*Wizard War*, p. 458).

THE BALANCE SHEET

Air Marshall Arthur Harris, chief of RAF Bomber Command during the war, was wont to refer to "those damn silly rockets" and he reminded the War Cabinet that his aircraft could do more damage to a single German city in a single night than all of the rockets combined (*Bomber Command*, p. 331). He was certainly correct. Ironically, one of the reasons Hitler needed the V-weapons was his Luftwaffe had failed to develop a fleet of heavy bombers capable of the devastation wrought in Germany by RAF Bomber Command and the USAAF Eighth and Fifteenth Air Forces.

"The Federal Statistical Offices in Wiesbaden computed after the war that 593,000 German civilians died and 3.37 million dwellings were destroyed, including 600,000 in Berlin alone, from 1939 to 1945" (*Bomber Command*, p. 410). Weighed against the power of thousands of heavy bombers, the damage potential of the V-Weapons pales into insignificance. Their major impacts devolved to engendering fear and showing the way to the future of war, all BECAUSE Allied intelligence identified them, allowing countermeasures to blunt their effect.

Certainly both the V-weapons and Allied countermeasures had effect on the conduct of the war. "One of the most obvious results of the V-weapon campaign was that it caused the Allied air forces to turn aside from their primary offensive mission and commit part of their forces to essentially defensive operations. This commitment was very substantial" (*USSBS*, p. 27-29). During the peak "*Crossbow*" offensive (August 1943 to August 1944), the effort amounted to 11.1% of Eighth AF sorties, 17.4% for the RAF and 16.7% for Tactical Air Forces (Ninth AF and 2nd TAF). RAF Fighter Command devoted as much as 79% of its sorties to "*Crossbow*" from November 1944 to March 1945.

"Thus, in contrast to the Allied

"Bomber" Harris was right. Thousands of sorties by four-engine aircraft were carrying bomb loads to Germany far in excess of anything the V-weapons programs could deliver. Mainz, after the war.

MAINZ

BREMEN

Bremen after the war. The effect of strategic bombing speaks for itself. The Allies paid a terrible price, but accepted high losses of aircraft and aircrew to do this level of damage to their enemy.

"*Crossbow*" effort, which had an insignificant effect on our prosecution of the war as a whole, the German preoccupation with the development and use of long range weapons absorbed important quantities of technical ability, labor, materials, industrial capacity and armaments, nearly all of which could have been used to strengthen the flagging defenses of the Reich. This valuable part of Germany's war potential was staked on a race against time and Allied countermeasures. The race was lost and the V-weapon campaign failed – failed to prevent or delay the invasion, failed to shatter Allied morale and failed to change the course of the war" (*USSBS*, p. 36).

Nothing the Luftwaffe or V-weapons were able to do to the Allies could equal what RAF Bomber Command and the USAAF were doing to Germany after the late fall of 1943.

AN ASSESSMENT

The entire German failure in the Second World War could be summed up by Dornberger's "too little-too late". The V-weapons are not an exception. The Nazi Vengeance weapons programmes were overly ambitious, overly complex, and insufficiently produced, in part because of mercurial and arbitrary meddling by an absolute dictator. But that can also be said about their late-generation U-boats and jet fighters. Deployed earlier and in greater numbers, any of those weapons might have been decisive—at least significant. But then, if the Luftwaffe had produced a fleet of bombers with the capacity of a Lancaster in 1938, the Blitz in 1940-41 might have turned out differently. If the Luftwaffe had remained focused on RAF Fighter Command in the Battle of Britain instead of shifting to London…. The history of war is strewn with "what ifs". It must be remembered that the Germans dominated the war until the summer of 1940. From 1942 on they didn't control the war and badly needed something to regain the initiative—dramatically new technology seemed to be the answer.

RAF fighters did a good job of protecting Britain against the best Goring could send over but the Luftwaffe couldn't stop Bomber Command and the Eighth Air Force from reaching urban and industrial targets in occupied Europe. Allied convoys and escorts braved the submarine blockade and brought the wealth of the new world in men and material to the battle while Germany couldn't replace losses at the same rate. Air attacks on installations building German planes, submarines, and V-weapons, made those programmes slow or stumble. Allied intelligence got better and better at finding threats and directed destruction upon them.

It is easy to say today, "Those weapons could never have been decisive", or, "There weren't enough of them", or "They weren't accurate enough". Those often heard comments ignore the dynamic of Allied intervention on both aspects. War is not one-sided. It is punch and counter punch. Static analysis of a single factor won't disclose what happened or why. It certainly won't explain how and what the public and leadership in London were going through—and the hard decisions they had to make. People on both sides reacted in 1943 based upon what they knew in 1943, not what we know today. The Allies probably feared the V-weapons too much, but then we always fear the unknown. Some on the other side expected far too much from them. But the damage done by the V-1 and V-2 would undoubtedly been much greater, the loss of life much higher, if the Allies hadn't found, understood and destroyed or damaged the means to produce and launch more of the weapons—and, the way I see it, photo interpreters were instrumental in that success.

"In 1944 Germany, though hard-pressed, was by no means finished. Not only was her war production still increasing. She was also preparing new weapons—fast U-boats equipped with "schnorkel", jet-aircraft, pilotless aeroplanes, and rockets—weapons which the Allies could not have answered, or only after another long period of setbacks and delays. Allied unity and the resolution of the Allied peoples, particularly of the British, would have been dangerously strained. As it was, Germany's new weapons came too late. The fast U-boats and the jet-aircraft never operated on any large scale. The use of the pilotless aeroplanes and of the rockets was delayed, first by bombing the stations where they were being prepared and then by bombing their launching sites in France. Both weapons came into action, with much suffering to the inhabitants of London, but only after D-day, and the Allies, advancing through France, overran most of the launching sites before life in London became intolerable. The final victory of May 1945 came only just in time. It was touch-and-go, not a foregone conclusion" (*England 1914 – 1945*, p. 501).

Even looking at it from this distance it is easy to see that aerial photoreconnaissance and photo interpretation played a major role in the Allied victory. In the Pantheon of World War II Intelligence, mission N860, the 540 Squadron Mosquito out of Leuchars, Scotland that photographed Peenemünde from 24,000 feet on 23 June 1943 must rank as one of the most significant intelligence collection events of the war. Albeit not all recognized at the same time, those clear, sharp images disclosed the horizontal and erected V-2 rocket, the V-1 and the Me 163. Spotting the tiny P20 at Peenemünde, on photos taken five months earlier, in particular led to a complete understanding of the flying bomb threat within a few days of its identification when it was seen on a launch ramp. That in turn led to a flurry of countermeasures that delayed and blunted the enemy attack just in time to negate the V-1 as an influence on the Normandy Invasion.

Could the flying bomb have had an impact on the invasion? I say yes. Beyond question, Allied bombing of launch sites delayed the V-1 assault, denying that influence. I believe Professor Jones' actions to deceive the Germans as to firing distances actually did result in changes to the V-1 flight profile, causing them to be less effective. Rapidly improving accuracy of the V-1 is evident on radar tracking (see Chapter VI). Half of the fourteen bombs plotted just a month before D-Day, fell within a circle of about twelve miles, and closer to eight miles deviation in azimuth. Of course when action on the ground pushed launch sites back and air-launches began, impact variances were much greater—to the point of being random.

It seems Professor Jones' deception on V-1 impacts, devised to save London, has deceived some people writing about flying bomb accuracy ever since. From the German viewpoint both V-weapons were needed in their time, and deemed worthwhile. After late 1942, Hitler had no reliable way to destroy targets in England, while his own cities and factories were being savaged. Both the V-1 and V-2 seemed to have the potential to do what the Luftwaffe could not. It is interesting that because of range limitations, both V-weapons were operationally predicated on continued German control of the launch zone. It is ironic that the V-1 units fired a few days after the most critical time of the invasion that they might have influenced, and thereafter could only abandon site after site as the Allied invasion lodgment expanded.

STRENGTHS AND WEAKNESSES OF THE WEAPONS

It is easy to say, six decades later, that the weapons didn't have the accuracy, or they couldn't carry the payload necessary to be decisive. In reality, they were wondrous, well ahead of their time and frighteningly destructive, particularly the rocket, because it gave no warning and couldn't be stopped once launched. It is no accident that we use weapons today that evolved from the V-2.

One author recently characterized the German rocket programme as a "boondoggle", far too complex and expensive to be viable, let alone decisive.[3] If that's true, you could say the same thing about IRBM/ICBM development, and indeed several of the NASA space programmes.

I've only been directly involved in two military Research and Development projects but I know that author should have understood that waste, back-tracking and false starts are unfortunate siblings of cutting-edge technology. More importantly, I know military officers and how they think. Their focus is always on success of any task assigned and they will tirelessly pursue the intended result. Add to that increasing loss of control of the air space over Germany in 1944 and a steady increase of heavy bomber raids and the V-weapons became necessary as straws to grasp. As much as weapons of vengeance, by the time they went operational they were weapons of desperation—because nothing else was working for the Nazis and they knew it.

The actual internal state of the V-weapons programme was irrelevant to the actions and decisions required of the Allies in the face of the new threat—they had to act based on what they knew at the time. I submit that the reason the V-weapons had so little effect on the war was more a function of what Allied intelligence and Allied air power accomplished than the admitted convoluted shambles of the Nazi V-weapons programme. While true that the V-2 was expensive, a bomber was thirty times more expensive. The Battle of Britain proved that the He 111s and Do 17s could drop only six to eight tons of bombs before being destroyed. This, plus the increasing shortage of aircrews, made the rocket cost effective—at least it seemed so in 1940-41 ("*Astronautix*", p. 4). Thus, while the rocket may have been wasteful, it certainly didn't seem unnecessary to the Nazi leadership in 1942. It could hardly have been a programme undertaken for personal or political gain for to fail, and fail with great expense, in Nazi Germany was not a good career move. The rocket was undoubtedly "oversold", but hopes of the unstoppable devastation were unquestionably attractive. The fact that Germany was pushing too far out on the edge of "state-of-the-art" caused many delays.

This same author referenced above also maintained that the rocket only became a viable weapon when mated with a nuclear warhead (ie after the war). That too is simplification and revisionist. Having had military duties in the early 1960s that considered long-range rockets from the standpoint of both offense and defence, I know many of our early ICBM targets were "population centres" because we didn't yet have the accuracy to go after hardened ICBM silos (the real targets). What we were forced to plan on doing was no different than what the Germans (or our bombers) were doing in the Second World War, just on a larger scale. We also planned to use shorter-range ballistic rockets with conventional warheads with the same long-range artillery concepts the Germans had. I submit that, aside from obvious range improvements, the difference that makes ballistic and cruise missiles the threat they are today is guidance systems that can strike small targets. That technology was almost two decades beyond anything available to Dornberger and Von Braun.

A shorter launch rail, better guidance system (and more flexible or variable flight path) would have made the V-1 a more potent weapon. Still, had the flying bomb been available earlier, and in larger numbers as planned, the V-1 might well have been decisive—perhaps not in changing the outcome of the war but in altering its path to conclusion.

The V-2 was brilliantly devised for launch simplicity, making it almost impossible to detect and stop once in the field. Its major weaknesses were complexity and a vulnerable infrastructure from manufacture to field. The V-1, on the other hand, was cheaper and easier to produce but needed a large, relatively easily located launching system. The inability to make the flying bomb go anywhere but where the elaborate ramp pointed was also a serious limitation. Though impressive for their day, both systems suffered from a lack of range.

Allied intelligence, in particular the work at Medmenham, caused both V-weapons to be exposed to the might of Allied air power and that blunted their impact and eventually eliminated them as a threat.

"The air photograph, then, was our main source. Fortunately we could take photographs where and when we wished as the enemy were never able to close an area to us. Having got the photographs and repeated them at intervals where necessary, we had a factual objective piece of data which we could study as long as we needed to, employing as many experts as we wished and from which we could make detailed measurements and deductions. Admittedly we could not see everything but in the jungle it is not necessary to see the whole elephant to know that the elephant is there. Camouflage was, and is, totally ineffective against the air camera and merely serves to emphasize the importance of the object being hidden" (*Kendall*, Spring 2008 Medmenham Club Newsletter, p. 25).

One final observation from an "old Intel Analyst" that I haven't seen mentioned anywhere else: The V-1 ground launching was from an arc east to south of England. "Short rounds" went into the sea or relatively sparsely populated Kent. "Longs" had plenty of enemy land to drop into but with few targets. Rockets and air-launched "buzz-bombs" were fired from north-east, crossing the North Sea, giving a difficult azimuth problem and a very narrow range-window to strike anything of value. Since V-2 launch sites were always moving, I suspect the rocket accuracy problem was also exacerbated by lack of a refined survey linking launch sites in The Netherlands to targets in England (as had been carefully done in France for the V-1).

The V-weapons turned out to be more vulnerable, less numerous and less accurate than needed to be decisive, but the Allies had no way of knowing that until well after the attacks began. By the fall of 1944 they had "identified Waldo" and knew where to find him.

The Allies turned out to be a lot better at locating and destroying the V-weapons than the Germans imagined possible.

Thanks largely to aerial photoreconnaissance and hard work at Medmenham, the Allies knew enough, early enough, to blunt the assault and deny the V-weapons the timing and opportunity to be decisive.

---

1   Albert Speer, Minister for Armaments; General Karl Koller, Chief of the Luftwaffe operations staff; Karl Frydag, member of the Industrial Council responsible for coordinating work between leading companies and sub-contractors.

2   There is considerable debate over why the main V-2 production facilities were not destroyed. This was largely because they were not all located; because they were extremely "hard" targets; because they were staffed with thousands of slave-labour workers; because some were at extreme range for Allied bombers; and/or because bombers were heavily committed to "Air Superiority" and post-D-Day targets.

3   Boondoggle is defined as a **wasteful pursuit**: an activity or project that is unnecessary and wasteful of time or money, especially one undertaken for personal or political gain.

BIBLIOGRAPHY

Babington Smith, Flight Officer Constance, WAAF. *Air Spy.* New York, N.Y.: Ballantine Books, 1957. Paperback ed. Quoted with kind permission from the copywrite holder. Originally published in the UK as *Evidence In Camera*, this book inspired me to become an aerial photo interpreter, and my copy was so often used it wore out and I had to buy another. The most recent edition of the book was published by Stroud: Sutton in 2004.

Becker, Cajus. *The Luftwaffe War Diaries*. New York, N.Y.: Ballantine Books, 1969.

Bowman, Martin. *Mosquito Photo-Reconnaissance Units of World War 2*. Botley, Oxford, England: Osprey Publishing, 1999.

Bowyer, Chaz. *The Encyclopedia of British Military Aircraft*. London, England: Bison Books, Ltd., 1982.

Breuer, William B. *Secret Weapons of World War II*. New York, N.Y.: John Wiley & Sons, Inc., 2000.

Brookes, Andrew J. *Photo Reconnaissance*. London, England: Ian Allan Ltd., 1975.

Brown, Anthony Cave. *Bodyguard of Lies*. New York, N.Y.: Bantam Books, Inc., 1975.

Budiansky, Stephen. "The Man on the Trail of the Nazi A-Bomb." Leesburg, VA, October 2007 World War II magazine.

Carter, Kit C. and Mueller, Robert, compilers. *Army Air Forces in World War II: Combat Chronology 1941-1945*. Washington, DC: Office of Air Force History, 1973.

Churchill, Sir Winston S. *Closing the Ring*. Cambridge, Mass.: Houghton Mifflin Co., 1951.

———— *Triumph and Tragedy*. Cambridge, Mass.: Houghton Mifflin Co., 1951. Both Churchill books quoted with kind permission of Houghton Mifflin Harcourt.

Cooksley, Peter. *Flying Bomb*. New York, N.Y.: Charles Scribner's Sons, 1979. Quoted with kind permission from the author and Hale Books.

Craven, Wesley F. and Cate, James L. T*he Army Air Forces in World War II*, vol. 3. Washington, D.C.: Office of Air Force History, 1983.

Der Zweite Weltkrieg Im Bild, Band II. Baden-Baden, GR: Eilebrect (compilation of photos included as sales inducements in cigarette packages), circa late 1940s.

Dornberger, Major Gen. Walter R., German Army. *V-2*. New York, N.Y.: Ballantine Books, Inc., 1954.

Eisenhower, General of the Armies Dwight D., U.S. Army. *Crusade in Europe*. Garden City, N. Y.: Doubleday & Company, Inc., 1948. Quoted with permission of the copyright holder, Random House, Inc.

"Encyclopedia Astronautica" *www.astronautix.com/sites/peenemunde/htm*

Esposito, Brigadier General Vincent J., U.S. Army. *The West Point Atlas of American Wars, vol. II*. New York, N.Y.: Praeger Publications, 1959.

"Evidence In Camera," ACIU magazine, March 1945 special edition reprinted by Medmenham Club.

Faber, Harold (ed.). *Luftwaffe: A History*. New York, N.Y.: Times Books, 1977.

Ford, Brian. *German Secret Weapons: Blueprint For Mars*. New York, N.Y.: Ballantine Books Inc., 1969.

Freeman, Roger A. *Mighty Eighth War Diary*. London, UK: Jane's Publishing Company Ltd., 1981.

Garlinski, Jozef. *Hitler's Last Weapons*. New York, N.Y.: Times Books, 1978.

Hallion, Dr. Richard P. "Bombs That Were Smart Before Their Time." Leesburg, VA, September 2007 World War II magazine.

Halter, Jon C. *Top Secret Projects of WW II*. New York, N.Y.; Wanderer Books, 1978.

Hastings, Max. *Bomber Command*. New York, N.Y.: The Dial Press, 1979.

Haswell, Jock. *D-Day Intelligence and Deception*. New York, N.Y.: Times Books, 1979.

Henshall, Philip. *Hitler's Rocket Sites*. New York, N.Y.: St. Martin's Press, 1985.

Hinsley, F. H. *British Intelligence in the Second World War*, vol. 2 & 3. New York, N.Y.: Cambridge University Press, 1981 & 1984. Footnoted as *Brit Intel*. Quoted with permission from the Office of Public Sector Information.

H?lsken, Dieter. *V-Missiles of the Third Reich the V-1 and V-2*. Sturbridge, Mass: Monogram Aviation Publications, 1994. Footnoted as *V-Missiles*. Quoted with permission from Eagle Monogram Publications. I do not agree with all the author's conclusions but this book is a MUST for anyone serious about the V-Weapons.

Hogg, Ian V. *German Secret Weapons of the Second World War*. Mechanicsburg, Penn.: Stackpole Books, 1999. Reproduced by kind permission of the publisher from German Secret Weapons of the Second World War by Ian Hogg, published by Greenhill Books, London, 1999.

Infield, Glenn B. *Unarmed and Unafraid*. New York, N.Y.: The Macmillan Company, 1970.

"Interpretation of Military Installations." Development of Photographic Intelligence, vol. V: 325th Photographic Wing, Reconnaissance, (probably, Mt. Farm, circa 1945). Courtesy of Capt. Herman J. Bendfeldt, USAF (ret.)

Irving, David. *The Mare's Nest*. London, England: William Kimber, 1964.

Isaacson, Walter. "Einstein and the Bomb." Leesburg, VA, June 2007 World War II magazine.

Ivie, Thomas G. *Aerial Reconnaissance*. Fallbrook, CA: Aero Publishers, Inc., 1981.

Johnson, Brian. *The Secret War*. New York, N.Y.: Methuen, 1978.

Johnson, David. *V-1 V-2*. Briarcliff Manor, N.Y.: Stein And Day, 1981.

Jones, R. V. *Reflections on Intelligence*. London: Heinemann, 1989.

——— MOST SECRET WAR: BRITISH SCIENTIFIC INTELLIGENCE 1939-1945. London: Hamish Hamilton, 1978 Copyright (c). American release as *The Wizard War*. New York, N.Y.: Coward, McCann & Geoghegan, Inc., 1978. Quoted by kind permission of Penguin Books Ltd. I don't agree with everything the author said or did but this is another "must read" from a brilliant man who was central to a number of "intelligence coups."

Keegan, John. *Intelligence in War*. New York, N.Y.: Vintage Books, 2004

Keen, Patricia F. *Eyes of the Eighth*. Sun City, AZ: CAVU Publishers, L.L.C., 1996.

Kendall, Wing Commander Douglas N., OBE, OC, RAF (Ret'd). Extracts from unpublished work "A War of Intelligence," circa. 1957. Quoted through the courtesy of the Medmenham Collection and Trustees. All rights reserved. Invaluable comments and insight by a man who was at the center of things.

King, Benjamin & Kutta, Timothy. *Impact*. Rockville Centre, N.Y.: Sarpedon, 1998.

Klee, Ernst and Merk, Otto. *Damals in Peenemunde*. Oldenburg and Hamburg, Germany: Gerhard Stalling Verlag, 1963.

Kreis, John F. (Gen Ed.). *Piercing the Fog*. Washington, D.C., Air Force and Museums Program, 1996.

Leaf, Edward. *Above All Unseen*. Yeovil, Somerset, UK; Patrick Stephens Limited, 1997.

Lewin, Ronald. *Ultra Goes to War*. New York, N.Y.: Pocket Books, 1978.

Marks, Leo. *Between Silk and Cyanide*. New York, N.Y.: The Free Press, 1998.

Memoirs of Field-Marshal the Viscount Montgomery of Alamein, K.G. New York, N.Y.: Signet Books, 1958.

Miller, Donald L. *Masters of the Air*. New York, N.Y.: Simon & Shuster, 2006.

Nesbit, Roy Conyers. *Eyes of the RAF*. Phoenix Mill, Gloucestershire, England: Alan Sutton Publishing Limited, 1996.

Neufeld, Michael J. *The Rocket and the Reich*. Cambridge, Mass.: Harvard University Press, 1996.

Ordway, Frederick I, III and Sharp, Mitchell. *The Rocket Team*. New York, N.Y.: Thomas Y. Crowell, Publishers, 1979.

Photo Interpretation of Underground Installations. Washington, D.C.: Headquarters U.S. Air Force, Directorate of Intelligence Collection Operations Division, Reconnaissance Branch, circa 1947.

Physical Damage Division Report (ETO). Washington, DC: United States Strategic Bombing Survey (USSBS) vol. 134b, April 1947. Footnoted as USSBUS.

Powys-Lybbe, Flight Officer Ursula, WAAF. *The Eye of Intelligence*. London, England: William Kimber & Co. Limited, 1983. Footnoted as Eye. I had been in the PI business for years when this book was published and I found it had a familiarity, a "ring of truth." Page after page I kept thinking "she's telling it like it is."

Price, Dr. Alfred. *Targeting the Reich*. London, England: Greenhill Books, 2003.

Ramsey, Winston G. (ed.). *The Blitz Then and Now (vol 1)*. London, England: Battle of Britain Prints International Limited, 1987.

Rise and Fall of the German Air Force 1933-1945, The. New York, N.Y.: St. Martin's Press, 1983.

Shirer, William L. *Rise and Fall of the Third Reich*. New York, N.Y.: Simon & Schuster, 1960. Quoted with permission from the publisher.

Showalter, Dennis. "Book Review." Leesburg, VA, October 2004 World War II magazine. Quoted with permission from The Weider History Group.

Simon, Major General Leslie E., US Army. *Secret Weapons of the Third Reich*. Old Greenwich, Conn.: WE, Inc., Publishers, 1971.

Staesck, Chris, ed. *Allied Photo Reconnaissance of World War Two*. San Diego, CA: Thunder Bay Press, 1998.

Stanley, Col. Roy M. II, USAF (ret.). *To Fool A Glass Eye*. Shrewsbury, UK: Airlife Publishing Ltd., 1998.

———— *World War II Photo Intelligence*. New York, N.Y.: Charles Scribner's Sons, 1981.

Taylor, A. J. P. *England 1914 – 1945*. London, England: The Folio Society, 2000. Quoted by permission of Oxford University Press.

*V-Weapons (*Crossbow*) Campaign*. Washington, DC: United States Strategic Bombing Survey (USSBS) vol. 60, November 1945.

Wagner, Ray and Nowarra, Heinz. *German Combat Planes*. Garden City, N.Y.: Doubleday & Company, 1971.

Webster, Sir Charles and Frankland, Noble. *The Strategic Air Offensive Against Germany 1939-1945* (four volumes). London, England: Her Majesty's Stationary Office, 1961.

Welchman, Gordon. *The Hut Six Story*. New York, N.Y.: McGraw-Hill Book Company, 1982.

Wood, Tony & Gunston, Bill. *Hitler's Luftwaffe*. London, England: Salamander Books, Ltd., 1978.

Young, Richard Anthony. *The Flying Bomb*. New York, N.Y.: Sky Books Press, 1978.

Ziegler, Mano. *Rocket Fighter*. New York, N.Y.: Bantam Books, 1984.

INDEX